Sok le Boy

THE ROWTE

THE GLINNES

Castle Balan
Lough Guil
Lo. Hardwarnes

Bellomogy

Mc GUILLY

COUNTYE
Carrogh

Knock Mullagh

Brienhcarrogh
Grange

La Boy

Tisane Cast

ANTRYM

Clayton a hardwory

Red Bag Cast
Red Bay

Dromonork

Owenbigh

Glenarme
Glenarme Bay
The Maydres

Oldeflote haven
Kneiland

Skivrik

Raney

Craig Castle

Stone over

The Nether
Clan de Boy

Carrine
Tohove

Adaflote

Nagis
Bey

Kow

Blackhead

Lean

Crosse

Capla

Kelly

Kelles Mt

Conor a Bish. [en.

Dundough [carrick] tofe
a bryen

Mc Macomer

Mc Mefarnah

Starbar

Doh Andery
Bencoll

Knockferfus

White Ho.

Bennodi

Mc Banger

Hollywoods Ab

COUNTYE

Lough Neaugh

Eres Goule

Drumboe

Sidney Iland

Knockerahollye

L. Dar

Carmacan

Mahonegall

Belfast

Freyfaene

Columbill

Rough

Connor

South Clan de Boy

Derry

Blare

Mc Conber

Slut Mc THE
O'Neale KELLES
DUFFRE S. Brides

Knockstedal
Derry

Seotrick

Knockstredal

ARDES

THE

Kilmltagh

Bandes
Aghagh Ilon

Clan
Brasil

L. Ryle

Kilwarlin

Maharta COUNTYE

Revyhed

Fallragh

Donachdu

Dromon

Lo. Afere

Whites Cast

Smithes Cy

Darkins O.

Mc Aryam

B. Tally

Newcastle
Sauage

Portine
ferry

Dundorlin

Delgen fte

L. Boyne

Fullash

Legan fte

Mahonby

Patrick

L. Knock Tormy

L. Shenshan

Dundram

Inch

Mahore

The Fort

LECALE

Mc Sall
Doane

Ardglass

Argles haven

Argles

Aguaderny

Idc

Ca. Lough
Brackley

Knock Baah

Downmore

BAGNALL

Anaghelome

DOWNE

Kilcor
way

L. Kena

Dromduly

IRIS

SCOTS-IRISH LINKS
1575–1725

PART THREE

by
David Dobson

CLEARFIELD

Printed for
Clearfield Company, Inc. by
Genealogical Publishing Co., Inc.
Baltimore, Maryland
2001

Reprinted for
Clearfield Company, Inc. by
Genealogical Publishing Co., Inc.
Baltimore, Maryland
2002, 2003

International Standard Book Number: 0-8063-5102-0

Made in the United States of America

INTRODUCTION

The Plantation of Ulster by Scots in the seventeenth century is a well - established fact. Genealogists, however, require very specific reference material which is generally missing from the published accounts of the migration of up to 100,000 Scottish Lowlanders to northern Ireland at that time.

Part Three of *Scots Irish Links, 1575 - 1725* attempts to identify some of these Scots settlers and is based mainly on contemporary primary source material in Ireland, Scotland and England. Sometimes the individuals listed are described as 'Scots or of the Scotch nation' and on other occasions their identification is circumstantial and based on surname, place and time. Many of the early Scots listed have been granted, or have applied for, 'denization'. This was a direct result of the legal position that many of the original Scots found themselves in that it was illegal for them as 'aliens' to buy and eventually bequeath land in Ireland. Consequently, most of them applied to be declared denizens of Ireland, which in effect naturalised them and enabled them to grant or purchase land there. Between 1603 and 1634 a number of residents of Ireland, particularly Ulster, *"all of the Scotch nation or descent"* were recorded in the Irish Patent Rolls as having been granted denization. For example on November 22, 1605 there was recorded *"the Grant of English liberty to Sir Hugh Montgomery, of Scotland, and his issue, to be of free state and condition, and from all yoke of servitude, Scotch, Irish, or otherwise, quit and free, to use and and enjoy the English laws, pre-eminences, rights and customs, with permission to acquire lands and possessions"*.

While it is generally assumed that these settlers were Protestants, it should be noted that many of the initial wave of emigrants were more inclined to Episcopalianism; but from about 1640 the settlers were overwhelmingly Presbyterian, while a few seem to have converted to Catholicism.

Their descendants, within a few generations, emigrated in significant numbers across the Atlantic where, as the Scotch-Irish, they made a major contribution to the settlement and development of Colonial America.

David Dobson
St Andrews, Scotland, 2000

REFERENCES

ARCHIVES

BM   =   British Museum, London
NAS =   National Archives of Scotland, Edinburgh
NEHGS   New England Historic Genealogical Society, Boston
PROI=   Public Record Office of Ireland, Dublin
PRONI   Public Record Office of Northern Ireland, Belfast
TCD =   Trinity College, Dublin

PUBLICATIONS

APS =   Acts of the Parliament of Scotland
ActsPCCol   Acts of the Privy Council, Colonial, series
C   =   Census of Ireland circa1659, [Dublin, 1939]
CA   =   Chronicles of Atholl & Tullibardine, [Edinburgh, 1908]
Cal.SP.Ire   Calendar of State Papers, Ireland, series
Carew=   Calendar of Carew MS
CEG =   Catalogue of Edinburgh Graduates, [Edinburgh, 1868]
CTB =   Calendar of Treasury Books, series
CTP =   Calendar of Treasury Papers, series
EPR =   English Patent Rolls
ERA =   Edinburgh Register of Apprentices
F   =   Fasti Ecclesiae Scoticanae, [Edinburgh, 1915]
FI   =   Fasti of the Irish Presbyterian Church,[Belfast,1951]
GBR =   Glasgow Burgess Register
IPR   =   Irish Patent Roll
IWD =   Index of Will Abstracts in the Genealogical Office, Dublin
KCA =   Officers & Graduates of King's College, [Aberdeen, 1893]
MCA =   Records of Marischal College, [Aberdeen, 1898]
MUG =   Matriculation Albums of the University of Glasgow, [Glasgow, 1913]
PHS =   Presbyterian Historical Society, Belfast
PU   =   The Plantation of Ulster...,[Belfast, 1877]
RGS =   Register of the Great Seal of Scotland, series
RPCS   Register of the Privy Council of Scotland, series

SBT   =   Plantation of Ulster in Strabane barony, County
               Tyrone 1600-1641, [Coleraine, 1982]
SPDom   State Papers, Domestic, series
SPIre   State Papers, Ireland
UJA   =   Ulster Journal of Archaeology, series

SCOTS-IRISH LINKS, 1575-1725.

[Part Three]

ABERCORN, JAMES, Earl of, was granted Irish denization and a
   grant of Strabane in the barony of Strabane, County Tyrone, 15
   August 1610, [IPR]; with 1000 acres at Strabane, 2000 acres at
   Doaghlong, and 1500 acres at ....., County Tyrone, 28 March
   1619. [Carew Mss#211/122, 124]

ABERCORN, Lady MARION, Countess of, was granted Irish
   denization 12 May 1620. [IPR]

ABERCROMBY, THOMAS, was granted Irish denization on 5 July
   1631. [IPR]

ABERCROMBY, WILLIAM, was granted Irish denization on 20
   July1610. [IPR]

ACHESON, ALEXANDER, in Tonnybeague, County Fermanagh,
   1710. [IWD]

ACHESON, ARCHIBALD, of Glencarny, and his son Patrick, was
   granted Irish denization 12 February 1618. [IPR]

ACHESON, ARCHIBALD, with 1000 acres at Corrodownan, County
   Cavan, 28 March 1619. [Carew#211/35]

ACHESON, ARCHIBALD, with 1000 acres in the barony of
   Tulleknough, County Cavan, appeared at a muster in 1618 with
   24 men, 1 musket, 3 calivers, 14 pikes, and 22 swords.
   [Cal.SP.Ire, 1618/501][BMAddMS#18735]

ACHESON, ARCHIBALD, with 2000 acres in the barony of Fues, County Armagh, appeared at a muster in 1618 with 48 men, 4 muskets, 14 calivers, 17 pikes and 40 swords. [Cal. SP.Ire.1618/501]

ACHESON, Sir GEORGE, in Lower Fewes, County Armagh, 1659. [C]

ACHESON, HENRY, gentleman from Edinburgh, applied for 2000 acres in Ulster on 25 July 1609, [PU#141]; was granted Irish denization 30 July 1610, grant of Coolemalish in the barony of Fewes, County Armagh, 30 July 1610, [TCD.ms#N2/2] [IPR]; Undertaker in Precinct of Fewes, County Armagh, 1611, with 1000 acres in the barony of Fues, appeared at a msuter in 1618 with 24 men, 2 muskets, 8 calivers, 10 pikes and 18 swords. [Cal.SP.Ire.1611/384; 1612/452; 1618/501]; with 1000 acres at Coolemalsh, Precinct of Fewes 28 March 1619. [Carew Mss#211/169]

ACHESON, or LINDSEY, JANET, of Tullaghoge, was granted Irish denization 12 February 1618. [IPR]

ACHESON, Mr JOHN, sometime of Newtonleys, to bring writs from Ireland, 19 March 1629. [RPCS.III.101]

ACHESON, THOMAS, son of James Acheson HM servant for the Mint in Ireland, imprisoned in the Gatehouse during 1625. [Cal.SP.Ire.1625/1421]

ACHMUTY, ALEXANDER, was granted Irish denization 24 June 1610. [IPR][TCD.ms#N2/2]; Undertaker of the Precinct of Tullochone, County Cavan, 1611. [Cal.SP.Ire.1611/384]; grant of Drumheada in the barony of Tullocouch, County Cavan, 24 June 1610. [IPR]

AUCHMUTY, JAMES, of Drumbarry, was granted Irish denization 12 February 1618. [IPR]

ACHMUTY, JOHN, was granted Irish denization 27 June 1610. [IPR]; Undertaker of the Precinct of Tullochone, County Cavan, 1611. [Cal.SP.Ire.1611/384]; grant of Keylagh, in the barony of Tullocouch, County Cavan, 24 June 1610. [IPR][TCD.ms#N2/2]

ADAIR, ALEXANDER, Captain of the Earl of Lindsay's Regiment, in Bangor 1642. [PRO.SP.28.120]

ADAIR, ALEXANDER, gentleman in Killughe, County Down, 1720. [IWD]

ADAIR, ANN, relict of Mr Thomas Kennedy, later in Newtown, Ireland, 6 September 1688. [NAS.GD135.889]

ADAIR, ARCHIBALD, justice of the peace for County Donegal, 1629. [Cal.SP.Ire.1629/1437]

ADAIR, BENJAMIN, grandson of John McCubbin of Dunamuy, parish of Rashee, County Antrim, 1690. [NAS.GD180#216]

ADAIR, CHARLES, Cornet of Pearce's Dragoons, 1711. [IWD]

ADAIR, MARIAN, wife of William Houston jnr., was granted Irish denization 28 November 1624. [IPR]

ADAIR, PATRICK, a Presbyterian minister in Northern Ireland who petitioned the Queen in 1691. [CTB.#/III.1207, 1258]

ADAIR, PATRICK, born in 1675, son of William Adair in Corgie, Galloway, educated at the universities of Glasgow and Edinburgh, graduated MA from Glasgow University in 1694, minister of Carrickfergus from 1702, died 12 June 1717. [FI#89]

ADAIRE, ROBERT, of Ballemeachan, son of William Adaire, was granted Irish denization 28 November 1624. [IPR]

ADAIR, ROBERT, of Ballymena, High Sheriff of County Antrim, 1632. [UJA.11.1.79]

ADAIR, Sir ROBERT, a Cavalry officer in Ulster 27 January 1646. [SP.Ire]

ADAIR, Sir ROBERT, of Kinhilt, father of Alexander Adair of Drummoir husband of Margaret Agnew, 1 July 1698. [NAS.GD135.903]

ADAIR, ROBERT, of Ballimanoch, County Antrim, 6 September 1688. [NAS.GD135.889]; High Sheriff of County Antrim in 1696. [UJA.11.1.79]

ADAIR, Sir ROBERT, of Ballymena, High Sheriff of County Antrim in 1726. [UJA.11.1.79]

ADAIR, WILLIAM, of Ballemeachan, gentleman, was granted Irish denization 28 November 1624. [IPR]

ADAIR, WILLIAM, son of William Adair of Ballemeachan, was granted Irish denization 28 November 1624. [IPR]

ADAIR, WILLIAM, in Ballymanagh, County Antrim, 1666. [IWD]

ADAIR, WILLIAM, master of the Prosperity of Belfast at the port of Ayr 9 November 1689. [NAS.E72.3.21]

ADAIR, WILLIAM, a Presbyterian minister in Northern Ireland who petitioned the Queen in 1691. [CTB.#/III.1207, 1258]

ADAIR, WILLIAM, born 1650, died during February 1698. [Antrim g/s]

ADAMS, DANIEL, of Ballemullin, was granted Irish denization on 28 November 1617. [IPR]

ADAM, WILLIAM, master of the Janet of Donaghadee at the port of Ayr 22 January 1690. [NAS.E72.3.20]

ADAMSON, JAMES, brother of Mr William Adamson of Graycrook, applied for 2000 acres in Ulster on 18 July 1609. [PU#140]

ADARE, ARCHIBALD, Dean of Raphoe, was granted Irish denization 28 November 1617. [IPR]; 1622, [TCD.ms.E#3/6]; Bishop of Killala by 10 April 1640, [SP.Ire.#258/34]; appointed as Bishop of Waterford and Achonry on 7 June 1641. [SP.Dom.Sig.Off.III#464]

ADARE, GILBERT, of Ardehine, was granted Irish denization 20 May 1617. [IPR]

ADAIR, PATRICK, matriculated at St Salvador's College, University of St Andrews, 1640, graduated MA there 1642, a student at Glasgow University 1643, minister at Cairncastle 1646, and in Belfast 1674. [UJA#13/15]

ADAIR, ROBERT, settled in Ulster, returned to Scotland in 1639, accused of signing the National Covenant in Scotland in June 1639 and later plotting a Scottish invasion of Ireland with a rising at Ballymena, County Antrim, found not guilty and pardoned. [SP.Dom.Sig.Off.III#447/8]

ADARE, ROBERT, son and heir of William Adare of Ballymanagh, County Antrim, 30 December 1661. [Cal.S.P.Ire.1661]

ADAM, JAMES, master of the James of Donaghadee at the port of Irvine 14 June 1686. [NAS.E72.12.13]

ADAM, WILLIAM, a Scots-Irish student at Glasgow University 1707. [MUG#187]

AGNEW, ALEXANDER, master of the Charles of Strangford at the port of Irvine 23 June 1691. [NAS.E72.12.18]

AGNEW, ALEXANDER, of Belymaglach, died 29 August 1700, his wife Jane McQuoid, born 1652, died 7 December 1723. [Comber g/s]

AGNEW, ANDREW, of Carnie, was granted Irish denization 20 May 1617. [IPR]

AGNEW, ANDREW, a merchant in Belfast, 1695. [NAS.RD2.78.724]

AGNEW, ANDREW, a Scots-Irish student at Edinburgh University 1715, later an Anglican priest in Essex. [CEG]

AGNEW, ANN, a widow in Cross, parish of Ballymony, 1686. [IWD]

AGNEW, FRANCIS, in Mabuy, 1681. [IWD]

AGNEW, JAMES, in Ballymoney, 1709. [IWD]

AGNEW, PATRICK, a tenant farmer of 25 acres on the Agnew estate in 1645. [NAS.GD154/514]

AGNEW, PATRICK, of Ballygally, High Sheriff of County Antrim in 1668. [UJA.11.1.79]

AGNEW, PATRICK, in Kilwaghter, County Antrim, 1725. [IWD]

AGNEW, THOMAS, of Grayabbey was granted Irish denization on 20 May 1617. [IPR]

AGNEW, WILLIAM, in Donaghadee, 1727, [NAS.GD10#410]; cnf 1734 Commissariot of Wigtown

AICKEN, JOHN, of Donaghadie, was granted Irish denization on 20 May 1617. [IPR]

AIKIN, ROBERT, a minister in the diocese of Raphoe, 1622. [TCD.ms.E#3/6]

AIKENHEAD, JOHN, in Donaghadee on 1 Janaury 1647. [SP.Ire#263/3]

AIRTH, DAVID, born in Scotland, graduated MA from Edinburgh University in 1657, minister of Glenavy from 1683 to 1694, died in Scotland on 5 June 1697. [FI#51]

AITKEN, HUGH, servant of Thomas Schairpe of Houstoun, to Ireland 1702. [NAS.GD30.2213]

ALEXANDER, Reverend ANDREW, settled in Ulster, married Dorothea, daughter of Reverend Mr Caulfield, 16... [PU#577]

ALEXANDER, CHRISTOPHER, burgess of Stirling, and his son Robert, applied for 1000 acres in Ulster on 4 August 1609. [PU#143]

ALEXANDER, JAMES, born in Aberdeenshire, educated at King's College, Aberdeen, from 1666-1670, minister at Raphoe from 1677, husband of Marian Shaw. [FI#57]

ALEXANDER, JOHN, a Scots-Irish student at Glasgow University 1701. [MUG#172]

ALEXANDER, JOHN, a gentleman in Dublin, burgess and
guildsbrother of Glasgow 13 June 1718. [GBR]

ALEXANDER, W., petitioner in June 1624. [Cal.SP.Ire.1624/1226]

ALEXANDER, WALTER, in County Longford, 23 January 1624.
[SP.Ire.#238/8]

ALGOE, ROBERT, Leckpatrick parish, County Tyrone, gentleman,
was granted Irish denization 19 July 1631. [IPR]

ALLEN, JOHN, tenant of John Hamilton of Edenagh, Precinct of
Fewes, 1618. [PU#567]

ALLAN, JOHN, merchant aboard the Merchant of Larne at the port
of Irvine, Ayrshire, on 22 December 1682. [NAS.E72.12.7]

ALLAN, JOHN, master of the Anna of Larne at the port of Irvine,
Ayrshire, on 1 January 1669. [NAS.E72.12.1]

ALLEN, ROBERT, of Raphoe, was granted Irish denization 28
November 1617. [IPR]

ALLEN, ROBERT, tenant of John Hamilton of Edenagh, Precinct of
Fewes, 1618. [PU#567]

ALLAN, ROBERT, a merchant in Belfast, 1725. [NAS.AC7/32/116]

ALLARDYCE, WILLIAM, born in Aberdeen, settled in Ireland
before 18 February 1671.   [IPR]

ALLISON, ROBERT, master of the Two Brothers of Belfast at the
port of Irvine, Ayrshire, on 13 December 1683.
[NAS.E72.12.8]

ANBURRY, CHARLES, a merchant in Dublin, 1701.
[NAS.RD3.98.135]

ANDERSON, AGNES, wife of John Braynen, died 17 December
1680. [Comber g/s]

ANDERSON, ALEXANDER, of Glasdiomoe, was granted Irish denization on 13 May 1634. [IPR]

ANDERSON, DAVID, of Castle Canvarie, was granted Irish denization on 28 November 1617. [IPR]

ANDERSON, JOHN, burgess of Edinburgh, applied for 1000 acres in Ulster on 4 July 1609. [PU#139]

ANDERSON, JOHN, born in 1629, son of Reverend Alexander Anderson in Auchtergaven, graduated MA from Edinburgh University in 1649, minister in Glenarm from 1671, in Antrim from 1685, returned to Scotland in 1688, died during February 1708. [FI#57]

ANDERSON, JOHN, merchant aboard the Blessing of Donaghadee at the port of Ayr 20 March 1673. [NAS.E72.3.3]

ANDERSON, NINIAN, in Waterford, Ireland, 1677. [Glasgow Records.III.228]

ANDERSON, ROBERT, Londonderry, was granted Irish denization 17 August 1616. [IPR]

ANDREW, JAMES, of Strabane, was granted Irish denization 20 May 1617. [IPR]

ANDREW, JOHN, a tenant farmer of 15 acres on the Agnew estate in 1645. [NAS.GD154/514]

ANSTRUTHER, Sir ROBERT, was granted Irish denization 2 June 1617. [IPR]

ARBUCKLE, JAMES, born in Scotland, educated in Glasgow during 1684, a minister in Dublin from 1703, died in 1721. [FI#89]

ARBUCKLE, JAMES, a merchant in Belfast, 1722. [NAS.AC9/849]

ARBUTHNOTT, ALEXANDER, chamberlain of Galway, 4 August 1718. [NAS.GD10.867]

ARBUTHNOTT, ROBERT, in Lessnadyne, County Down, serviced as heir to his brother Robert Arbuthnott a clothier in Edinburgh, on 20 August 1709. [NAS.SH]

ARCHIBALD, JOHN, a tenant farmer of 15 acres on the Agnew estate in 1645. [NAS.GD154/514]

ARKLES, DAVID, tenant of John Hamilton of Edenagh, Precinct of Fewes, 1618. [PU#567]

ARMORE, JOHN, born 1601, late tanner in Bangor, died 20 June 1672. [Bangor Abbey g/s]

ARMSTRONG, ALEXANDER, in County Cavan, 1703. [IWD]

ARMSTRONG, ALEXANDER, in Carrickmakiggen, County Leitrim, 1720, 1721. [IWD]

ARMSTRONG, ANDREW, in Drunmurry, 1698. [IWD]

ARMSTRONG, ANDREW, in Ballycumber, King's County, 1717. [IWD]

ARMSTRONG, ANDREW, in Mauriston, County Kildare, will subscribed on 19 January 1721, probate 22 January 1723 Dublin

ARMSTRONG, ARCHIBALD, the king's fool, was granted Irish denization 9 July 1612. [IPR]

ARMSTRONG, CHRISTOPHER, in the barony of Tireagh, County Sligo, 1659. [C]

ARMSTRONG, GEORGE, of Kinmont, a refugee in Ireland, 1679. [RPCS.VI.159]

ARMSTRONG, JOHN, in County Fermanagh, 1659. [C]

ARMSTRONG, JOHN, Lieutenant of the Earl of Donegal's Regiment of Foot, 1705. [IWD]

ARMSTRONG, JOHN, in Macosquin parish, Londonderry, 1715. [NAS.RD4.117.856]

ARMSTRONG, JOHN, born 1768, died 1722. [Drumbo g/s]

ARMSTRONG, JOHN, in Rakeivan, Killan parish, 1729. [IWD]

ARMSTRONG, LANCELOT, in Crulan, Templecarne, 1700. [IWD]

ARMSTRONG, MARTIN, in Killaconkill, County Leitrim. 1693. [IWD]

ARMSTRONG, ROBERT, in Largindarrock, parish of Cleenish, County Fermanagh, 1680. [IWD]

ARMSTRONG, ROBERT, in Legewell, County Cavan, 1725. [IWD]

ARMSTRONG, SIMON, in Aghamore, County Leitrim, 1721. [IWD]

ARMSTRONG, Sir THOMAS, was granted the monopoly of farthing-making in Ireland for 21 years on 5 November 1660. [Cal.S.P.Ire.1660]

ARMSTRONG, THOMAS, in Longsfield, County Leitrim, 1699. [IWD]

ARMSTRONG, ..., a tenant of Viscount Conway and Killuta, 1669. [Cal.SP.Ire]

ARMSTRONG, ..., died in 171-, aged 77. [Drumbog g/s]

ARNOTT, ANDREW, was granted Irish denization on 17 August 1616; in Strabane, County Tyrone, 1617. [IPR][SBT#22]

ARNOT, Sir CHARLES, Captain of Robert Home of the Heugh's Regiment, in Carrickfergus, 1642. [PRO.SP.18.120]

ARNOT, CHARLES, Captain of Major General Robert Monro's Regiment, in Carrickfergus 1642. [PRO.SP.18.120]

ARNET, JAMES, of Gartnederragh, County Fermanagh, a juryman in Inniskillen on 28 February 1624. [Cal.SP.Ire.1624#1157]

ARNOT, JAMES, in Clownish, County Fermanagh, 1659. [C]

ARSKIN, JOHN, a Scots-Irish student at Glasgow University in 1710. [MUG#195]

ATCHESON, WILLIAM, in Skeagh, parish of Cleenish, 1656. [IWD]

ATKINSON, JAMES, a Scots-Irish student at Glasgow University in 1712. [MUG#198]

AUCHENLECK, Reverend JAMES, in Ballyvelan, Cleenish, County Fermanagh, 1685. [IWD]

AUCHMUTY, ALEXANDER, grant of part of Dromheada, barony of Tullocouch, County Cavan, 24 June 1610. [EPR.8.16]

AUCHMUTY, JOHN, grant of part of Keylagh, barony of Tullocouch, County Cavan, 24 June 1610. [EPR.8.21]

AUCHMUTY, JOHN, a gentleman in Newtown, County Longford, will subscribed on 19 May 1726, probate 13 August 1726 Dublin.

AUCHTERLONIE, ("Atherlawney"), Sir JAMES, servant of the king, was granted Irish denization 13 July 1618. [IPR]

AUSTIN, GEORGE, in the barony of Ardes, County Down, 1659. [C]

AYTON, RICHARD, a schoolmaster in Raphie 1673. [BM.Sloane#202]

AYTON, Sir ROBERT, servant of the king, was granted Irish denization 26 February 1616. [IPR]

BAILLIE, ALEXANDER, in the barony of Ardes, County Down, 1659. [C]

BAILLIE, EDWARD, born 1635, second son of Alexander Baillie of Inishargie, Ringdufferin. [Killaresy g/s, County Down]

BAILLIE, EDWARD, in the barony of Ardes, County Down, 1659. [C]

BAILLIE, EDWARD T., born 1673, minister of Drumbo 1699-1703, died 26 June 1703. [Drumbo g/s]

BAILLIE, JOHN, in the barony of Ardes, County Down, 1659. [C]

BAILLIE, PHILIP, in Dungannon on 8 March 1667.
[Cal.SP.Ire.348/8]

BAILEY, ROBERT, granted lands of Drummore in the parish of Clonchy, County Cavan, on 14 May 1628.
[SP.Dom.Sig.Off.#I/238]

BAILLIE, ROBERT, of Ballyhebrowe, was granted Irish denization 13 May 1634. [IPR]

BAILLIE, WILLIAM, was granted Irish denization and a grant of Toneregin in the barony of Clanchy, County Cavan, 6 August 1610. [IPR]

BAILLIE, WILLIAM, was granted Irish denization 22 June 1629.
[IPR]

BAIRD, JOHN, merchant in Dublin, 1702. [NAS.RD2.86.1.264]

BAIRD, ROBERT, a gentleman in St Johnston, County Donegal, subscribed to his will on 19 December 1713, reference to his son Thomas, his grandson Charles McFarland, Archibald Woods in Transalleagh, County Donegal, Archibald Cunningham a gentleman in Londonderry, William Cowan, son of John Cowan, and his tenants in Strabane - Patrick Bedlow in Church Street, Andrew Park in Castle Street, Alexander Jameson and Claud Scott, probate 21 June 1714 Dublin

BALCONQUALL, WALTER, clerk, was granted Irish denization 25 June 1618. [IPR]

BALFOUR, BARTHOLEMEW, in County Fermanagh, 1659. [C]

BALFOUR, CHARLES, in County Fermanagh, 1659. [C]

BALFOUR, CHARLES, in Lisnaskey, Inniskilling, 1696.
[CTP.vol#42]

BALFOUR, Sir JAMES, 1000 acres at Carawshee and 2000 acres in Legan, County Fermanagh, 1619. [Carew#211/40]

BALFOUR, Lord JAMES, Baron of Clanawly, was granted Irish denization 19 May 1626. [IPR]; 1634 [IWD]

BALFOUR, JOHN, a Scots-Irish student from Inniskillin, at Glasgow University 1720. [MUG#217]

BALFOUR, MICHAEL, Lord Burley, eldest son of Sir James Balfour of Pittendreich and Montquhannie in Fife and Margaret Balfour, grant of Legan and Carowshee, County Fermanagh, 29 June 1610. [PRO.Signet Office Docquet Book, Privy Seal Chancery #21]; was granted Irish denization 29 June 1610. [IPR]

BALFOUR, Sir WILLIAM, in Achahurdur, County Fermanagh, 1659. [C]

BALLENDINE, JAMES, Captain of the Lifeguard of Horse in Carrickfergus on 10 September 1642. [PRO.SP.16.539.1/105]

BAMBER, THOMAS, an Anglo-Irish student at Glasgow University 1711. [MUG#196]

BANN, JAMES, an Anglo-Irish student at Glasgow University in 1714. [MUG#203]

BANNATYNE, ANNE, wife of Reverend John Campbell of Dunoon, minister in Cairncastle, County Antrim, 1714. [NAS.RD4.115.337]

BANNERMAN, ALEXANDER, Captain of Lord Sinclair's Regiment, in Newry, 1642. [PRO.SP.18.120]

BANNERMAN, Mr JAMES, sometime minister at Baltimore, Ireland, fled to Scotland 1643. [SLT#150]

BARBER, JOHN, a preacher, was granted Irish denization 12 February 1618. [IPR]

BARCLAY, ALEXANDER, Major of the Earl of Glencairn's Regiment, in Carrickfergus 1642. [PRO.SP.18.120]

BARCLAY, DAVID, leased lands from Sir William Stewart on 1 November 1622 for 19 years. [PU#545]

BARCLAY, DAVID, of Ladyland, was granted Irish denization on 18 February 1622. [IPR]

BARCLAY, DAVID, clerk in Killaloe, 1715. [IWD]

BARCLAY, GAVIN, chanter of St Patrick's, Cashel, 1664. [IWD]

BARCLAY, GEORGE, Major of Major General Robert Monro's Regiment, in Carrickfergus 1642. [PRO.SP.18.120]

BARCLAY, HUGH, a minister in the Diocese of Clogher, 1634. [TCD.ms.T#1/10]

BARCLAY, HUGH, of Annacley, was granted Irish denization 13 May 1634. [IPR]

BARCLAY, ISOBEL, born 1674, died 26 November 1734. [Dromara g/s]

BARKLAY, JAMES, of Belyselloch, born 1646, died 17 August 1710, father of James, born 1675, a divinity student, died 16 July 1693, Alexander born 1677, a consel at law, diedon 28 October 1705, and Ann born 1683, died 20 February 1705. [Old Abbey Church g/s, Bangor]

BARCLAY, JOHN, of Ballyrolly, was granted Irish denization on 20 May 1617. [IPR]

BARCLAY, Sir MAURICE, grant of 2000 acres in Precinct of Liffer, County Donegal, by 1612. [Cal.SP.Ire.1612/608]

BARCLAY, ROBERT, of Figart, was granted Irish denization 28 November 1617. [IPR]

BARCLAY, ROBERT, Dean of Clogher, 1622, [TCD.msE#3/6]; Was granted Irish denization 13 May 1634. [IPR]

BARCLAY, WILLIAM, burgess of Newton Ards, County Down, 1612. [Cal.SP.Ire.1613/614]

BARCLAY, WILLIAM, in the barony of Ardes, County Down, 1659. [C]

BARR, GAVIN, of Ballymagarachan, born 1654, died 5 March 1730. [Magheralin g/s]

BARR, ROBERT, a merchant in Carrickfergus. [PRONI#T828/4]

BARRY, JAMES, of Raphoe, was granted Irish denization 28 November 1617. [IPR]

BATHURST, JOHN, in Urney, barony of Strabane, County Tyrone, probate 1630

BAXTER, JOHN, of Crossgate, born 1640, died 16 November 1713. [Dromara g/s]

BAXTER, Mrs SARAH, wife of John Barclay, born 1639, died 16 October 1727. [Dromara g/s]

BAYLIE, EDWARD, of Lissgarr, was granted Irish denization on 5 July 1631. [IPR]

BAYLIE, WILLIAM, of Finnyston, in the precinct of Clankee, County Cavan, 3 May 1610. [TCD.ms#N2/2]; Undertaker of the Precinct of Clanchy, County Cavan, 1611; with 1000 acres, appeared at a muster in 1618 with 24 men, 4 muskets, 6 calivers, 8 pikes and 18 swords. [Cal.SP.Ire.1611/384; 1618/501][BMAddMS#18735]

BAYRE, ROBERT, merchant in Dublin, admitted as a burgess and guildsbrother of Glasgow on 11 July 1712. [GBR]

BEATON, JOHN, master of the Hopewell of Larne at the port of Glasgow 11 October 1672. [NAS.E72.10.3]

BEERS, WILLIAM, a Scots-Irish student at Glasgow University in 1714. [MUG#203]

BELL, ANDREW, tenant of John Hamilton of Edenagh, Precinct of Fewes, 1618. [PU#567]

BELL, ANDREW, Major of the Earl of Eglinton's Regiment, in Bangor 1642. [PRO.SP.18.120]

BELL, JAMES, of Bellystockert, born during 1642, died on 8 April 1715. [Comber g/s]

BELL, JOHN, of Balykighe, born 1619, died 27 December 1701, his wife Barbara Dixon, born 1614, died 18 May 1686. [Comber g/s]

BELL, JOHN, of New Comber, born during 1648, died on 1 April 1721. [Comber g/s]

BELL, WILLIAM, tenant of John Hamilton of Edenagh, Precinct of Fewes, 1618. [PU#567]

BELLENDINE, JOHN, son of Sir Lewis Bellendine the Justice Clerk, applied for 2000 acres in Ulster on 25 July 1609. [PU#142]

BELLENDINE, WILLIAM, son of Sir Lewis Bellendine, applied for 2000 acres in Ulster on 13 July 1609. [PU#139]

BENNET, KENTIGERN, a minister in Ireland, a student at Edinburgh University 1650. [CEG]

BENT, JOHN, an Anglo-Irish student at Glasgow University 1712. [MUG#199]

BIGGAR, WILLIAM, born in Scotland, graduated MA from Edinburgh University in 1691, minister in Limerick from 1697 to 1704, in Bangor from 1704 to 1729, died in Scotland during May 1738.[FI#90]

BIGGART, ALEXANDER, of Coleraine, County Londonderry, merchant, was granted Irish denization 19 July 1631. [IPR]

BINTHILL, DAVID, was granted Irish denization 22 June 1615. [IPR]

BIRKBY, OLIVER, a Scots-Irish student at Edinburgh University 1718. [CEG]

BIRSBANE, WILLIAM, Captain of the Earl of Eglinton's Regiment, in Bangor 1642. [PRO.SP.18.120]

BISHOP, JAMES, of Island Taggart, born 1659, died 17 June 1739. [Killinchy g/s, County Down]

BLACKBURN, ANDREW, in Carrickena, County Roscommon, 1708. [IWD]

BLACKBURN, JOHN, a merchant in Londonderry, 1710. [IWD]

BLACKWOOD, JAMES, born 1591, merchant and late provost of Bangor, died on 22 May 1663. [Old Abbey Church g/s, Bangor]

BLACKWOOD, JOHN of Ballyleidy, born 1662, died 11 July 1720. [Old Abbey Church g/s, Bangor]

BLAIR, ALEXANDER, was granted Irish denization 22 June 1615. [IPR]

BLAIR, ALEXANDER, of Bangor, was granted Irish denization 28 November 1617. [IPR]

BLAIR, ALEXANDER, in Maghera, barony of Loghinshoun, County Londonderry, 1659. [C]

BLAIR, BRYCE, Captain of the Earl of Eglinton's Regiment, in Bangor 1642. [PRO.SP.18.120]

BLAIR, BRICE, merchant in Belfast, 1699. [NAS.RD2.82.1050]

BLAIR, HUGH, of Ballyshenog, was granted Irish denization 28 November 1617. [IPR]

BLAIR, JAMES, was granted Irish denization 22 June 1615. [IPR]

BLAIR, JAMES, Captain of the Earl of Leven's Regiment, in Carrickfergus, 1642. [PRO.SP28/120]

BLAIR, JOHN, of Carrickballidonie, was granted Irish denization 20 May 1617. [IPR]

BLAIR, JOHN, born 1680, died 27 October 1720, his wife Janet Lin born 1675, died 20 January 1730. [Kilbride g/s, Antrim]

BLAIR, ROBERT, born in Irvine, Ayrshire, during 1593, sixth son of John Blair of Windyedge, a merchant in Irvine, and Beatrix Mure of Rowallan, educated at Glasgow University, graduated MA in 1614, minister in Bangor from 1623 to 1634, died in Aberdeen on 27 July 1666, husband of (1) Beatrix, daughter of Robert Hamilton a merchant in Edinburgh, who died in 1633, and (2) Catherine, daughter of Hugh Montgomery of Busby. [PHS]; a minister in the diocese of Down, 1634. [TCD.ms.T#1/10]

BLAIR, ROBERT, in Aughandowey, barony of Coleraine, County Londonderry, 1659. [C]

BLAIR, ROBERT, Captain of the Earl of Leven's Regiment, in Carrickfergus, 1642. [PRO.SP28/120]

BLAIR, Sir WILLIAM, Captain of Major General Robert Monro's Regiment, in Carrickfergus 1642. [PRO.SP.18.120]

BLAIR, WILLIAM, in Aughandowey, barony of Coleraine, County Londonderry, 1659. [C]

BLANEY, THOMAS, was granted Irish denization 12 February 1618. [IPR]

BLOOD, WILLIAM, merchant in Dublin, burgess and guildsbrother of Glasgow 20 February 1724. [GBR]

BOOTH, BENJAMIN, merchant aboard the Speedwell of Glenarme at the port of Irvine, Ayrshire, on 22 November 1688. [NAS.E72.12.14]

BORTHWICK, DAVID, chamberlain of Newbattle, Midlothian, applied for 2000 acres in Ulster on 25 July 1609. [PU#141]

BORTHWICK, THOMAS, Captain of the Earl of Lindsay's Regiment, in Bangor 1642. [PRO.SP.28.120]

BORTHWICK, WILLIAM, Major of the Earl of Lindsay's Regiment, in Bangor 1642. [PRO.SP.28.120]

BOSWELL, DAVID, was granted Irish denization 18 August 1607.
[IPR]

BOSWELL, JAMES, was granted Irish denization 18 August 1607.
[IPR]

BOULD, ARCHIBALD, of Ardie, was granted Irish denization 28
November 1617. [IPR]

BOWES, R., a minister in Leck, Leiterkennie County Donegal, 1697.
[NAS.GD22.2.91]

BOWIE, JAMES, Sergeant of H. M. wine cellar, was granted Irish
denization 28 May 1621.[IPR]

BOYD, ANDREW, in Ballymcilluannan, born 1678, died 20
November 1734. [Ballywillin g/s, County Antrim]

BOYDE, ARCHIBALD, of Carntulloch, County Antrim, was granted
Irish denization 28 November 1617. [IPR]

BOYDE, DAVID, of Glasroche, was granted Irish denization 20 May
1617. [IPR]

BOYD, Colonel DAVID, purchased lands from Sir Hugh
Montgomery of the Ardes, which were forfeit on his death to
the Crown as he was not a denizen of Ireland, were granted to
his son and heir Robert Boyd 'for good and faithful services' on
22 March 1624. [Cal. SP.Ire.1624/1173, 1392]

BOYD, DAVID, merchant in Dublin, was admitted as a burgess and
guildsbrother of Glasgow on 24 July 1717. [GBR]

BOYD, FRANCIS, a merchant in Portaferry, County Down, 7
January 1709. [NAS.GD25, SEC.8/862]

BOYD, GEORGE, Captain of the Earl of Eglinton's Regiment, in
Bangor 1642. [PRO.SP.18.120]

BOYD, GEORGE, ship carpenter in Dublin, 1654. [IWD]

BOYD, JAMES, son of James Boyd in Racharie, Ireland, a trooper of
HM Life Guards in Linlithgow 5 June 1678. [CA.1.xxxviii]

BOYD, JOHN, in Drumnavoddy, Seapatrick, County Down, 1659.
[C]

BOYD, JOHN, master of the Mary of Coleraine at the port of
Glasgow 12 August 1670. [NAS.E72.10.2]

BOYD, JOHN, master of the Two Brothers of Coleraine at the port of
Irvine 11 September 1689. [NAS.E72.12.14]

BOYD, JOHN, master of the Elizabeth of Belfast at the port of Ayr 2
April 1690. [NAS.E72.3.24]

BOYD, JOHN, in Telyhubert, born 1640, died 27 December 1707.
[Comber g/s]

BOYD, JOHN, a gentleman in Rathmore, will subscribed on 25 April
1720, reference to his wife, son James, daughters Jane and
Elizabeth, son in law John McDowell, James Crawford, John
McDowell, and Alexander Adair, probate 11 August 1721
Dublin

BOYD, MARY, a widow in Dublin, 1707. [IWD]

BOYD, Lady MARY, widow of Thomas Boyd, in Dublin 1727.
[NAS.GD8#991]

BOYD, ROBERT, son of Colonel David Boyd who had bought land
in Ulster from Lord Hugh Montgomery but had since died. He
'prays that he and his heirs might be made free denizens of
Ireland", 26 June 1626. [Cal.SP.Ire.1626/364][SP.Ire#242/364;
243/377]

BOYD, ROBERT, a merchant in Belfast. [PRONI#SL19/74]

BOYD, ROBERT, master of the James of Londonderry at the port of
Irvine 24 July 1682. [NAS.E72.12.6]

BOYD, ROBERT, master of the Margaret of Larne at the port of
Irvine 15 August 1681. [NAS.E72.12.5]

BOYD, ROBERT, merchant, late of Londonderry, admitted as a
burgess and guildsbrother of Glasgow on 18 January 1715.
[GBR]

BOYD, ROBERT, in Carrickfergus, [PRONI#T828/4]

BOYD, THOMAS, was granted Irish denization 29 January 1611.
[IPR]; Undertaker in Precinct of Strabane, County Tyrone,
1611. [SP.Ire.1611/384]

BOYD, THOMAS, of Crownerston, was granted Irish denization 20
May 1617. [IPR]

BOYD, THOMAS, of Ballehackett, a farmer, was granted Irish
denization 9 February 1625. [IPR]

BOYD, THOMAS, in the barony of Ardes, County Down, 1659. [C]

BOYD, THOMAS, a merchant in Dublin, imprisoned on 22 May
1663. [Cal.SP.Ire.345/149]

BOYD, THOMAS, merchant aboard the Mary of Glenarme at the
port of Irvine 8 July 1682. [NAS.E72.12.5]

BOYD, WILLIAM, a Scots-Irish student at Glasgow University
1709. [MUG#191]

BOYES, JAMES, master of the Janet of Donaghadee at the port of
Irvine 26 July 1681. [NAS.E72.12.3]

BOYLE, ARCHIBALD, was granted Irish denization 20 January
1622. [Privy Seal Chancery, file 1930]

BOYLE, JAMES, master of the Marion of Glenarme at the port of
Irvine 27 September 1685. [NAS.E72.12.9]

BOYLE, JOHN, of Moill, County Donegal, was granted Irish
denization 17 August 1616. [IPR]

BOYLE, JOHN, graduated MA from Edinburgh University in 1596,
to Ireland after 1610, curate of Killyleagh, [PHS]; a minister in
the diocese of Down, 1634. [TCD.ms.T#1/10]

BOYLE, JOHN, master of the St Andrew of Donaghadee at the port of Ayr 8 June 1689. [NAS.E72.3.18]

BOYLE, ROBERT, of Drumfad, was granted Irish denization 20 May 1617. [IPR]

BOYLE, ROBERT, of Morlegh, gentleman, was granted Irish denization 28 November 1624. [IPR]

BOYLE, THOMAS, sr., was granted Irish denization 22 June 1615. [IPR]

BOYLE, WILLIAM, gentleman in County Donegal, was granted Irish denization 17 August 1616. [IPR]

BOYLE, WILLIAM, master of the James of Larne at the port of Irvine 27 March 1691. [NAS.E72.12,18]

BRACKLEG, NINIAN of Newton Donaghadee, was granted Irish denization 20 May 1617. [IPR]

BRADNER, JOHN, student of divinity in Dromore, County Down, husband of Christian Colville, 1714. [NAS.RD4.115.340]

BRICE, JAMES, Captain of the Earl of Eglinton's Regiment, in Bangor 1642. [PRO.SP.18.120]

BRICE, WILLIAM, died on 26 April 1696; his wife Jane Kelso died on 12 October 1697; his sons Arthur died in March 1691 and William died in January 1696. [Drumbeg g/s, County Down]

BRISBANE, ELIZABETH, wife of John Shaw of Ballygelly, was granted Irish denization on 9 February 1625. [IPR]

BRISBANE, JOHN, of Gortlosh, gentleman, was granted Irish denization 9 July 1616; possibly a merchant in Strabane, County Tyrone, ca.1617. [IPR][SBT#29]

BRISBANE, WILLIAM, of Strabane, County Tyrone, was granted Irish denization 19 July 1631. [IPR]

BROCK, Mr WILLIAM, Captain of the John and Thomas of Londonderry, admitted a a burgess and guildsbrother of Glasgow on 22 April 1717. [GBR]

BROWN, ALEXANDER, an Irish student at Edinburgh University in 1697. [CEG]

BROWN, DAVID, born in Stirlingshire, graduated MA from Glasgow University in 1663, minister in Urney from 1677, died at the Siege of Londonderry in 1689. [FI#58]

BROWN, DAVID, a yeoman in Magheragall, County Antrim, 1687. [IWD]

BROWN, HEW, merchant, former apprentice to James Hepburn a merchant burgess, admitted as a burgess and guildsbrother of Glasgow 2 February 1643, settled in Ireland by 1655. [GBR]

BROWN, JAMES, in Connor, County Antrim, 1711. [IWD]

BROWN, JOHN, of Gorgie Mill, applied for 2000 acres in Ulster on 18 July 1609, [PU#140]; was granted Irish denization 23 July 1610, grant of 1000 acres at Carrodownan in the barony of Tullochouche, County Cavan, 23 July 1610, [IPR] [TCD.ms#N2/2]; Undertaker of the Precinct of Tullochone, County Cavan, 1611. [Cal.SP.Ire.1611/384; 1612/608]

BROWN, JOHN, tenant of John Hamilton of Edenagh, Precinct of Fewes, 1618. [PU#567]

BROWN, JOHN, gentleman, servant of the king, was granted Irish denization 24 July 1619. [Privy Seals Chancery, file 1904]

BROWN, JOHN, a merchant in Strabane, County Tyrone, ca.1617. [SBT#29]

BROWN, JOHN, master and merchant of the Crystal of Donaghadee at the port of Irvine, Ayrshire, on 24 June 1669. [NAS.E72.12.1]

BROWN, JOHN, in Carnaglish, County Antrim, 1695. [IWD]

BROWN, JOHN, was granted Irish denization 9 July 1616. [IPR]

BROWN, ROBERT, master of the <u>Anna Helena of Belfast</u> at the port of Irvine, Ayrshire, on 28 May 1689. [NAS.E72.12.14]

BROWN, ROBERT, an Irish student at Glasgow University in 1705. [MUG#183]

BROWN, WILLIAM, in the barony of Ardes, County Down, 1659. [C]

BROWN, WILLIAM, in Coleraine, 1691. [IWD]

BROWN, WILLIAM, a Scots-Irish student at Glasgow University in 1715. [MUG#205]

BROWN, WILLIAM, a Scots-Irish student at Glasgow University in 1719. [MUG#215]

BRUCE, ALEXANDER, son of Sir George Bruce of Carnock, was granted Irish denization 9 November 1613. [IPR]

BRUCE, ALEXANDER, born in 1637, son of Robert Bruce in Kennet, Clackmannanshire, graduated MA from Edinburgh University in 1657, minister in Donaghadie from 1694 to 1697, in Vineash from 1697, died on 16 April 1704, father of Alexander - died 1715, James - a judge in Barbados who died 1749, Marion, Margaret and Rachel, [FI#91]; a minister in Vinecash, County Antrim, formerly of Garland, husband of Margaret Cleland, 1701. [NAS.RD2.85.494]; minister in County Armagh, relict of Margaret Cleland, 1715. [NAS.RD2.105.523]

BRUCE, ALEXANDER, son of Reverend Alexander Bruce and Margaret Cleland in Vinecash, County Antrim, 1701. [NAS.RD2.85.609]

BRUCE, Sir GEORGE, of Carnock, was granted Irish denization on 9 November 1613. [IPR]

BRUCE, GEORGE, son of Sir George Bruce of Carnock, was granted Irish denization on 9 November 1613. [IPR]

BRUCE, JOHN, of Dromekine, was granted Irish denization on 28 November 1617. [IPR]

BRUCE, JOHN, in Shandon, County Cork, 1631. [IWD]

BRUCE, Reverend MICHAEL, minister of Killinchy 1657 to 1661 and 1670 to 1689, died and buried in Scotland during 1693, husband of Jane ..., father of Robert born 1669, died June 1684; Michael born 1670 died June 1672; and Anna died 18 January 1683. [Killinchy g/s, County Down]

BRUCE, ROBERT, was granted Irish denization on 9 November 1613. [IPR]

BRUCE, THOMAS, a clerk, was granted Irish denization on 22 September 1619. [IPR]; archdeacon of Raphoe 1622. [TCD.ms.E#3/6]

BRUCE, WILLIAM, Captain of Sir Mungo Campbell of Lawers' Regiment, in Temple Patrick, 1642. [PRO.SP.18.120]

BRUCE, WILLIAM, a Scots-Irish student at Glasgow University in 1718. [MUG#213]

BRUGES, JAMES, was granted Irish denization on 20 January 1622. [Privy Seal Chancery, file 1930]

BRYCE, ARCHIBALD, merchant in Dublin, later in Glasgow, cnf 1 August 1691 Commissariot of Glasgow

BRYCE, EDWARD, ordained by the Presbytry of Dunbarton in 1595, minister of Broadisland, Ballycarry, in 1613, a minister in the diocese of Connor, 1634. [TCD.ms.T.1/10]

BRYCE, RANDALL, of Kilroot, High Sheriff of County Antrim in 1675. [UJA.11.1.79]

BRYDEN, ANDREW, Captain of Major General Robert Monro's Regiment, in Carrickfergus 1642. [PRO.SP.18.120]

BUCHANAN, JOHN, of Coleraine, was granted Irish denization on 20 May 1617. [IPR]

BUCHANAN, MAURICE, a minister in the Diocese of Clogher, 1622. [TCD.ms.E#3/6]

BUCHANAN, ROBERT, of Glenaquoyn, County Donegal, gentleman, was granted Irish denization on 22 February 1634. [IPR]

BUCHANAN, WILLIAM, burgess of Newton Ards, County Down, 1612. [Cal.SP.Ire.1613/614]

BUCHANAN, WILLIAM, of Donan, was granted Irish denization 28 November 1617. [IPR]

BUCHANAN, JOHN, in the barony of Ardes, County Down, 1659. [C]

BURNE, JAMES, was granted Irish denization 9 July 1616. [IPR]

BURNE, JAMES, of Ramullin, was granted Irish denization 28 November 1617. [IPR]

BURNETT, ANDREW, Scots-Irish, formerly a student at Dublin University, graduated MA at King's College, Aberdeen, 30 August 1725. [KCA#227]

BURNETT, DUNCAN, was granted Irish denization on 10 January 1613. [IPR]

BURNETT, THOMAS, a physician, was granted Irish denization on 26 February 1616. [IPR]

BURNETT, WALTER, gentleman in Dublin, 1695. [IWD]

BURNSIDE, JOHN, a merchant in Silver Street, Londonderry, 1659. [C]

BUTHELL, DAVID, matriculated at St Leonard's College, University of St Andrews, 1632, graduated MA there 1636, minister at Ballymena, County Antrim, 1645. [UJA#13/15]

BUTLER, PETER, an Anglo-Irish student at Glasgow University in 1708. [MUG#190]

BUTTLE, ARTHUR, a Scots-Irish student at Glasgow University in 1719. [MUG#216]

CADOU, JOHN, a Scots-Irish student at Glasgow University in 1715. [MUG#205]

CALDERWOOD, WILLIAM, of Ballyfrenzies, was granted Irish denization on 20 May 1617. [IPR]

CALDWELL, Sir JAMES, father of Captain Hugh Balfour and Elizabeth Balfour, petitioned for the lands of Ballynoone, Ballylour, Oldtown, etc. in Ireland, on 7 December 1695. [CTP.vol.35]

CALDWELL, JOHN, master of the St Andrew of Donaghadee at the port of Irvine, Ayrshire, on 6 February 1690. [NAS.E72.12.16]

CALDWELL, THOMAS, in County Kildare, October 1625. [SP.Ire.Docquets#13/2212]

CALDWELL, Mr WILLIAM, sometime Keeper of the Register of Sasines for Ayrshire, later a minister at Tamin, County Armagh, 13 December 1673. [RPCS.IV.13]

CALLANDER, AGNES, only daughter of the deceased George Callander minister in Glenarme, County Antrim, entered a marriage contract with Andrew Bruce, son of the deceased Alexander Bruce of West Abden, on 2 February 1655. [NAS.RH9.7.43]

CALLANDER, GEORGE, minister in Glenairn, Ireland, husband of Agnes Ricarton, sister of Lieutenant Colonel James Ricarton, 1714. [NAS.RD.4.114.690]

CALLENDAR, WILLIAM, burgess of Newton Ards, County Down, 1612. [Cal.SP.Ire.1613/614]

CALLINEL, JAMES, merchant in Cork, admitted as a burgess and guildsbrother of Glasgow 29 June 1719. [GBR]

CALUM, ARCHIBALD, a Scot, April 1625. [SP.Ire#241/16]

CAMERON, Reverend WILLIAM, in Ballingray, Limerick, serviced as heir to his father James Cameron minister at Strangfoord, on 9 October 1716. [NAS.SH]

CAMPBELL, AGNES, spouse to William McClearne at Auldston, Ireland, 1623. [see John Campbell's testament, Comm. Glasgow]

CAMPBELL, ALEXANDER, minister at Drumore, Ireland, husband of Christian Thomson, father of Christian, 1715. [NAS.RD4.116.49]

CAMPBELL, ALEXANDER, of Barraphaile, surgeon in Coleraine, County Londonderry, admitted as a burgess of Inveraray, Argyll, on 14 January 1718. [Inveraray Burgess Roll]

CAMPBELL, ARCHIBALD, in Camus, Strabane, County Tyrone, probate 1623

CAMPBELL, ARCHIBALD, Captain of Sir Mungo Campbell of Lawers' Regiment, in Temple Patrick, 1642. [PRO.SP.18.120]

CAMPBELL, ARCHIBALD, in Dublin, 1689. [IWD]

CAMPBELL, ARCHIBALD, in Ballyrelie near Rosecrea, King's County, Ireland, in 1725. [NAS.SC54.22.32]

CAMPBELL, CHARLES, of Balsarrache, at Kilrout, County Antrim, 7 May 1628. [NAS.RD429]

CAMPBELL, CHARLES, in the barony of Ardes, County Down, 1659. [C]

CAMPBELL, CHARLES, Justice of the Peace in Louth and Meath, 23 May 1712. [NAS.GD10#498]

CAMPBELL, COLIN, of Ramullin, was granted Irish denization on 28 November 1617. [IPR]

CAMPBELL, COLIN, of Moyres, County Donegal, gentleman, was granted Irish denization on 19 July 1633. [IPR]

CAMPBELL, COLIN, of Balleherring, Ireland, 1636. [NAS.RD494]

CAMPBELL, COLIN, Major of Sir Mungo Campbell of Lawers' Regiment, in Temple Patrick, 1642. [PRO.SP.18.120]

CAMPBELL, COLIN, Captain of the Marquis of Argyll's Regiment, in Dunluce, 1642. [PRO.SP.16.492.58]

CAMPBELL, COLIN, of Belliechem, Ireland, husband of Geills Stewart, 1702. [NAS.RD2.86.2.17]

CAMPBELL, DAVID, in Ireland 1623, brother of John Campbell burgess of Ayr. [see John Campbell's testament 1623 Comm.Glasgow]

CAMPBELL, DOUGALL, a minister in the diocese of Raphoe, 1634. [TCD.ms.T#1/10]

CAMPBELL, Sir DUNCAN, of Auchenbreck, Lieutenant Colonel of the Marquis of Argyll's Regiment, in Dunluce, 1642. [PRO.SP.16.492.58]

CAMPBELL, DUNCAN, of Dunans, Captain of the Marquis of Argyll's Regiment, in Dunluce, 1642. [PRO.SP.16.492.58]

CAMPBELL, DUNCAN, of Inverliver, Captain of the Marquis of Argyll's Regiment, in Dunluce, 1642. [PRO.SP.16.492.58]

CAMPBELL, DUNCAN, Murogh, County Wicklow, 1663. [IWD]

CAMPBELL, DUNCAN, born in Scotland during 1635, graduated MA from Glasgow University in 1655, minister of Killybegs and at Inver from 1673 to 1676, returned to Scotland in 1679, died on 12 November 1707. [FI#58]

CAMPBELL, HEW, chapman, and his elder brother John Campbell, sons of George Campbell portioner of Cluives, accused of money-clipping in Ayrshire, fled to Ireland in July 1637. [RPCS.VI.691]

CAMPBELL, HUGH, son of Josias Campbell in Ireland, apprenticed to Samuel Hay a wright burgess of Edinburgh, for 6 years, on 21 July 1687. [NAS.RH9.17.276]

CAMPBELL, JANET, natural daughter in Ireland of John Campbell
merchant in Ayr who died in February 1623. [see John
Campbell's testament with Commissariot of Glasgow, 1623]

CAMPBELL, JOHN, of Ballehering, was granted Irish denization on
28 November 1617. [IPR]

CAMPBELL, JOHN, of Ballycastle, County Londonderry,
gentleman, was granted Irish denization on 19 July 1633. [IPR]

CAMPBELL, JOHN, Captain of the Marquis of Argyll's Regiment, in
Ballycastle, 1642. [PRO.SP.16.492.58]

CAMPBELL, ['Cumbill'], JOHN, a tenant farmer of 10 acres on the
Agnew estate in 1645. [NAS.GD154/514]

CAMPBELL, JOHN, gentleman in the parish of Donoghmare,
County Down, 1659. [C]

CAMPBELL, JOHN, born in Loudoun, Ayrshire, graduated MA from
Glasgow University in 1674, minister at Carncastle from 1677
to 1714, husband of Agnes Cunningham. [FI#59]

CAMPBELL, JOHN, merchant aboard the Mary of Glenarme at the
port of Irvine on 13 November 1684. [NAS.E72.12.9]

CAMPBELL, JOHN, Captain of Denoon, formerly a minister at
Carncastle, County Antrim, husband of (1) Agnes
Cunningham, (2) Anna Bannatyne, 1715.
[NAS.RD2.104.520/548]

CAMPBELL, JOHN, a merchant from Ballinton, Argyll, now
resident in Londonderry on 15 June 1713. [Argyll Sheriff Court
Book. Vol.6, 4.3.1718]

CAMPBELL, JOSIAS, in Dublin, subscribed to his will on 17 March
1720, probate 2 November 1722 Dublin

CAMPBELL, LAUCHLAN, born in 1675, son of John Campbell in
Kildaloig, Argyll, educated in Glasgow around 1691, a minister
in Dublin from 1707, died on 6 October 1708. [FI#92]

CAMPBELL, MARGARET, relict of James Muir a skipper in Belfast, petitioned the Privy Council on 28 August 1690. [RPCS.15.413]

CAMPBELL, MATTHEW, Captain of the Marquis of Argyll's Regiment, in Ballymoney, 1642. [PRO.SP.16.492.58]

CAMPBELL, PATRICK, in County Mayo, was proclaimed as a robber on 29 April 1669. [Cal.SP.Ire.309#254/60]

CAMPBELL, ROBERT, born in Argyll, educated at Glasgow University in 1663, a minister in Scotland and Ireland from 1671 to 1719, died on 5 October 1722. [FI#59]

CAMPBELL, THOMAS, in Drumcore, barony of Kenaght, County Londonderry, 1659. [C]

CAMPBELL, WILLIAM, Major of the Marquis of Argyll's Regiment, in Ballycastle, 1642. [PRO.SP.16.492.58]

CAMPBELL, WILLIAM, minister at Carnecastle, Ireland, 28 June 1715. [NAS.RS.Bute/4/253]

CAMPSIE, JOHN, in Bishop Gate Street, Londonderry, 1659. [C]

CANNON, WILLIAM, master of the James of Portaferry at the port of Irvine, Ayrshire, on 17 November 1688. [NAS.E72.12.14]

CANNON, WILLIAM, a Scots-Irish student at Glasgow University in 1715. [MUG#206]

CARCAT, ADAM, was granted Irish denization on 12 February 1618. [IPR]

CARCAT, WILLIAM, of Drumcrowe, was granted Irish denization on 12 February 1618. [IPR]

CARMICHAEL, DAVID, son of James Carmichael of Pottieshaw, applied for 1000 acres in Ulster on 6 July 1609. [PU#139]

CARMICHAEL, JAMES, August 1627. [SP.Ire#245/765]

CARMICHAEL, RACHEL, was granted Irish denization on 5 July 1631. [IPR]

CARMICHAEL, WILLIAM, of Island McHugh, was granted Irish denization on 17 August 1616. [IPR]

CARMICHAEL, WILLIAM, was granted Irish denization on 6 February 1619. [IPR]

CARMICHAEL, WILLIAM, Captain of the Earl of Leven's Regiment, in Carrickfergus, 1642. [PRO.SP28/120]

CARR, ARCHIBALD, parson of Dromore, on 24 July 1631. [SP.Ire#252/2003]

CARR, EDWARD, of Ramullin, was granted Irish denization on 28 November 1617. [IPR]

CARR, Sir JAMES, of Crailing Hall, was granted Irish denization on 15 April 1613. [IPR]

CARR, JAMES, of Ramullin, was granted Irish denization on 28 November 1617. [IPR]

CARR, JOHN, of Ramullin, was granted Irish denization on 28 November 1617. [IPR]

CARR, Sir ROBERT, of Ancrum, was granted Irish denization on 15 April 1613. [IPR]

CARR, W., a petitioner in June 1624. [Cal. SP.Ire.1624/1226]

CARRUTHERS, FRANCIS, a tenant of John Hamilton of Edenagh, Precinct of Fewes, in 1618. [PU#567]

CARSON, JOHN, born in Scotland during 1650, graduated MA from Edinburgh University in 1670, a minister at Longford Corboy from 1675 to 1689, died on 18 May 1719. [FI#59]

CASSIDY, PATRICK, an Anglo-Irish student at Glasgow University in 1710. [MUG#195]

CATHCART, ADAM, agent for Ludovick Hamilton, in Devonish, County Fermanagh, 1659. [C]

CATHCART, ALEXANDER, in Devonish, County Fermanagh, 1659. [C]

CATHCART, ALLAN, in Enniskillen, County Fermanagh, will subscribed on 25 December 1705, reference to his wife Anna, Captain Charles Hamilton, William Hamilton, and John Fulton, probate 8 May 1721 Dublin. [IWD]

CATHCART, GABRIEL, in Devonish, County Fermanagh, 1659. [C]

CATHCART, JAMES, of Ballirogan, County Down, was granted Irish denization on 20 May 1617. [IPR]

CATHCART, JOHN, of Ballygreachine in Upper Claneboyne, County Down, subscribed to a lease by James Cathcart of Barneill, Scotland, on 4 October 1617. [NAS.GD180#196]

CATHCART, ROBERT, of Ballymanock, County Tyrone, was was granted Irish denization on 20 May 1617. [IPR]

CATHCART, ROBERT, in Devonish, County Fermanagh, 1659. [C]

CATHERWOOD, ANDREW, a merchant aboard the Anthony of Glenarme at the port of Irvine, Ayrshire, on 11 December 1689. [NAS.E72.12.16]

CATHERWOOD, WILLIAM, a Scots-Irish student at Glasgow University in 1715. [MUG#206]

CAWDOR, JAMES, in Urney, barony of Strabane, County Tyrone, probate 1635

CAWDOR, WILLIAM, was granted Irish denization on 9 July 1616. [IPR]

CHALMERS, ALEXANDER, a merchant in Belfast, 16 May 1729. [NAS.SC20.33.11]

CHAMBERS, Dr JAMES, one of H. M. Physicians, was granted Irish denization on 14 December 1619. [IPR]

CHAMBERS, JAMES, merchant in Belfast, 1714, [NAS.RD4.114.49]

CHALMERS, ALEXANDER, in Belfast, 29 May 1729. [NAS.SC20.33.11]

CHERRY, GEORGE, an Anglo-Irish student at Glasgow University in 1717. [MUG#210]

CHIRNSIDE, DAVID, Captain of Lord Sinclair's Regiment, in Newry, 1642. [PRO.SP.18.120]

CHRISTIAN, JAMES, minister in Badonie, Derry, testament confirmed in 1720 with the Commissariot of Wigtown. [NAS]

CLARK, ALEXANDER, was granted Irish denization on 8 January 1618. [IPR]

CLARK, HENRY, was demised lands in the Precinct of Mountjoy by Sir Robert Hepburn on 10 May 1620. [PU#547]

CLARK, MOSES, a Scots-Irish student at Glasgow University in 1706. [MUG#184]

CLERK, THOMAS, of Drumrainey, a juryman at a Coroner's inquest held at Duncanalley, County Donegal, on 15 September 1660. [Cal.S.P.Ire.1660]

CLEGHORN, JAMES, was granted Irish denization on 8 March 1621. [IPR]

CLELAND, JAMES, DD, was granted Irish denization 28 September 1618. [IPR]

CLELAND, JOSEPH, minister in Ahoghill, Ireland, formerly in Dalserf, husband of Mary Muirhead, 1701. [NAS.RD4.37.762/842]

CLELAND, MARY, relict of Alexander Bruce a minister in County Armagh, 1715. [NAS.RD2.105.523]

CLEPHANE, JAMES, in the precinct of Strabane, County Tyrone, 28 April 1610, [TCD.ms#N2/2]; Undertaker in Precinct of Strabane, County Tyrone, 1611. [Cal.SP.Ire.1611/384]

CLERK, MATHEW, minister in Kilrea, Londonderry, 19 May 1701. [NAS.GD18.5241]

CLOGGIE, JOHN, of Carnetooagh, County Donegal, was granted Irish denization on 17 August 1616.   [IPR]

COCHRANE, BRYCE, Captain of the Earl of Glencairn's Regiment, in Carrickfergus 1642. [PRO.SP.18.120]

COCHRANE, H., a Lieutenant Colonel in Antrim on 19 May 1645. [SP.Ire#260/137]

COCHRANE, HUGH, in the barony of Ardes, County Down, 1659. [C]

COCHRAN, MATTHEW, a Scots-Irish student at Glasgow University in 1707. [MUG#186]

COCHRAN, NINIAN, an Irish student at Glasgow University in 1706. [MUG#185]

COCHRANE, WILLIAM, Major of Robert Home of the Heugh's Regiment, in Carrickfergus, 1642. [PRO.SP.18.120]

COCKBURN, WILLIAM, accused of murdering Sir John Wemyss, failed to appear at the Court of the Chief Place in Ireland during 1627. [SP.Ire.Docquet#14]

COLDEN, Mr ROBERT, a minister, and his family, fled from Ireland to Dunbar during 1643. [SLT#148]

COLLYER, PATRICK, of Ballycubedell, County Antrim, gentleman, was granted Irish denization on 27 June 1634. [IPR]

COLQUHOUN, Sir ALEXANDER, of Corkagh, County Donegal, was granted Irish denization on 20 May 1617. [IPR]

COLQUHOUN, ANDREW, of Droughedonan, was granted Irish denization on 28 November 1617. [IPR]

COLQUHOUN, DANIEL, of Corkie, was granted Irish denization on 20 May 1617. [IPR]

COLQUHOUN, JOHN, of Kenmure, fled to Ireland during 1680. [NAS.GD61/71]

COLQUHOUN, MALCOLM, a burgess of Glasgow, applied for 2000 acres in Ulster on 11 July 1609. [PU#139]

COLQUHOUN, MATTHEW, in Carrickfergus, on 18 November 1642. [NAS.GD164.1600]

COLQUHOUN, PETER, of Droughedonan, was granted Irish denization on 28 November 1617. [IPR]

COLQUHOUN, ROBERT, was granted Irish denization on 14 July 1630. [IPR]

COLTE, ADAM, tenant of John Hamilton of Edenagh, Precinct of Fewes, in 1618. [PU#567]

COLTHARD, JOHN, a minister in Ireland, a student at Edinburgh University in 1647. [CEG]

COLVILLE, ALEXANDER, of Ballymony, County Antrim, clerk, was granted Irish denization on 9 August 1633. [IPR]

COLVILLE, ALEXANDER, born in Scotland, graduated MA from Edinburgh University in 1689, minister of Newtonards from 1696 to 1700, and in Dromore, County Down, from 1700, died on 1 December 1719, [FI#93]; minister in Dromore, Ireland, 1714, [NAS.RD4.115.340]; husband of Christian Thomson and father of Christian, 1715. [NAS.RD4.116.49]

COLVILL, ARCHIBALD, gentleman, was granted Irish denization on 9 July 1616. [IPR]

COLVILLE, CHRISTIAN, daughter of Reverend Alexander Colville in Dromore, County Down, wife of John Bradner, student of divinity, 1714. [NAS.RD4.115.340]

COLVILLE, JAMES, incorporator of Strabane 1613, freeholder in 1622. [SBT#32]

COLVILLE, Sir ROBERT, of Galcorm, High Sheriff of County Antrim in 1670. [UJA.11.1.79]

COLVILLE, WILLIAM, of Ardstraw, High Sheriff of County Tyrone in 1628, Provost of Strabane in 1636. [SBT#32]

COMYNE, ALEXANDER, of Killan, was granted Irish denization on 13 May 1634. [IPR]

CONYNGHAM, ROBERT, minister of Taboyne, in 1652. [IWD]

COOPER, JAMES, in Strabane, County Tyrone, was granted Irish denization on 17 August 1616. [IPR][SBT#22]

COPELAND, WILLIAM, in Monaghan, 1714. [IWD]

CORBET, JOHN, a clerk, 10 August 1639. [Cal.SP.Ire.1639/vol.257]

CORBET, SAMUEL, in Culraine, Ireland, 1702. [NAS.RD4.91.565]

CORNWALL, GABRIEL, matriculated at St Mary's College, University of St Andrews, 1640, a minister at Ballywillan. [UJA#13/15]

CORRY, JAMES, in Derryvollan, County Fermanagh, 1659. [C]

CORRY, JAMES, a Scots-Irish student at Edinburgh University in 1699. [CEG]

CORRY, JOHN, in Derryvollan, County Fermanagh, 1659. [C]

CORRY, WALTER, in Glen, County Monaghan, 1699. [IWD]

CORSAN, DONALD, master of the Hopewell of Larne at the port of Irvine, Ayrshire, 28 September 1685. [NAS.E72.12.9]

CORSLAW, MATHEW, in Strabane, was granted Irish denization on 17 August 1616; in Strabane, County Tyrone, 1617. [IPR][SBT#22]

COGHLAN, THOMAS, of Littekenny, County Donegal, merchant, was granted Irish denization on 19 July 1630. [IPR]

COULSON, JOHN, was demised lands in the Precinct of Mountjoy by Sir Robert Hepburn on 10 May 1620. [PU#547]

COULTER, ALEXANDER, butler of the King's hospital in Oxmanton, 1701. [IWD]

COUTIS, ROBERT, of Corswoods, applied for 1000 acres in Ulster on 4 July 1609; resident agent of Lord Ochiltree on his estate in the precinct of Mountjoy, 1611. [PU#139/546]

COWAN, DANIEL, master of the Katrine of Larne at the port of Glasgow on 1 October 1672; master of the Seaflower of Larne at the port of Irvine, Ayrshire, on 2 November 1683; master of the Swallow of Carrickfergus at the port of Irvine on 11 August 1690. [NAS.E72.10.3; E72.12.8/16]

COWAN, JOHN, merchant in Londonderry, admitted as a burgess and guildsbrother of Glasgow on 15 October 1712. [GBR]

COWAN, JOHN, Alderman of Londonderry, admitted as a burgess of Inveraray, Argyll, on 20 October 1712. [Inveraray Burgess Roll]

COX, WILLIAM, graduated MA from Glasgow University in 1662, minister at Clonmel from 1672, died in 1690. [FI#59]

COWPER, JAMES, of Ballichosta, was granted Irish denization on 20 May 1617. [IPR]

CRAIG, ALEXANDER, was granted Irish denization on 17 August 1616; in Strabane, County Tyrone, 1617. [IPR][SBT#22]

CRAIG, ARCHIBALD, an Irish student at Glasgow University in 1718. [MUG#212]

CRAIG, HUGH, a shopkeeper in Coleraine, County Londonderry, 1659. [C]

CRAIG, Sir JAMES, with 2000 acres in the barony of Tulleknoughe, County Cavan, appeared at a muster in 1618 with 45 men, 7 muskets, 6 calivers, 24 pikes, 2 halberds, and 37 swords. [Cal.SP.Ire.1618/501]; with 2000 acres at Dromheda, County Cavan, 28 March 1619. [Carew#211/34]; 1626. [SP.Ire#242/237]

CRAIG, JAMES, Undertaker of the Plantation of Ulster, grant in Magheryentrim, barony of Fues, County Armagh, 24 June 1610. [EPR.8.21][TCD.ms#N2/2]; Undertaker in Precinct of Fewes, County Armagh, 1611. [Cal.SP.Ire.1611/384; 1612/452]; with ... acres in the precinct of Fewes 28 March 1619. [Carew Mss#211/169]

CRAIG, JOHN, a minister in the diocese of Derry, 1622. [TCD.ms.E#3/6]

CRAIG, JOHN, a merchant in Diamond Street, Londonderry, 1659. [C]

CRAIG, JOHN, master of the Providence of Portaferry at the port of Irvine, Ayrshire, 29 July 1681. [NAS.E72.12.3]

CRAIG, JOHN, a merchant in Belliehoun, County Antrim, and his son John, 1702. [NAS.RD2.86.2.4]

CRAIG, JOHN, a merchant in County Antrim, father of John and Robert, nephew of John Craig a merchant in Glasgow, 1715. [NAS.RD3.145.453]

CRAIGE, MICHAEL, of the Redene, was granted Irish denization on 20 May 1617. [IPR]

CRAIG, ROBERT, maltman, admitted as a burgess and guildsbrother of Glasgow on 2 August 1649, husband of Jean Sempill, settled in Ireland during 1655. [GBR]

CRAIG, WILLIAM, master of the Good Intention of Knock at the port of Irvine, Ayrshire, 4 May 1682. [NAS.E72.12.6]

CRAIGHEAD, ROBERT, a Presbyterian minister in Northern Ireland who petitioned the Queen in 1691. [CTB.#/III.1207, 1258]

CRAIGHEAD, THOMAS, a Scots-Irish student at Edinburgh University in 1691. [CEG]

CRANFORD, ROBERT, merchant aboard the Rose of Belfast at the port of Irvine, Ayrshire, on 15 October 1691. [NAS.E72.12.18]

CRANSTON, THOMAS, was granted Irish denization on 12 February 1618. [IPR]

CRAWFORD, DANIEL, goldsmith in Edinburgh, applied for 2000 acres in Ulster on 4 July 1609. [PU#139]

CRAWFORD, DAVID, son of Owen Crawford in Donegal, butler to the Earl of Tyrconnell, 1609. [PU#151]

CRAWFORD, DAVID, son of Andrew Crawford of Badlair, applied for 1000 acres in Ulster on 4 July 1609. [PU#139]

CRAWFORD, GEORGE, of Lochnories, Ayrshire, was granted Irish denization and a grant of Tullelegan in the precinct of Mountjoy, 29 August 1610. [IPR]

CRAWFORD, GEORGE, master of the George of Strangford at the port of Glasgow on 2 January 1666 and on 23 February 1670. [NAS.E72.10.1/2]

CRAFFORD, HENRY, in Sligo 1659. [C]

CRAWFORD, HUGH, born in 1628, sixth son of Patrick Crawford in Auchenames, Ayrshire, graduated MA from Glasgow University in 1648, a minister in Glenarm from 1685 to 1688, died in May 1692. [FI#60]

CRANSTOUN, NATHANIEL, son of Reverend Michael Cranstoun in Cramond, applied for 1500 acres in Ulster on 13 July 1609. [PU#140]

CRAWFORD, HUGH, master of the Joan of Carrickfergus at the port of Glasgow on 14 August 1666; master of the Venture of Glenarme at the port of Ayr, Ayrshire, on 30 October 1673. [NAS.E72.10.1; E72.3.3]

CRAWFORD, JAMES, a goldsmith burgess of Edinburgh, applied for 2000 acres in Ulster on 6 July 1609. [PU#139]

CRAWFORD, JAMES, of Donnelonge, County Tyrone, gentleman, was granted Irish denization on 19 July 1631. [IPR]

CRAFFORD, Major JAMES, in Ballyniskrean, barony of Loghinshoun, County Londonderry, 1659. [C]

CRAWFORD, JAMES, master of the George of Strangford at the port of Glasgow on 5 March 1666. [NAS.E72.10.1]

CRAWFORD, JOHN, of Bearcroft, applied for 2000 acres in Ulster on 25 July 1609. [PU#142]

CRAWFORD, JOHN, of Ballyaquart, was granted Irish denization on 20 May 1617. [IPR]

CRAWFORD, JOHN, Captain of the Earl of Glencairn's Regiment, in Carrickfergus 1642. [PRO.SP.18.120]

CRAWFORD, JOHN, in Wexford, 1660. [IWD]

CRAWFORD, JOHN, master of the Nightingale of Donaghadee at the port of Ayr, Ayrshire, on 19 November 1677. [NAS.E72.3.4]

CRAWFORD, LAURENCE, son of Major General Laurence Crawford of the Scots Army who was killed at the Siege of Hereford in September 1645, settled in Cavancarragh, County Fermanagh.

CRAWFORD, MALCOLM, Captain of the Earl of Glencairn's Regiment, in Carrickfergus 1642. [PRO.SP.18.120]

CRAWFORD, MATHEW, servant of James, Earl of Abercorn, 9 July 1616; in Strabane, County Tyrone, 1617. [IPR][SBT#22]

CRAWFORD, OWEN, father of David Crawford, in Donegal around 1609. [PU#151]

CRAWFORD, PATRICK, Scottish army officer sent to Ulster in 1608, later settled in Donegal, first Provost of Strabane 1613, killed in 1614. [SBT#30]

CRAFFORD, PATRICK, born 1591, signed an affidavit on 20 April 1631. [SP.Ire#252/1928]

CRAWFORD, ROBERT, of Possil, applied for 2000 acres in Ulster on 25 July 1609. [PU#142]

CRAWFORD, ROBERT, in Ballysallagh, County Down, 1658. [IWD]

CRAWFORD, THOMAS, graduated MA at Edinburgh University 1646, matriculated at St Leonard's College, University of St Andrews, 1646, a minister in Donegore 1655. [CEG][UJA#13/15]

CRAWFORD, THOMAS, an Irish student at Glasgow University in 1718. [MUG#212]

CRAWFORD, WILLIAM, of Cunningburn, was granted Irish denization on 20 May 1617. [IPR]

CRAWFORD, WILLIAM, of Droughedonan, was granted Irish denization on 28 November 1617. [IPR]

CRAWFORD, WILLIAM, in the barony of Ardes, County Down, during 1659. [C]

CRAWFORD, WILLIAM, merchant aboard the Anna of Larne at the port of Irvine, Ayrshire, on 1 November 1669. [NAS.E72.12.1]

CRAWFORD, WILLIAM a tailor in Dublin, 1702. [IWD]

CRAFFORD, WILLIAM, in Belfast, County Antrim, subscribed to his will on 22 May 1716, reference to his wife Janet, his only son David, grandson William Crafford, granddaughter Ann Crafford, daughter Helenor, wife of Roger Haddock, grandson John Haddock, sister Grissell McCologh, George McCartney in Belfast, Reverend John Kirkpatrick, Robert Donaldson attorney, Robert Stevenson, Hugh Moore, witnesses John Chalmers and Benjamin Patterson merchants, and William King servant to Samuel McClinton innkeeper, all in Belfast, probate 11 October 1716 Dublin.

CREICHTOUN, ABRAHAM, brother of Creichton of Brunstoun, applied for 2000 acres in Ulster on 6 July 1609. [PU#139]

CREIGHTON, ABRAHAM, in County Fermanagh, 1659. [C]

CREITON, ALEXANDER, of Aghalaghan, County Fermanagh, a juryman in Inniskillen on 28 February 1624. [Cal.SP.Ire.1624#1157]

CREICHTON, ALEXANDER, in Dungannon on 15 March 1667. [Cal.SP.Ire.348/8]

CREICHTON, GEORGE, of Virginia, was granted Irish denization on 13 May 1634. [IPR]

CREIGHTOWN, ISABEL, wife of John Creightown in Tullylegan, County Tyrone, was granted Irish denization on 27 June 1634. [IPR]

CREIGHTOWN, JAMES, was granted Irish denization on 29 April 1622. [IPR]

CREIGHTOWN, JOHN, of Tullylegan, County Tyrone, gentleman, was granted Irish denization on 27 June 1634. [IPR]

CREIGHTON, JOHN, in Crum, County Fermanagh, will subscribed to on 14 November 1715, reference to David Creighton of Lifford, County Donegal, and his eldest son Abraham, sister Mary, aunt Marianna Willoughby, Sir Gustavus Home, Sir Raplh Gore, Brigadier david Creighton, executors James Hamilton in Brownhall and his brother Abraham Hamilton, witnesses Robert Hamilton, Robert Richardson and William Armstrong, probate 14 January 1716 Dublin

CRERIE, ANDREW, of Findewoyre, County Tyrone, weaver, was granted Irish denization on 17 August 1616. [IPR]

CRIGHTON, ABRAHAM, of Drumboorie, County Fermanagh, was granted Irish denization on 17 August 1616. [IPR]

CRIGHTON, DAVID, in Ireland, 13 April 1638; 31 August 1643. [NAS.RS25.27.146; RS.25.31.449]

CRIGHTON, EDWARD, of Duncandle, a juryman at a Coroner's inquest held at Duncanalley, County Donegal, on 15 September 1660. [Cal.S.P.Ire.1660]

CRIGHTON, GEORGE, a minister in Ireland, 31 August 1643. [NAS.RS26.31.449]; in Ireland 25 February 1659. [NAS.GD18/1473]

CRIGHTON, JAMES, of Aughelane, County Fermanagh, was granted Irish denization on 17 August 1616. [IPR]

CRICHTON, JOHN, in Dungannon on 15 March 1667. [Cal.SP.Ire.348/8]

CRICHTON, JOHN, born in Ireland, son of Alexander Crichton of Leslenan, a trooper in HM Life Guards in Linlithgow 5 June 1678. [CA.1.xxxix]

CREICHTOUN, THOMAS, of Brunstoun, applied for 2000 acres in Ulster on 20 July 1609. [PU#141]

CRIGHTON, THOMAS, agent for Lord Aubigny, William Dunbar, William Bayley, and John Ralston, 29 July 1611. [Cal.SP.Ire.1611/204]

CRIGHTON, THOMAS, of Aghehan, County Donegal, was granted Irish denization on 17 August 1616. [IPR]

CRIGHTON, THOMAS, of Aghaloue, County Fermanagh, was granted Irish denization on 28 November 1617. [IPR]

CRIGHTON, WILLIAM, Lord Sanquhar, was granted Irish denization on 6 March 1620. [IPR]

CROOKS, HENRY, a minister at Minimar, County Derry, father of Ann 8 October 1736. [NAS.RS.Argyll.7.215]

CROZIER, JOHN, in Magherydunbar, 1717. [IWD]

CRUICKSHANK, RICHARD, master of the Rowberry of Londonderry at the port of Irvine, Ayrshire, on 4 April 1690. [NAS.E72.12.16]

CRUMP, JOHN, a Scots-Irish student at Glasgow University in 1718. [MUG#213]

CUDBERT, JOHN, of Bellybunan, born 1656, died 20 October 1717, father of David born 1688, died 16 May 1711, and Michael born 1697, died 12 March 1718. [Killinchy g/s, County Down]

CUFFIES, JOHN, died on 2 April 1688. [Tullymacnous g/s, County Down]

CUFFIES, WILLIAM, died on 2 April 1688. [Tullymacnous g/s, County Down]

CUNNINGHAM, ADAM, of Ballegin, was granted Irish denization on 28 November 1617. [IPR]

CUNNINGHAM, ADAM, master of the Anna of Coleraine at the port of Irvine, Ayrshire, on 9 November 1668, and of the Agnes of Coleraine at the port of Irvine on 10 May 1669. [NAS.E72.12.1]

CUNNINGHAM ALEXANDER, minister in Enver, County Donegal, was granted Irish denization on 17 August 1616. [IPR]; a minister in the diocese of Raphoe, 1622. [TCD.ms.E#3/6];

CUNNINGHAM, ALEXANDER, of Powton, Sorbie, Wigtonshire, applied for 2000 acres in Ulster on 25 July 1609, [PU#142]; gentleman, was granted Irish denization and a grant of Moynargan in the barony of Boylagh and Bonnagh, County Donegal, on 29 August 1610, [IPR] [TCD.ms#N2/2]; Undertaker in the Precinct of Boylagh, County Donegal, 1611. [Cal.SP.Ire.1611/384]; with 1000 acres at Moynagan, County Donegal, 28 March 1619. [Carew Mss#211/82]

CUNNINGHAM, ALEXANDER, of Ballesallagh, gentleman, was granted Irish denization on 28 November 1624. [IPR]

CUNNINGHAM, ALEXANDER, was granted Irish denization on 5 June 1629. [IPR]

CUNNINGHAM, ALEXANDER, Captain of the Earl of Glencairn's Regiment, in Carrickfergus 1642. [PRO.SP.18.120]

CUNNINGHAM, ANDREW, a planter on the London Plantation 20 March 1627. [SP.Ire#244/616]

CUNNINGHAM, Mr ANDREW, Dean of Raphoe, 1630. [SP.Ire#251/1758]

CUNNINGHAM, BERNARD, a settler on the Grocers' Property on the London Plantation 20 March 1627. [SP.Ire#244/616]

CUNNINGHAM, CLAUD, Donoghdie, was granted Irish denization on 20 May 1617. [IPR]

CUNNINGHAM, CUTHBERT, was granted Irish denization and grant of Coole McItriers in the precinct of Portalagh in the barony of Raffoe, County Donegal, on 19 September 1610. [IPR] [TCD.ms#N2/2]; Undertaker in Precinct of Portlogh, County Donegal, 1611. [Cal.SP.Ire.1611/384]; with 1000 acres at Dromagh, Prcinct of Portlough, 28 March 1619. [Carew Mss#211/86]

CUNNINGHAM, DAVID, of Drumfad, was granted Irish denization on 20 May 1617. [IPR]

CUNNINGHAM, Reverend DAVID, and wife Anna Kerr, in Connor, 1696. [NAS.RD4.79.124]; born in Ayrshire, graduated MA from Glasgow University in 1667, a minister in Antrim and Connor from 1671 to 1689, died in Scotland on 21 May 1697. [FI#60]

CUNNINGHAM, GABRIEL, of Tulliscanly, was granted Irish denization on 12 February 1618. [IPR]

CUNNINGHAM, HUGH, of Castlespick, was granted Irish denization on 20 May 1617. [IPR]

CUNNINGHAM, Sir JAMES, of Glengarnoch, was granted Irish denization on 20 July 1610. [IPR]; grant of Dacrosscroose, barony of Raffoe, on 20 July 1610. [EPR.8.10][TCD.ms#N2/2]; with 2000 acres at Darastrosse and Portlough, Precinct of Portlough, 28 March 1619. [Carew Mss#211/85]

CUNNINGHAM, JAMES, was granted Irish denization on 9 July 1616. [IPR]

CUNNINGHAM, JAMES, of Ballyachan, County Donegal, was granted Irish denization 17 August 1616. [IPR]; Undertaker in Precinct of Portlogh, County Donegal, 1611. [Cal.SP.Ire.1611/384;1612/608]; with 1000 acres at Moyege in the Precinct of Portlough on 28 March 1619, [Carew Mss#211/84]

CUNNINGHAM, JAMES, was granted Irish denization 29 May 1629. [IPR]

CUNNINGHAM, JAMES, graduated MA at the University of Glasgow 1654 or possibly at the University of St Andrews in 1648, minister in Antrim 1659-1670. [UJA#13/15]

CUNNINGHAM, JANE, wife of John Symington, in County Tyrone, was granted Irish denization 27 June 1634. [IPR]

CUNNINGHAM, JEANET, of Portalough, County Donegal, widow, was granted Irish denization 19 July 1631. [IPR]

CUNNINGHAM, Lady JOAN, wife of John Cunningham, was granted Irish denization 28 November 1624. [IPR]

CUNNINGHAM, JOHN, of Rawis, applied for 2000 acres in Ulster on 20 July 1609. [PU#141]

CUNNINGHAM, JOHN, of Crafield, gentleman, was granted Irish denization 16 July 1610. [IPR]; Undertaker in Precinct of Portlogh, County Donegal, 1611. [Cal.SP.Ire.1611/384]; grant of Donboy, precinct of Portelogh, barony of Raffoe, County Donegal, 16 July 1610. [EPR.8.10][TCD.ms#N2/2]; with 1000 acres at Dunboy, Precinct of Portlough, 28 March 1619. [Carew Mss#211/84]

CUNNINGHAM, JOHN, of Homill, a Scot, granted of part of Moyegh, precinct of Porteleugh, barony of Raffoe, County Donegal, on 19 July 1610. [EPR8.40][TCD.ms#N2/2]; was granted Irish denization on 16 July 1610. [IPR]

CUNNINGHAM, JOHN, of Rinchrivie, was granted Irish denization on 20 May 1617. [IPR]

CUNNINGHAM, JOHN, of Loughrissone, was granted Irish denization on 9 February 1625. [IPR]

CUNNINGHAM, JOHN, St Michael's Lane, Dublin, 1629. [SP.Ire#249/1504]

CUNNINGHAM, Sir JOHN, was granted Irish denization on 23 May 1629. [IPR]

CUNNINGHAM, JOHN, merchant in the City of Londonderry, was granted Irish denization on 19 July 1631. [IPR]

CUNNINGHAM, JOHN, a merchant freeman of Newton, County Down, sometime provost of Newtown, 1644. [Hunter of Hunterstone MS#9]

CUNNINGHAM, JOHN, Lieutenant Colonel in Antrim on 19 May 1645. [SP.Ire#260/137]

CUNNINGHAM, JOHN, of Bedland, a rebel in 1666, apprehended in Ireland, to be returned to Scotland via Ayr or Greenock, then imprisoned in Dunbarton Castle, 4 February 1669. [RPCS.II.595]

CUNNINGHAM, JOHN, born in Ayrshire, graduated MA from Glasgow University in 1665, a minister in Donaghadee, died in March 1689. [FI#60]

CUNNINGHAM, JOHN, a Scots-Irish student at Glasgow University 1708. [MUG#190]

CUNNINGHAM, Lady KATHERINE, was granted Irish denization 17 August 1627. [IPR]

CUNNINGHAM, MARION, in Glasgow, relict of Reverend Hew Vasse in Duluce, Ireland, cnf 30 September 1670 Commissariot of Glasgow

CUNNINGHAM, MICHAEL, Justice of the Peace for Tyrone, 1630. [SP.Ire#257/1144]

CUNNINGHAM, PATRICK, of Portlough, was granted Irish
denization on 28 November 1617. [IPR]

CUNNINGHAM, PATRICK, of Imlegh, gentleman, was granted
Irish denization on 28 November 1624. [IPR]

CUNNINGHAM, ROBERT, a minister in the diocese of Down, 1622.
[TCD.ms.E#3/6]; a minister in Raphoe 1630.
[SP.Ire#251/1758]; born in Ayrshire, graduated MA from
Glasgow University in 1608, minister in Ireland from 1615 to
1636, died in Irvine, Ayrshire, on 29 March 1637, husband of
Isabel, daughter of Hugh Montgomery of Busby, father of
Robert later minister of Broadisland from 1646 to 1697, James
later minister in Antrim from 1656 to 1670, Margaret, Janet,
etc.[PHS]

CUNNINGHAM, ROBERT, born in Ayrshire, educated at Glasgow
University 1621, graduated MA in 1624, a minister in Ulster
from 1627 to 1647, died in June 1654, buried at Taughboyne,
probate 5 July 1654, husband of Frances Cunningham, father of
Hugh, William and Elizabeth. [PHS]

CUNNINGHAM, ROBERT, Captain of the Earl of Glencairn's
Regiment, in Carrickfergus 1642. [PRO.SP.18.120]

CUNNINGHAM, ROBERT, matriculated at St Salvador's College,
University of St Andrews, 1640, graduated MA there 1643,
minister at Templecorran. [UJA#13/15]

CUNNINGHAM, ROBERT, in the barony of Ardes, County Down,
1659. [C]

CUNNINGHAM, ROBERT, in Dungannon on 8 March 1667.
[Cal.SP.Ire.348/8]

CUNNINGHAM, Major THOMAS, a surgeon. [IWD]

CUNNINGHAM, WILLIAM, was granted Irish denization on 9 July
1616. [IPR]

CUNNINGHAM, WILLIAM, of Donaghdie, was granted Irish
denization on 20 May 1617. [IPR]

CUNNINGHAM, WILLIAM, of Drumcrowe, was granted Irish denization on 12 February 1618. [IPR]

CUNNINGHAM, WILLIAM, of Gortinleane, gentleman, was granted Irish denization on 28 November 1624. [IPR]

CUNNINGHAM, WILLIAM, of Rathmullin, County Donegal, clerk, was granted Irish denization 19 July 1631. [IPR]; a minister in the dioces of Raphoe, 1622, 1634. [TCD.ms.E#3/6; ms.T#1/10]; Justice of the Peace for County Donegal in 1629. [Cal.SP.Ire.1629/1437]

CUNNINGHAM, WILLIAM, of Carnony, County Tyrone, was granted Irish denization 19 July 1631. [IPR]; Justice of the Peace for Tyrone 1630s. [SP.Ire#257/1144]

CUNNINGHAM, WILLIAM, in Articlare, County Londonderry, 1635. [NAS.RH15.91.61]

CUNNINGHAM, WILLIAM, Lieutenant Colonel of the Earl of Glencairn's Regiment, in Carrickfergus 1642. [PRO.SP.18.120]

CUNNINGHAM, WILLIAM, Captain of the Earl of Glencairn's Regiment, in Carrickfergus 1642. [PRO.SP.18.120]

CURROUGH, PETER, a yeoman of Scaboe in the parish of Newton, County Down, leased 40 acres of Ballinebarns, from Sir Hugh Montgomery on 4 April 1610. [NAS.GD180#194]

CUTHBERT, THOMAS, an Irish student at Glasgow University 1718. [MUG#212]

CUTHBERT, ALLAN, merchant, eldest son of John Cuthbert a fisher burgess, admitted as a burgess and guildsbrother of Glasgow 17 February 1641, settled in Ireland by 1655. [GBR]

CUTHBERT, Mr THOMAS, Dublin, admitted as a burgess and guildsbrother of Glasgow on 16 June 1721. [GBR]

CUTHBERTSTON, THOMAS, was granted Irish denization on 17 August 1616, a merchant in Strabane, County Tyrone, 1617. [IPR][SBT#22]

DALLAWAY, ROBERT, in Dublin, 1699. [NAS.RD3.92.375]

DALRYMPLE, JAMES, brother to Dalrymple of Stair, applied for 2000 acres in Ulster on 6 July 1609. [PU#139]

DALYELL, THOMAS, Captain of Major General Robert Monro's Regiment, in Carrickfergus 1642. [PRO.SP.18.120]

DALZIEL, JAMES, in the barony of Castlereagh, County Down, 1659. [C]

DALZIEL, WILLIAM, graduated MA from Edinburgh University in 1597, a minister in Donaghery and Stewartstown, County Tyrone, from 1614 to 1634, [PHS]; minister in Diocese of Armagh during 1622. [TCD.msE#3/6]

DANIELSTON, CHARLES, of Proveston, was granted Irish denization on 20 May 1617. [IPR]

DARROCH, JOHN, born in Argyll, educated at Edinburgh University around 1665, minister in Glenarm and Cushendall from 1688 to 1690, died in Scotland on 6 May 1730. [FI#61]

DARRAGH, WILLIAM, of Dirrelowran, County Tyrone, clerk, was granted Irish denization 19 July 1633. [IPR]

DAVIDSON, JOHN, tenant of John Hamilton of Edenagh, Precinct of Fewes, 1618. [PU#567]

DAVIDSON, JOHN, master of the Happy Return of Portaferry at the port of Ayr 25 March 1673. [NAS.E72.3.3]

DAVIDSON, ROWIE, and his son William Davidson in Dalincover, Carrick, thieves, who fled to Ireland 1628. [RPCS.I.444]

DAVIE, JAMES, master of the Elizabeth of Larne at the port of Glasgow 24 July 1666. [NAS.E72.10.1]

DAVIE, WALTER, merchant in Dublin, admitted as a burgess and guildsbrother of Glasgow on 20 February 1724. [GBR]

DEAN, JOHN, tenant of John Hamilton of Edenagh, Precinct of Fewes, 1618. [PU#567]

DEAN, WILLIAM, master and merchant of the Margaret of Larne at the port of Irvine, Ayrshire, in April 1669. [NAS.E72.12.1]

DEMPSTER, JANE, a tenant of Sir William Stewart, around 1620. [PU#545]

DENNISTON, GEORGE, a merchant in Dublin, subscribed to his will on 20 March 1717, reference to his wife Jane Craigie, son William, witnesses William Johnston in Finglassbridge, County Dublin, Margaret Denniston and Barnaby Rider, probate 8 May 1818 Dublin

DENISTON, WALTER, of Tawnagh, County Donegal, gentleman, was granted Irish denization on 19 July 1631. [IPR]

DENNISTON, WILLIAM, a Scots-Irish student at Glasgow University 1715. [MUG#205]

DENNY, JOHN, a merchant in Pomp Street, Londonderry, 1659. [C]

DEWAR, DAVID, matriculated at St Leonard's College, University of St Andrews, 1622, curate in Glenarm, Connor, 1634. [UJA#13/15]

DEWAR, ROBERT, matriculated at St Leonard's College, University of St Andrews, 1650, graduated MA there 1653, minister at Connor 1658. [UJA#13/15]

DICK, JAMES, of Raphoe, was granted Irish denization on 28 November 1617. [IPR]

DICK, ROBERT, was granted Irish denization on 22 June 1615. [IPR]

DICKSON, JAMES, passenger on the James of Belfast at the port of Ayr 13 October 1673. [NAS.E72.3.3]

DICKSON, JOHN, born 1666, died 27 September 1728. [Blaris g/s, County Down]

DOISH, ALEXANDER, master of the Providence of Coleraine at the port of Ayr 2 July 1686. [NAS.E72.3.16]

DONALDSON, JOHN, of Glenarm, High Sheriff of County Antrim in 1633 and 1665. [UJA.11.1.79]

DONALDSON, JOHN, of Maghermorne, was granted Irish denization on 13 May 1634. [IPR]

DONALDSON, NEHEMIAH, a Scots-Irish student at Glasgow University in 1706. [MUG#184]

DONALDSON, ROBERT, master of the Janet of Portaferry at the port of Irvine, Ayrshire, 18 July 1683. [NAS.E72.12.7]

DONINGE, JOHN, 'rufus', was granted Irish denization on 17 August 1616; in Dunnalong, barony of Strabane, County Tyrone, 1617. [IPR][SBT#23]

DONNON, ANDREW, a Scots-Irish student at Glasgow University 1708. [MUG#189]

DOOK, ALEXANDER, master of the Providence of Coleraine at the port of Irvine, Ayrshire, on 27 February 1686. [NAS.E72.12.11]

DOUGALL, ALEXANDER, of Ramullin, was granted Irish denization on 28 November 1617. [IPR]

DOUGLAS, ANDREW, master of the Providence of Coleraine at the port of Irvine, Ayrshire, on 3 May 1683. [NAS.E72.12.8]

DOUGLAS, ARCHIBALD, son of Sir James Douglas, was granted Irish denization in April 1611. [IPR]

DOUGLAS, GEORGE, of Sheill, applied for 2000 acres in Ulster on 20 July 1609. [PU#141]

DOUGLAS, Sir GEORGE, was granted Irish denization in January 1611. [IPR]

DOUGLAS, GEORGE, son of Sir George Douglas, was granted Irish denization in January 1611. [IPR]

DOUGLAS, JAMES, of Clapperton, applied for 2000 acres in Ulster on 25 July 1609. [PU#142]

DOUGLAS, JAMES, son of Sir George Douglas, was granted Irish denization in January 1611. [IPR]

DOUGLAS, Sir JAMES, of Spott, East Lothian, was granted Irish denization on 23 July 1610, grant of Clancarney in the barony of Fewes, County Armagh, 23 July 1610, [IPR][TCD.ms#N2/2]; Undertaker in Precinct of Fewes, County Armagh, 1611. [Cal.SP.Ire.1611/384]

DOUGLAS, JOHN, an Irish student at Glasgow University 1718. [MUG#212]

DOUGLAS, JOSEPH, of Pumpharstoun, applied for 2000 acres in Ulster on 25 July 1609. [PU#142]

DOUGLAS, Sir ROBERT, Treasurer of the Prince's Household, was granted Irish denization on 31 May 1621. [Historical Manuscript Commission#3/23]

DOUGLAS, WILLIAM, of Ballyhallaghan, was granted Irish denization 27 June 1634. [IPR]

DRUMMOND, ALEXANDER, Captain of the Earl of Lothian's Regiment, in Carrickfergus in 1642. [PRO.SP.28.120]

DRUMMOND, DAVID, of Mylnab, born ca.1612, eldest son of James Drummond and Marion Murray, educated at St Andrews University, minister in Crieff 1635-1649, Episcopal Rector of Omagh 1668, killed at Clogher 1676, husband of Isabel Sibbald, father of John and David. [F4.265]

DRUMMOND, Sir JOHN, of Bordland, Menteith, Undertaker of the Plantation of Ulster, grant in Ballymagoiech, barony of Strabane, County Tyrone, 3 June 1610.
[EPR.8.16][TCD.ms#N2/2] ; Undertaker in Precinct of Strabane, County Tyrone, 1611; with 1000 acres in Strabane appeared at a muster in 1618 with 21 men.
[Cal.SP.Ire.1611/384; 1612/501, 608]; with 1000 acres at Ballymeyna, County Tyrone, on 28 March 1619. [Carew

Mss#211/130]; in The Rathe, County Tyrone, 1625. [IWD]

DRUMMOND, JOHN, Captain of Sir Mungo Campbell of Lawers'
Regiment, in Temple Patrick, 1642. [PRO.SP.18.120]

DRUMMOND, MALCOLM, of Ballewitticocke, gentleman, was
granted Irish denization 28 November 1624. [IPR]

DRUMMOND, MALCOLM, was granted Irish denization on 29 May
1629. [IPR]

DRUMMOND, ROBERT, Captain of the Earl of Lindsay's Regiment,
in Bangor 1642. [PRO.SP.28.120]

DRUMMOND, THOMAS, a non-conformist minister imprisoned at
Lifford in 1669. [Cal.SP.Ire]

DRUMMOND, WILLIAM, Captain of Major General Robert
Monro's Regiment, in Carrickfergus 1642. [PRO.SP.18.120]

DUCHALL, JAMES, a Scots-Irish student at Glasgow University
1710. [MUG#194]

DUDGEON, JAMES, a merchant in Dublin, and James Dudgeon, a
merchant burgess of Inverkeithing, Fife, on 20 April 1698.
[NAS.GD10.842]

DUN, PETER, merchant aboard the John of Portaferry at the port of
Irvine, Ayrshire, on 14 August 1682. [NAS.E72.12.5]

DUNBAR, ALEXANDER, of Egernes, Galloway, applied for 2000
acres in Ulster on 13 July 1609, [PU#139]; was granted Irish
denization and a grant of Killkerhan in the barony of Bannagh,
County Donegal, on 19 September 1610,
[IPR][TCD.ms#N2/2]; Undertaker in the Precinct of Boylagh,
County Donegal, 1611. [Cal. SP.Ire.1611/384]

DUNBAR, ALEXANDER, was granted Irish denization on 12
February 1618 [IPR]

DUNBAR, ALEXANDER, a minister in the Diocese of Clogher,
1622. [TCD.ms.E#3/6]

DUNBAR, DAVID, of Coronary, Ireland, 1715. [NAS.RD2.105.820]

DUNBAR, GEORGE, was granted Irish denization on 12 February 1618. [IPR]

DUNBAR, GEORGE, a minister in Ayrshire from 1599 to 1622, to Ireland in 1624, a preacher in Carrickfergus, Ballymena and Larne, died in Scotland during December 1641, husband of (1) Jean Crawford, (2) Margaret Wallace, father of Samuel, George, Margaret and Marian, [PHS]; a minister in Connor by September 1631. [SP.Ire#252/2020]

DUNBAR, JOHN, of Avoch, applied for 2000 acres in Ulster on 25 July 1609. [PU#142]

DUNBAR, JOHN, Wigtonshire, an Undertaker in the Precinct of Magheraboy, County Fermanagh, 1611. [Cal.SP.Ire.1611/384] [TCD.ms#N2/2]; with 1000 acres at Drumcro, precinct of Magheraboy, 28 March 1619. [Carew Mss#211/73]

DUNBAR, JOHN, of Knockfergus, was granted Irish denization on 28 November 1617. [IPR]

DUNBAR, JOHN, and his son James, were granted Irish denization on 12 February 1618. [IPR]

DUNBAR, Sir JOHN, agent in County Fermanagh for Sir Jeremy Lindsay, 1632. [SP.Ire#253/2090]

DUNBAR, JOHN, in Lanesborough, County Longford, son of George Dunbar of Knockmuir, ca.1681. [NAS.RS37.5.102/198]

DUNBAR, ROBERT, a minister in the diocese of Connor, 1622 and 1634. [TCD.ms.E#3/6; ms.T#1/10]; rector of Kilraghts 1631. [SP.Ire#252/1931]

DUNBAR, THOMAS, a schoolmaster in Enniskillen, Diocese of Clogher, 1673. [BM.Sloane#202]

DUNBAR, WILLIAM, of Enterkin, was granted Irish denization and a grant of 1000 acres at Dromuck, County Cavan, 29 August 1610. [IPR] [TCD.ms#N2/2]; Undertaker of the Precinct of Clanchy, Co. Cavan, 1611. [Cal.SP.Ire.1611/384; 1612/608]

DUNBAR, WILLIAM, in Magheryacross, County Fermanagh, 1659. [C]

DUNCAN, JAMES, master and merchant of the Margaret of Larne at the port of Irvine, Ayrshire, on 30 September 1669. [NAS.ER72.12.1]

DUNCAN, MARGARET, who had been crippled in both hands by the Irish rebels, given one dollar on 29 March 1644 by the Kirk Session of Elgin, Morayshire. [Elgin Kirk Session Records]

DUNDAS, Captain ALEXANDER, was granted land by Sir Patrick Agnew in 1635. [NAS.GD154.509.5]

DUNDAS, HUGH, gentleman, in the barony of Castlereagh, County Down, 1659. [C]

DUNLOP, ALEXANDER, a tenant farmer with 33 acres on the Agnew estate in 1645. [NAS.GD154/514]

DUNLOP, DAVID, master and merchant of the ..... of Larne at the port of Irvine 9 June 1669. [NAS.E72.12.1]

DUNLOP, HUGH, of Mullaghes, a yeoman, was granted Irish denization on 9 February 1625. [IPR]

DUNLOP, WILLIAM, was granted Irish denization on 29 January 1611. [IPR]

DUNN, PATRICK, educated at Marischal College, Aberdeen, 1658, MD of Dublin and of Oxford, founded a hospital in Dublin. [MCA.2.226]

DUNSMOOR, SAMUEL, merchant aboard the Anthony of Carrickfergus at the port of Irvine, Ayrshire, on 26 July 1682. [NAS.E72.12.5]

DURHAM, JAMES, Captain of Robert Home of the Heugh's Regiment, in Carrickfergus, 1642. [PRO.SP.18.120]

DURY, ROBERT, matriculated at St Leonard's College, University of St Andrews, 1628, graduated MA there 1631, curate of Ardquin. [UJA#13/15] minister at Blaris 1628. [UJA#13/15]

DYER, HUGH, master of the John and Ann of Coleraine at the port of Irvine, Ayrshire, on 25 January 1691. [NAS.E72.12.17]

DYKES, ANDREW, of Londonderry, was granted Irish denization on 28 November 1617. [IPR]

ECCLES, GILBERT, in Clownish, County Fermanagh, 1659. [C]

ECHLIN, JOHN, of Ercham, a farmer, was granted Irish denization 9 February 1625. [IPR]

ECHLIN, JOHN, Chancellor of Down 1629. [UJA#13/15]

ECHLIN, JOHN, of Ballyphillip, County Down, clerk, was granted Irish denization 9 August 1633. [IPR]

ECHLIN, MARGARET, wife of Reverend Robert Maxfield, Was granted Irish denization 9 February 1625. [IPR]

ECHLIN, ROBERT, Was granted Irish denization 18 May 1613. [IPR]; MA University of St Andrews 1596, Bishop of Down and Connor 1613-1635. [UJA#13/15]

ECHLIN, ROBERT, matriculated at St Leonard's College, University of St Andrews, 1625, graduated MA there 1628, Chancellor of Down 1642. [UJA#13/15]

EDMONDSON, JAMES, was granted Irish denization on 18 August 1607. [IPR]

EDMONDSON, WILLIAM, of Dimthriffe, was granted Irish denization 18 August 1607. [IPR]; arrived in County Down with Sir Hugh Montgomery, settled in Ballybrian, moved to Braid, County Antrim, in 1609. [NAS.GD.97.1.328]

EDMONSTON, ALEXANDER, of Ardfracknen, was granted Irish denization 28 November 1617. [IPR]

EDMISTON, ARCHIBALD, of Redhall, High Sheriff of County
Antrim in 1669. [UJA.11.1.79]

EDMONSTON, ARCHIBALD, of Ballybrian, was granted Irish
denization 5 July 1631. [IPR]; Archibald Edmonston, son of
William Edmonston in Stirlingshire, settled on Braiden Island,
County Antrim, died 25 March 1636

EDMONSTONE, CATHERINE, daughter of John Edmonstone of
Bellibentroe, 23 November 1710. [NAS.GD26.4.469]

EDMONSTONE, ELIZABETH, daughter of Archibald Edmonstone
of Duntreath, wife of James Montgomery of Rosemount,
County Down, 1699. [NAS.RD3.92.375]; married in 1687,
[Grey Abbey g/s]

EDMONDSTON, JAMES, of Broad Island, County Antrim,
gentleman, was granted Irish denization on 9 August 1633.
[IPR]

EDMONSTON, ROBERT, was demised lands in the Precinct of
Mountjoy by Sir Robert Hepburn on 10 May 1620. [PU#547]

EDMONSTON, ROBERT, of Alfraknes, was granted Irish denization
on 13 May 1634. [IPR]

EDMONSTON, WILLIAM, merchant aboard the Anthony of
Carrickfergus at the port of Irvine, Ayrshire, on 9 August 1682.
[NAS.E72.12.5]

EDWARD, GILBERT, master of the Katrine of Larne at the port of
Glasgow 16 November 1670. [NAS.E72.10.2]

EDWARDS, HUGH, an Anglo-Irish student at Glasgow University
1719. [MUG#215]

EDWARDS, THOMAS, master of the Merchant of Larne at the port
of Irvine, Ayrshire, on 13 February 1682. [NAS.E72.12.6]

EGLISHAME, WILLIAM, master of the Margaret of Belfast at the
port of Irvine, Ayrshire, on 23 August 1682. [NAS.E72.12.5]

ELDER, JOHN, a Scots-Irish student at Glasgow University 1715. [MUG#205]

ELDER, THOMAS, a Scots-Irish student at Edinburgh University 1697. [CEG]

ELLIOT, Sir JOHN, with 400 acres at Mucken, County Cavan, 28 March 1619. [Carew#211/9]

ELLIOTT, ROBERT, tenant of John Hamilton of Edenagh, Precinct of Fewes, 1618. [PU#567]

ELLIOT, ROBERT, in County Fermanagh, 1659. [C]

ELLIOT, WILLIAM, in Rathmoran, County Fermanagh, 1696. [IWD]

ELPHINSTON, JAMES, was granted Irish denization on 19 May 1615. [IPR]

ELPHINSTONE, JOHN, Lord Balmerinoch, was granted Irish denization on 11 November 1614. [IPR]

ELPHINSTONE, MICHAEL, Captain of Robert Home of the Heugh's Regiment, in Carrickfergus, 1642. [PRO.SP.18.120]

ELPHINSTONE, Captain WILLIAM, a soldier in Cork, on 8 November 1626. [Cal.SP.Ire.1626/497][SP.Ire#253/489]

ERSKINE, ARCHIBALD, parson of Devenish, County Fermanagh, on 24 July 1631. [SP.Ire#252/2003]

ERSKINE, Sir JAMES, in castle and lands of Agher, County Tyrone, 1626. [SP.Ire#243/508]

ERSKINE, JOHN, in Muff, parish of Templemore, 1694. [IWD]

ERSKINE, JOHN, a Scots-Irish student at Edinburgh University 1697. [CEG]

ERVIN, JOHN, born 1599, died on 1 September 1699; his wife Elizabeth Jordan died 27 June 1697; his son Gawin born 1683, died on 3 December 1713 and his wife Jean Reid died on 18

June 1721. [Killyreagh g/s, County Down]

ERVIN, THOMAS, a merchant, born 1668, died 15 March 1725, his sons Robert born 1695, died in December 1697, and Andrew born 1695, died in April 1698. [Killyleagh g/s, County Down]

ERVIN, MARY, wife of James Ervin, born 1648, died 1 December 1683. [Killyleagh g/s, County Down]

ESPIE, JANE, alias Adaire, alias Getty, a widow in Maghera, County Londonderry, mother of John Getty a surgeon in Maghera and Elizabeth, 1694, prerogative grant. [PRONI]

EWING, FINLAY, of Coole McItean, County Donegal, yeoman, was granted Irish denization on 19 July 1631. [IPR]

EWING, JOHN, of Letterkenny, County Donegal, merchant, was granted Irish denization on 19 July 1631. [IPR]

EWING, ROBERT, an Irish student at Glasgow University 1705. [MUG#183]

FAIRBAIRN, JOHN, merchant aboard the John of Glenarme at the port of Irvine, Ayrshire, on 15 August 1682. [NAS.E72.12.5]

FAIRBAIRN, THOMAS, in the barony of Tarranney, County Armagh, 1659. [C]

FAIRFULL, DAVID, matriculated at St Leonard's College, University of St Andrews, 1607, graduated MA there 1608, precentor in County Down 1614. [UJA#13/15]; petitioner in June 1624. [Cal.SP.Ire.1624/1226]

FAIRFOUL, HUGH, cornet of Viscount Claneboy's troop of horse on 25 April 1642. [SP.Ire#260/63]

FAIRLIE, HANS, of Madero, born 1652, died on 13 July 1715; his children were Grisel, James, Hugh, John, James, Robert, Hans, James, and Grisel. [Saintfield g/s, County Down]

FAIRLEY, WILLIAM, in the barony of Castlereagh, County Down, 1659. [C]

FALCONER, JOHN, master of the James of Strangford at the port of Glasgow 13 September 1672. [NAS.E72.10.3]

FAW, GEORGE, and his wife Katherine Brown, and their daughter Margaret, William Baillie and his wife Helen Faw, plus Andrew Baillie and his wife Janet, to be released from Edinburgh Tolbooth and allowed to return to Ireland, 8 July 1630. [RPCS.III.599]

FEARID, THOMAS, master of the New Adventure of Glenarme at the port of Irvine, Ayrshire, on 5 November 1680. [NAS.E72.12.3]

FENTON, JOHN, a farmer in Urney, County Tyrone, will subscribed on 8 August 1721, probate 24 September 1723 Dublin

FENTON, WILLIAM, MA University of St Andrews 1612, curate of Cairncastle and Glenarm, County Antrim. [UJA#13/15]; Was granted Irish denization 9 February 1625. [IPR]

FERGUSON, ALEXANDER, born 1628, graduated MA from Glasgow University in 1650, a minister in Sorbie, Scotland, then in Killyleagh from 1670 to 1684, died on 6 November 1684; his wife Sarah died 12 November 1686. [Killyleagh g/s, County Down] [FI#61]

FERGUSON, ANDREW, born in Scotland, graduated MA from Edinburgh University in 1676, minister in Burt from 1690, died on 18 July 1725. [FI#61]

FERGUSON, ANDREW, a Scots-Irish student at Glasgow University 1717. [MUG#209]

FERGUSON, ARCHIBALD, matriculated at St Salvador's College, University of St Andrews, 1640, graduated MA there 1642, minister at Antrim 1645. [UJA#13/15]

FERGUSON, FINDEN, a sergeant-major in Antrim on 19 May 1645. [SP.Ire#260/137]

FERGUSON, JOHN, tenant of John Hamilton of Edenagh, Precinct of Fewes, 1618. [PU#567]

FERGUSON, ROBERT, tenant of John Hamilton of Edenagh, Precinct of Fewes, 1618. [PU#567]

FERRY, JAMES, of the Clary, County Tyrone, was granted Irish denization 28 November 1617. [IPR]

FINDLAY, ALEXANDER, a merchant in Londonderry (?) 1643. [SP.Ire#307/104]

FINGLASTON, JOHN, was granted Irish denization on 12 February 1618. [IPR]

FINLASON, Mr JOHN, of Killeith, applied for 2000 acres in Ulster on 27 July 1609. [PU#143]

FINNIE, ROBERT, master of the Sara of Londonderry at the port of Ayr 26 July 1686. [NAS.E72.3.17]

FISHER, JAMES, a merchant at the Diamond, Londonderry, 1659. [C]

FISHER, JOHN, with 2000 acres at Dromany, County Cavan, 28 March 1619. [Carew Mss#211/20]

FISHER, JOHN, master and merchant of the Mary of Belfast at the port of Irvine, Ayrshire, on 5 October 1683. [NAS.E72.12.8]

FITHIE, HENRY, MA University of St Andrews 1621, vicar of Ballylinny 1630. [UJA#13/15]

FLECK, FERGUS, tenant of John Hamilton of Edenagh, Precinct of Fewes, 1618. [PU#567]

FLEMING, JAMES, graduated MA at the University of Edinburgh 1646, matriculated at St Mary's College, University of St Andrews, 1647, minister at Glenarm 1658. [UJA#13/15]

FLEMING, JOHN, of Raphoe, was granted Irish denization on 28 November 1617. [IPR]

FLEMING, WILLIAM, a merchant in Leith, planning to settle in Ireland 12 March 1658. [Edinburgh Burgh Records]

FOOT, THOMAS, son in law of John McCubbin of Dunamuy, parish of Rashee, County Antrim, 1690. [NAS.GD180#216]

FORBES, ALEXANDER, matriculated at St Leonard's College, University of St Andrews, 1617, minister at Blaris 1628. [UJA#13/15]

FORBES, ARTHUR, was granted Irish denization on 1 April 1622. [IPR]

FORBES, Sir ARTHUR, at the Sign of Feathers, Castle Street, Dublin, 1661, [SP.Dom.Signet Office#357]; who had raised cavalry in Ireland and sent it to Scotland in 1648 to support King Charles I, petitioned the Scots Parliament for reimbursement in 1663. [APS]

FORBES, JAMES, gentleman, was granted Irish denization on 1 April 1622. [IPR]

FORBES, JOHN, from Ireland, graduated MA at King's College, Aberdeen, 1716. [KCA.1.226]

FORBES, ROBERT, gentleman, was granted Irish denization on 1 April 1622. [IPR]

FORBES, ROBERT, Captain of Major General Robert Monro's Regiment, in Carrickfergus 1642. [PRO.SP.18.120]

FORBES, SUSANNA, daughter of Reverend William Forbes, a distressed person from Ireland 1644. [SLT#167]

FORBES, TIMOTHY, a linen draper in Dublin, 1701. [NAS.RD4.89.923]

FORCHEADE, JOHN, of Costrewse, was granted Irish denization on 28 November 1617. [IPR]

FORRES, JOHN, in Dirlton, East Lothian, applied for 2000 acres in Ulster on 25 July 1609. [PU#141]

FORREST, GEORGE, master of the George of Holywood at the port of Irvine, Ayrshire, on 24 January 1691. [NAS.E72.12.17]

FORREST, ISAIAH, servant of the Earl of Clanbrasil, died on 17
May 1664; his son James was born 1650 and died 9 January
1722. [Killyleagh g/s, County Down]

FORREST, THOMAS, merchant in Dublin, admitted as a burgess and
guildsbrother of Glasgow on 1 March 1723. [GBR]

FORRESTER, ELIZABETH and WILLIAM, children of Reverend
Alexander Forrester in Londonderry, 14 August 1700.
[RGS#15.15]

FORSYTH, JAMES, clerk, was granted Irish denization on 7
November 1613. [IPR]

FORSTER, WILLIAM, in Leith, applied for 1000 acres in Ulster on
25 July 1609. [PU#141]

FORTUNE, JAMES, accused of murdering Sir John Wemyss, failed
to appear at the Court of the Chief Place in Ireland during
1627. [SP.Ire.Docquet#14]

FOULLER, WILLIAM, merchant burgess of Edinburgh, applied for
2000 acres in Ulster on 25 July 1609, [PU#141]; grant of
Moyglass, barony of Magheryboy, County Fermanagh, 11 July
1610. [EPR.8.17] [TCD.ms#N2/2]; Undertaker in the Precinct
of Magheraboy, County Fermanagh, 1611.
[Cal.SP.Ire.1611/384]; was granted Irish denization 11 July
1610. [IPR]

FRANCIS, HENRY, of Cloabicke, County Antrim, 15 April 1704.
[NAS.RS.Argyll.3.407]

FRASER, HEW, Lieutenant Colonel of Major General Robert
Monro's Regiment, in Carrickfergus 1642. [PRO.SP.18.120]

FRASER, JOHN, of Donaghadie, was granted Irish denization on 20
May 1617. [IPR]

FRASER, THOMAS, a minister in the diocese of Raphoe, 1622.
[TCD.ms.E#3/6]

FREELAND, JOHN, born in Scotland, graduated MA from Glasgow University in 1652, a minister in Antrim from 1674, died on 12 March 1716. [FI#61]

FRENCH, PATRICK, Scotus Hibernus, admitted as a member of the Scots Charitable Society of Boston in 1716. [NEHGS/SCS]

FREW, JOHN, of Ballow, died on 3 May 1723; his wife Janet Peterson was born 1656, died on 13 February 1718. [Killinchy g/s, County Down]

FRIZELL, ALEXANDER, master of the Elizabeth of Glenarme at the port of Irvine, Ayrshire, on 8 October 1683. [NAS.E72.12.7]

FRISELL, JAMES, a minister in the diocese of Down, 1622. [TCD.ms.E#3/6]

FRISSAL, THOMAS, born 1702, died 1 January 1710. [Comber g/s]

FROBISHER, ZACHARIAS, master of the Mary of Dublin at the port of Irvine, Ayrshire, on 16 February 1689. [NAS.E72.12.15]

FULLERTON, JOHN, agent for James Douglas, 29 July 1611. [Cal.SP.Ire.1611/203]

FULLERTON, WILLIAM, of Carncastle, County Antrim, clerk, was granted Irish denization 9 August 1633. [IPR]

FULLERTON, WILLIAM, clerk, was granted Irish denization on 13 May 1634. [IPR]

FULTON, JOHN, of Baltany, was granted Irish denization on 28 November 1617. [IPR]

FULTON, JOHN, in Clownish, County Fermanagh, 1659. [C]

FUTHIE, HENRY, of Ba....., County Antrim, clerk, was granted Irish denization on 9 August 1633. [IPR]

FUTHY, ROBERT, was granted Irish denization on 22 February 1615. [IPR]

GALBREATH, ANDREW, in Enniskeane, County Fermanagh, 1659. [C]

GALBRAITH, HUGH, of Roskawe, County Tyrone, gentleman, was granted Irish denization on 22 February 1634. [IPR]

GALBRAITH, HUMPHREY, a minister in the diocese of Clogher, 1622. [TCD.ms.E#3/6]

GALBRETH, JAMES, of Rateine, barony of Strabane, County Tyrone, was granted Irish denization on 17 August 1616. [IPR][SBT#23]

GALBREATH, HUMPHREY, accused of murdering Sir John Wemyss, failed to appear at the Court of the Chief Place in Ireland during 1627. [SP.Ire.Docquet#14]

GALBRETH, HUMPHREY, a clerk, 2 January 1641. [SP.Dom.Sig.Off#III, 407]

GALBRETH, JAMES, jr., of Rateine, barony of Strabane, County Donegal, was granted Irish denization on 17 August 1616. [IPR][SBT#23]

GALBRETH, JAMES, on the London Plantation 20 March 1627. [SP.Ire#244/616]

GALBRAITH, JAMES, a sergeant-major in Antrim on 19 May 1645. [SP.Ire#260/137]

GALBRAITH, JAMES, possibly in Armagh 1641. [SP.Ire#260/41]

GALBREATH, JAMES, in Clownish, County Fermanagh, 1659. [C]

GALBRAITH, JAMES, in Ramorane, County Fermanagh, 1673. [IWD]

GALBRAITH, JANE, a widow in Donish, County Donegal, 1675. [IWD]

GALBRAITH, JANE, in Ramorane, County Fermanagh, 1676. [IWD]

GALBRAITH, JOSIAS, in Crachadooey, County Donegal, 1676. [IWD]

GALBRAITH, ROBERT, of Ballilenan, County Donegal, gentleman, was granted Irish denization 22 February 1634. [IPR]

GALBREATH, ROBERT, in Enniskeane, County Fermanagh, 1659. [C]

GALBRAITH, THOMAS, in Up. Colladerry, County Donegal, 1720. [IWD]

GALBREATH, WILLIAM, accused of murdering Sir John Wemyss, failed to appear at the Court of the Chief Place in Ireland during 1627. [SP.Ire.Docquet#14]

GALD, WILLIAM, was granted Irish denization on 16 June 1615. [IPR]

GALT, JOHN, a shopkeeper in Coleraine, County Londonderry, 1659. [C]

GALT, WILLIAM, a shopkeeper in Coleraine, County Londonderry, 1659. [C]

GAMBLE, GEORGE, tenant of John Hamilton of Edenagh, Precinct of Fewes, 1618. [PU#567]

GAMBLE, MATTHEW, tenant of John Hamilton of Edenagh, Precinct of Fewes, 1618. [PU#567]

GAMBLE, or Gemmill, PATRICK, in Strabane, probate 1629

GAMBLE, WILLIAM, a Scots-Irish student at Glasgow University 1714. [MUG#203]

GARDINER, PATRICK, Lieutenant of Colonel Stanley's Foot in Ireland, husband of Mary Hodge, 1702. [NAS.RD3.99.45]

GARDNER, ROBERT, ofArdbrackan, County Meath, was granted Irish denization 20 May 1617. [IPR]

GARNER, RICHARD, skipper of the Isabel of Belfast, arrived in
Port Glasgow from Barbados October 1682. [NAS.E72.19.5]

GARTSHORE, JAMES, DD, minister in Ireland, formerly in Tranent,
1699. [NAS.RD3.91.247; RD4.84.503]

GARVEN, JOHN, in Kilmore, Ireland, husband of Marion Borland,
1714, [NAS.RD3.141.408]

GAULT, JOHN, an Irish student at Edinburgh University 1704.
[CEG]

GAY, WILLIAM, Captain of Colonel Burdwall's Regiment of Foot in
Ireland, 1702. [NAS.RD4.90.352]

GELSTON, SAMUEL, a Scots-Irish student at Glasgow University in
1706. [MUG#184]

GEMBLE, WILLIAM, was granted Irish denization on 17 August
1616. [IPR]

GEMMILL, JOHN, of Bally McCormoch, was granted Irish
denization on 28 November 1617. [IPR]

GETTY, Reverend ADAM, from Rosneath, Dunbartonshire,
graduated MA from Glasgow University in 1658, minister at
Ballymena, County Antrim, from 1666, died there in December
1674, will refers to his wife Jane, their children Elizabeth and
John, executors William Stiell, Robert Boyd a merchant in
Ballymena, overseers his brother John Gettie of Ballymena and
John Stewart of Ballymena, debtors James Adair of Dunagor,
my brother in law William Adair of Dunagor, John Wallace a
merchant in Ballymena, witnesses John Shaw and James
Abernethie, subscribed on 1 December 1674, proved 13 July
1675 Ballymena. [FI#62]

GETTY, CHARLES, master of the James of Larne 28 tons, 31
October 1718. [PRONI#T808/4799]

GETTY, DAVID, master of the Anthony of Larne at the port of
Irvine, Ayrshire, on 28 December 1689. [NAS.E72.12.16]

GETTY, JAMES, senior, a yeoman in Inver town, County Antrim, will refers to wife Agnes Roper, his brother Robert Getty in Inver, his nephew James Getty in Inver, creditors Andrew Young and John Wylly both in Inver, Edmund Davies of Carrickfergus, witnesses Andrew Young, John Getty and John Boyd, subscribed in Inver on 3 July 1673, proved 1 September 1673 Inver Town, County Antrim

GETTY, JANE, alias Espie alias Adaire, a widow in Maghera, County Londonderry, 1694. [IWD]

GETTY, MARGARET, of Larne, County Antrim, deceased, administrators her sons Samuel and John also of Larne, witnesses henry Smyth and William Carrell, 6 October 1719. [PRONI, Admin. Bond]

GETTY, ROBERT, senior, a merchant of Newtown of Inver, County Antrim, will refers to his wife Margaret Porter and their son Robert, witnesses James Getty and John Boyd, proved 7 April 1698, Inver parish, County Antrim, Connor will.

GETTY, ROBERT, of Black Key, Larne, County Antrim, his will refers to his wife Nell and their children, and to his sister Grissell, overseers Thomas Getty, John Getty, James Patrick, and Robert Boyd, subscribed on 17 September 1727, proved 27 November 1727, [PRONI.T808/4777-4811]

GETTY, Mr SAMUEL, minister in Larne, admitted as a burgess of Inveraray, Argyll, on 9 August 1718. [Inveraray Burgess Roll]; died on 27 February 1724. [PRONI]

GETTY, SAMUEL, of Mults, Larne, County Antrim, will refers to his wife Jean, their 4 children, overseers John Getty, Mrs Pettegrew and John McCulloch, witnesses John Getty and John McCulloch, subscribed on 27 February 1723, proved 1 July 1724, Connor will.

GIBB, JAMES, son of John Gibb a royal servant, was granted Irish denization and a grant of Dromra in the barony of Magheryboy, County Fermanagh, on 29 August 1610. [IPR][TCD.ms#N2/2]; Undertaker in the Precinct of Magheraboy, County Fermanagh, 1611. [Cal.SP.Ire.1611/384]

GIBB, JAMES, was granted Irish denization on 17 August 1616. [IPR]; in Strabane, County Tyrone, 1617, Provost there in 1630. [SBT#22]

GIBB, WILLIAM, merchant in Belfast, at the port of Ayr 22 October 1690. [NAS.E72.3.20]

GIBSON, GEORGE, burgess of Newton Ards, County Down, 1612. [Cal.SP.Ire.1613/614]

GIBSON, HENRY, Captain of Sir Mungo Campbell of Lawers' Regiment, in Temple Patrick, 1642. [PRO.SP.18.120]

GIBSON, JAMES, born 1560, Dean of Down, died 1623. [UJA#13/15]

GIBSON, JAMES, born around 1660s, died 20 July 1717. [Comber g/s]

GIBSON, JOHN, in Belykil, born 1620, died 27 December 1716, his wife Mary Anderson died 11 April 1706. [Comber g/s]

GIBSON, ROBERT, of Aughnahinchemore, County Fermanagh, was granted Irish denization on 17 August 1616. [IPR]

GIBSON, WILLIAM, of Belikiel, born 1670, died 3 November 1715, son of Janet Dickson born 1640, died 24 June 1712. [Comber g/s]

GIFFOLT, ANNE, a distressed Irish woman, sometime spouse to Mr William Murray a minister who had been crucified there by the rebels, given 5 dollars on 18 March 1643 by the Kirk Session of Elgin, Morayshire. [Elgin Kirk Session Records]

GIFFORD, JOHN, in Silver Street, Londonderry, 1659. [C]

GILCHRIST, WILLIAM, born in Scotland, graduated MA from Glasgow University in 1663, minister at Kilrea around 1680, died at the Siege of Londonderry during 1689. [FI#62]

GILLESPIE, HUGH, of Chirriebelly, Ireland, brother-in-law of Lord Rollo, 1715; husband of Susanna, daughter of Lord Andrew Rollo, 11 December 1717. [NAS.RD4.116.1310; GD56.102]

GILLESPIE, JOHN, was granted Irish denization on 26 September 1614. [IPR]

GILLIS, JOHN, master of the Bessie of Carrickfergus at the port of Irvine, Ayrshire, on 21 March 1681. [NAS.E72.12.3]

GILLIS, JOHN, master of the James of Larne at the port of Irvine, Ayrshire, on 23 July 1681. [NAS.E72.12.3]

GILMORE, ROBERT, tenant of John Hamilton of Edenagh, Precinct of Fewes, 1618. [PU#567]

GLADSTONE, THOMAS, a merchant in Dublin, admitted as a burgess and guildsbrother of Glasgow on 20 February 1724. [GBR]

GLASGOW, HUGH, passenger on the Venture of Glenarme at the port of Ayr 30 October 1673. [NAS.E72.3.3]

GLASGOW, JOHN, merchant on the John of Glenarme at the port of Irvine, Ayrshire, on 9 August 1682. [NAS.E72.12.5]

GLASSE, ALLASTER, of Raphoe, was granted Irish denization 28 November 1617. [IPR]

GLASS, ALEXANDER, born in 1653, son of Reverend Thomas Glass in Little Dunkeld, Perthshire. Graduated MA from Glasgow University in 1671, minister in Dunmurray from 1683 to 1689, died in Scotland. [FI#62]

GLEN, ELIZABETH, wife of Patrick Hamilton of Ballygrangahe, was granted Irish denization on 5 July 1631. [IPR]

GLEN, JAMES, of East Holywood, was granted Irish denization on 28 November 1617. [IPR]

GLENDENNING, JAMES, born in Scotland during 1583, matriculated at St Leonard's College, University of St Andrews, 1617, minister of Coole 1622 and Muckamore, County Antrim, 1626. [UJA#13/15]; a minister in the diocese of Down, 1622. [TCD.ms.E#3/6]; returned to Scotland by 1630. [PHS]

GLENN, JOHN, of Lifford, was granted Irish denization on 17 August 1616. [IPR]

GLOVER, JAMES, master of the Rose of Belfast at the port of Irvine, Ayrshire, on 29 February 1689. [NAS.E72.12.15]

GOOD, JOHN, master of the Margaret of Belfast at the port of Glasgow 20 May 1672. [NAS.E72.10.3]

GOODLAD, JAMES, in Strabrok, applied for 2000 acres in Ulster on 20 July 1609. [PU#140]

GOODLAD, JOHN, of Trewe, County Tyrone, gentleman, was granted Irish denization on 19 July 1633. [IPR]

GOODLAD, ROBERT, of Tirregallie, County Tyrone, gentleman, was granted Irish denization on 19 July 1633. [IPR]

GOODLATT, THOMAS, in Dungannon on 8 March 1667. [Cal.SP.Ire.348/8]

GORDON, AINEGIER, in Robertstown, 1723. [IWD]

GORDON, ALEXANDER, burgess of Newton Ards, County Down, 1612. [Cal.SP.Ire.1613/614]

GORDON, ALEXANDER, born in 1642, son of Alexander Gordon and Marjorie Geddes in Drainie, Aberdeenshire, graduated MA from King's College, Aberdeen, in 1659, minister at Rathfriland from 1673, died on 17 february 1709, buried at Drumballyroney. [FI#62]

GORDON, ALEXANDER, a Captain in Herbert's Regiment, 1691. [IWD]

GORDON, ALEXANDER, in Ardandreagh, County Longford, 1691. [IWD]

GORDON, ALEXANDER, in Lesise, parish of Dromballyroney, County Down, 1709. [IWD]

GORDON, GEORGE, Captain of the Earl of Leven's Regiment, in Carrickfergus, 1642. [PRO.SP28/120]

GORDON, JAMES, born in 1645, eldest son of Reverend James Gordon in Rothiemay, Aberdeenshire, graduated MA from King's College, Aberdeen, in 1663, minister at Bonevagh, Glendermott, from 1683, at the Siege of Londonderry in 1689, returned to Scotland, died on 16 May 1693. [FI#63]

GORDON, JAMES, minister in Comber, Ireland, 1714. [NAS.RD4.114.1075]

GORDON, MUNGO, born 1631, died 20 November 1696, his wife Sophia died 7 March 17..., aged 86. [Comber g/s]

GORDON, Sir ROBERT, born in Scotland, was granted Irish denization 2 December 1614. [IPR]; naturalisation of Sir Robet Gordon and grant of lands in County Donegal, 15 July 1614. [Cal.SP.Ire.1614/848]

GORDON, ROBERT, born 1605, died 1686, his wife Mary Shaw born 1645, died 7 March 1684, their son John born 1635, died in March 1682. [Comber g/s]

GOUDY, JOHN, born in Scotland during 1655, graduated MA from Edinburgh University in 1675, a schoolmaster in Bangor, then a minister at Ballee 1688, Ballywalter and Grey Abbey in 1693, died on 26 March 1733. [FI#63]

GOURDON, A., petitioner in June 1624. [Cal.SP.Ire.1624/1226]

GOWAN, THOMAS, born in Caldermuir during 1631, graduated MA from Edinburgh University in 1655, a minister in Glasslough and Antrim from 1658, died on 15 September 1683, buried in Antrim, father of Reverend Thomas Gowan in Drumbo from 1706 to 1716. [FI#37]

GRACE, WILLIAM, born 1700, died 16 March 1733. [Templepatrick g/s, County Antrim]

GRAEME, DICK, 1626. [SP.Ire.#252/299]

GRAHAM, ANDREW, in Castlecaffield, Ireland, 25 November 1686. [NAS.GD22.3.85]

GRAHAM, ANTHONY, 1682. [IWD]

GRAHAM, ARCHIBALD, tenant of John Hamilton of Edenagh, Precinct of Fewes, 1618. [PU#567]

GRAHAM, ARTHUR, in County Fermanagh, 1659. [C]

GRAHAM, Sir GEORGE, in barony of Tolehagh, County Cavan, 1611. [Cal.SP.Ire.1611/251]

GRAHAM, ISOBEL, an Irish woman, given 5 merks on 3 May 1644 by the Kirk Session of Elgin, Morayshire. [Elgin Kirk Session Records]

GRAHAM, JAMES, in Ballymore Allen, County Cork, 1718. [IWD]

GRAHAM, JOHN, a Scots-Irish student at Glasgow University 1714. [MUG#203]

GRAHAM, JOHN, 1657. [IWD]

GRAHAM, JOHN, in Ballygrane, Queen's County, 1667. [IWD]

GRAHAM, JOHN, an alderman in Drogheda, 1714. [IWD]

GRAHAM, JOHN, 1724. [IWD]

GRAHAM, PIERCE, in Orell, County Limerick, 1682. [IWD]

GRAHAM, Sir RICHARD, in the barony of Tolehagh, County Cavan, 1611. [Cal. SP.Ire.1611/251]

GRAHAM, RICHARD, master of the Mary of Holywood at the port of Glasgow 23 November 1666. [NAS.E72.10.1]

GRAHAM, ROBERT, in Balliheridon, County Armagh, 1680. [IWD]

GRAHAM, THOMAS, was granted Irish denization on 12 February 1618. [IPR]

GRAHAM, Major THOMAS, 1652/1666. [IWD]

GRANGER, ROBERT, of Dunelonge, barony of Strabane, County Tyrone, was granted Irish denization on 17 August 1616; there in 1617. [IPR][SBT#23]

GRANE, JOHN, tenant of John Hamilton of Edenagh, Precinct of Fewes, 1618. [PU#567]

GRANT, JANET, widow of Walter Grant, 1630. [SP.Ire#251/1812]

GRANT, JASPER, 1698. [IWD]

GRANT, MICHAEL, the Sheriff of Waterford, 1626. [SP.Ire#243/485]

GRAUNTON, PATRICK, tenant of John Hamilton of Edenagh, Precinct of Fewes, 1618. [PU#567]

GRAY, GAVIN, a minister in the diocese of Connor, 1622. [TCD.ms.E#3/6]

GRAY, GEORGE, was granted Irish denization on 9 July 1616. [IPR]

GRAY, JOHN, whose mother had been wet nurse to the king, was granted Irish denization, on 31 October 1616. [IPR]

GRAY, NEIL, born in Scotland, educated at Glasgow University, minister at Clogher and Taughboyne from 1665 to 1715, died on 3 March 1715, buried in Taughboyne, father of Reverend William Gray in Taughboyne. [FI#64]

GRAY, NEIL, master of the Adventure of Coleraine at the port of Irvine, Ayrshire, on 15 February 1689. [NAS.E72.12.14]

GREEN, ROBERT, merchant aboard the Mary of Glenarme at the port of Irvine, Ayrshire, on 13 November 1684. [NAS.E72.12.9]

GREENSHIELLS, WILLIAM, of Ballingrene, was granted Irish denization on 20 May 1617. [IPR]

GREER, JOHN, a Scots-Irish student at Edinburgh University in 1708. [CEG]

GREG, HUGH, merchant in Dublin, burgess and guildsbrother of Glasgow 22 August 1713. [GBR]

GREG, JOHN, a minister in the diocese of Clogher, 1622. [TCD.ms.E#3/6]

GREIG, JOHN, son of Reverend James Greig of Loudoun (1597-1635), graduated MA from Glasgow University in 1638, minister in Carrickfergus and Newtownards from 1646 to 1650, a prisoner in Carlingford Castle from 1663 to 1664, died on 20 July 1670. [FI#37]

GREGORY, WILLIAM, a merchant in Londonderry, 10 July 1718. [Argyll Sheriff Court Book, vol,6, 7.2.1719]

GRIER, ALEXANDER, tenant of John Hamilton of Edenagh, Precinct of Fewes, 1618. [PU#567]

GRIER, ANN, wife of William Grier a merchant in Killyleagh, died on 10 September 1680, aged 2--. [Killyleagh g/s, County Down]

GRIER, ARCHIBALD, tenant of John Hamilton of Edenagh, Precinct of Fewes, 1618. [PU#567]

GRIER, CUTHBERT, tenant of John Hamilton of Edenagh, Precinct of Fewes, 1618. [PU#567]

GRIER, DAVID, was granted Irish denization on 12 February 1618. [IPR]

GRIER, ELIZA, tenant of John Hamilton of Edenagh, Precinct of Fewes, 1618. [PU#567]

GRIER, JOHN, was granted Irish denization on 12 February 1618. [IPR]

GRINDALL, HENRY, tenant of John Hamilton of Edenagh, Precinct of Fewes, 1618. [PU#567]

GUION, DANIEL, a merchant in Dublin, admitted as a burgess and guildsbrother of Glasgow on 6 November 1716. [GBR]

HACKETT, RICHARD, a minister in the diocese of Down in 1622. [TCD.ms.E#3/6]

HADDOCK, Lieutenant JAMES, died in Mallon on 18 December 1657; his wife Arminele died on 23 March 1690. [Drumbeg g/s, County Down]

HADDOCK, JOHN, master of the Nightingale of Belfast, arrived in Glasgow 6 September 1627. [NAS: Glasgow Port Book]

HADDOWIE, ANDREW, in Strabane, County Tyrone, probate 1635

HAIG, JAMES, of Bemerside, Berwickshire, Undertaker in the Plantation of Ulster, a grant in fee farm of the small proportion of Tyremeunriertaghe in barony of Strabane, County Tyrone, 4 June 1610. [EPR.8.16] [TCD.ms#N2/2]; Undertaker in Precinct of Strabane, County Tyrone, 1611. [Cal.SP.Ire.1611/384]

HALDANE, ARCHIBALD, was granted Irish denization on 18 August 1607. [IPR]

HALDANE, HUMPHREY, of Broadland, was granted Irish denization on 13 May 1634. [IPR]

HALL, FRANCIS, in Ballynorus, Drumore, County Down, 1659. [C]

HALL, JAMES, of Raphoe, County Donegal, was granted Irish denization on 17 August 1616. [IPR]

HALL, JOHN, tenant of John Hamilton of Edenagh, Precinct of Fewes, 1618. [PU#567]

HALL, RALPH, master of the Tryall of Londonderry at the port of Ayr on 2 July 1686. [NAS.E72.3.16]

HALL, ROBERT, of Restady, County Fermanagh, was granted Irish denization on 17 August 1616. [IPR]

HALL, SIMON, of Tullaghbegg, County Tyrone, gentleman, was granted Irish denization on 19 July 1633. [IPR]

HALL, THOMAS, born in 1620, graduated MA from Glasgow
University in 1642, minister in Larne from 1646 to 1649 and
1654 to 1661, died in 1695, father of Gilbert and Jean. [FI#37]

HALLIBURTON, JOHN, in Ireland, formerly an advocate in
Edinburgh, husband of Katherine Adam, 1696.
[NAS.RD2.79.1124; RD80.347]

HALLIDAY, SAMUEL, born in Scotland during 1637, graduated
MA from Glasgow University in 1656, minister in Raphoe
from 1664 to 1677, in Longfield (Drumquin) and Drumraer
(Omagh) from 1677 to 1684, in Ardstraw from 1692 to 1694,
died on 18 February 1724. [FI#64]

HALTRIDGE, JOHN, born in Scotland, graduated MA from
Glasgow University in 1654, minister in Ballycarry,
Islandmagee, from 1672, died in 1697. [FI#65]

HALTRIDGE, MATTHEW, born in Scotland, graduated MA from
Glasgow University in 1669, minister in Glenavy from 1673 to
1675, in Ahogshill from 1676, died on 20 October 1705.
[FI#65]

HALYBURTON, or Wauchope, ELLEN, in The Cortyn, Barony
parish, County Tyrone, probate 1640

HALYBURTON, GEORGE, in The Cortyn, Barony Parish, Strabane,
County Tyrone, probate 1639

HAMBLETON, Sir CLAUDE, was granted Irish denization on 12
May 1620. [IPR]

HAMBLETON, ELIZABETH, wife of Alexander Cunningham of
Ballesallagh, was granted Irish denization on 28 November
1624. [IPR]

HAMBLETON, FRANCIS, of Castlekelagh, was granted Irish
denization on 12 February 1618. [IPR]

HAMILL, MATHEW, was granted Irish denization on 22 June 1615.
[IPR]

HAMILL, MATTHEW, a burgess of Irvine, now in Dunbog, Ireland, 1621. [see Jean Campbell's, wife of William Dunlop of Craig, testament 1621, Commissariot of Glasgow]

HAMILL, ROBERT, was granted Irish denization on 22 June 1615. [IPR]

HAMILTON, Sir ALEXANDER, of Innerwick, grant of Clankeine in the barony of Tullochouche, County Cavan, was granted Irish denization on 23 July 1610, [IPR][TCD.ms#N2/2]; Undertaker of the Precinct of Tullochone, County Cavan, 1611. [Cal.SP.Ire.1611/384; 1612/608]

HAMILTON, ALEXANDER, of Tullaghdonnell, was granted Irish denization on 28 November 1617. [IPR]

HAMILTON, Captain ALEXANDER, born 1613, second son of Patrick Hamilton of Innerwick, Scotland, sixth brother of James, Lord Viscount Claneboy, died in 1648. [Old Abbey Church g/s, Bangor]

HAMILTON, ALEXANDER, of Killyleagh, a merchant, died on 26 January 1676. [Killyleagh g/s, County Down]

HAMILTON, ANDREW, of Ballymulin, was granted Irish denization on 28 November 1617. [IPR]

HAMILTON, ARCHIBALD, of Bangor, County Down, brother of Sir James Hamilton, was granted Irish denization on 20 May 1617. [IPR]

HAMILTON, ARCHIBALD, was granted Irish denization on 24 March 1628. [IPR]

HAMILTON, ARCHIBALD, born in 1619, third son of Reverend Patrick Hamilton in Enderwick, graduated MA from Edinburgh University in 1638, married Jane, daughter of Reverend James Hamilton in Ballywalter during 1643, a minister in Bangor from 1670 to 1689, died in Wigtown, Scotland, on 29 June 1695. [FI#65]

HAMILTON, ARCHIBALD, in Killeleagh, barony of Kinallerly, County Down, 1659. [C]

HAMILTON, ARCHIBALD, born 1645, died 9 February 1725; his
wife Margaret, sister of Arthur Maxwell of Drum, was born in
1651 and died on 12 January 1736. [Drumbeg g/s, Co. Down]

HAMILTON, ARCHIBALD, minister in Bangor, late in Sorbie, 18
July 1677. [NAS.GD10.332]

HAMILTON, ARCHIBALD, son of Reverend James Hamilton,
graduated MA from Edinburgh University in 1653, minister in
Benburb from 1660 to 1673, in Armagh from 1673, and in
Killinchy from 1693, died in Belfast on 4 January 1699, buried
in Bangor, husband of Mary Kennedy, father of James, Hugh
and Jane. [FI#38]; a Presbyterian minister in Northern Ireland
who petitioned the Queen in 1691. [CTB.#/III.1207, 1258]

HAMILTON, CLAUD, of Creichnes, applied for 2000 acres in Ulster
on 25 July 1609. [PU#142]

HAMILTON, Sir CLAUD, of Lerleprivick, was granted Irish
denization and a grant of 1000 acres at Clovin in the barony of
Tullachouchoe, County Cavan, 14 August 1610,
[IPR][TCD.ms#N2/2]; Undertaker in Precinct of Strabane,
County Tyrone, 1611. [Cal.SP.Ire.1611/384]; Undertaker of the
Precinct of Tullochone, County Cavan, 1611; with 3000 acres,
appeared at a muster in 1618 with 62 men, 2 muskets, 9
calivers, 32 pikes, 3 halberds and 42 swords. [Cal.SP.Ire.
1611/384; 1612/608; 1618/501]; dead by 28 March 1619, had
owned 2000 acres at EdinKilliny, County Tyrone. [Carew
Mss#211/127]

HAMILTON, CLAUD, was granted Irish denization and a grant of
Edeneveagh in the precinct of Fewes, County Armagh, 29
August 1610, [IPR][TCD.ms#N2/2]; Undertaker in Precinct of
Fewes, County Armagh, 1611. [Cal.SP.Ire.1611/384]

HAMILTON, CLAUD, of Raphoe, County Donegal, was granted
Irish denization 17August 1616. [IPR]

HAMILTON, CLAUD, cleric in Clogher, County Tyrone, was
granted Irish denization 17 August 1616. [IPR]; a minister in
the diocese of Clogher, 1622. [TCD.ms.E#3/6]; parson of
Donacavey on 24 July 1631. [SP.Ire#252/2003]

HAMILTON, CLAUD, granted Strabane and Shean, County Tyrone, on 5 June 1634. [SP.Dom.Sig.Off.II#362/3]

HAMILTON, CLAUD, Captain of the Earl of Lindsay's Regiment, in Bangor 1642. [PRO.SP.28.120]

HAMILTON, CLAUD, a Scots-Irish student at Glasgow University in 1710. [MUG#194]

HAMILTON, DANIEL, merchant aboard the Catherine of Donaghadee at the port of Dumfries 1 September 1673. [NAS.E72.6.2]

HAMILTON, Sir FRANCIS, who had raised cavalry in Ireland and sent it to Scotland in 1648 to support King Charles I, petitioned the Scots Parliament for reimbursement in 1663. [APS]

HAMILTON, Sir FRANCIS, Castle Hamilton, County Cavan, subscribed to his will 19 January 1713, reference to wife Anne, his father Sir Charles Hamilton deceased, and his nephew Arthur Cecil, probate 25 February 1713 Dublin

HAMILTON, Sir FREDERICK, noble of the bedchamber, was granted Irish denization on 18 May 1630. [IPR]

HAMILTON, GAVIN, was granted Irish denization on 10 May 1605. [IPR]

HAMILTON, GAVIN, of Ballymulin, was granted Irish denization on 28 November 1617. [IPR]

HAMILTON, GAVIN, in the barony of Castlereagh, County Down, 1659. [C]

HAMILTON, Sir GEORGE, of Greenlaw, was granted Irish denization and a grant of Cloghognall in the barony of Strabane, Tyrone, on 6 August 1610, [IPR]; Undertaker in Precinct of Strabane, Tyrone, 1611. [Cal.SP.Ire.1611/384]; with 1500 acres at Largie Cloghognall, and 1000 acres at DerryWood, and acres at Terremurreath, Tyrone, 28 March 1619. [Carew Mss#211/125, 126, 128]; granted Downalong, Co Tyrone, on 5 June 1634. [SP.Dom.Sig.Off.II#362/3]

HAMILTON, GEORGE, of Binning, applied for 2000 acres in Ulster on 27 July 1609, [PU#143]; was granted Irish denization and a grant of Dirrywoon in the barony of Strabane, County Tyrone, on 29 August 1610, [IPR]; Undertaker in Precinct of Strabane, County Tyrone, 1611. [Cal.SP.Ire.1611/384; 1612/608]

HAMILTON, Sir GEORGE, patentee of the mines at Knockendrick, in the barony of Upper Ormond, County Tipperaray, 1660. [SP.Ire.#305/83]

HAMILTON, GILBERT, of Dunlady, Ireland, husband of Katherine Wardlaw, 1714. [NAS.RD2.103/1.622]

HAMILTON, HANS, Lieutenant of Viscount Claneboy's troop of horse on 25 April 1642. [SP.Ire#260/63]

HAMILTON, HANS, in Lower Fewes, County Armagh, 1659. [C]

HAMILTON, HUGH, of Moyagh, gentleman, was granted Irish denization on 9 July 1616. [IPR]

HAMILTON, HUGH, son of John Hamilton of Priestfield, Blantyre, Lanarkshire, of Lochneneas, Strabane, County Tyrone, merchant, was granted Irish denization on 9 July 1616. [IPR][SBT#22/29]; a merchant, leased 60 acres from the earl of Abercorn in January 1615. [PRONI#DOD.623/6]

HAMILTON, HUGH, of Ballygannoch, was granted Irish denization on 20 May 1617. [IPR]

HAMILTON, HUGH, merchant on the Christian of Carrickfergus at the port of Ayr 8 July 1678. [NAS.E72.3.4]

HAMILTON, HUGH, merchant on the Betty of Belfast at the port of Ayr 26 September 1681. [NAS.E72.3.9]

HAMILTON, HUGH, late of Bellybrettagh, County Down, born 1668, died 6 November 1728; his son Hugh Hamilton, born 1707, died 17 January 1729. [Killyleagh g/s, County Down]

HAMILTON, JAMES, was granted Irish denization on 22 June 1615, a merchant in Strabane, County Tyrone, 1617. [IPR][SBT#22]

HAMILTON, JAMES, gentleman, servant to the Earl of Abercorn, was granted Irish denization on 9 July 1616; in Strabane, County Tyrone, 1617. [IPR][SBT#22]

HAMILTON, JAMES, of Drumraye, County Fermanagh, was granted Irish denization on 17 August 1616. [IPR]

HAMILTON, JAMES, merchant in Strabane, was granted Irish denization on 17 August 1616. [IPR]

HAMILTON, Sir JAMES, with 3000 acres in the barony of Clankye, County Cavan, appeared at a muster in 1618 with 61 men, 3 muskets, 1 caliver, 22 pikes and 48 swords. [Cal. SP.Ire. 1618/501][BMAddMS#18735]

HAMILTON, JAMES, of Gortree, gentleman, was granted Irish denization on 28 November 1624. [IPR]

HAMILTON, JAMES, of Ballywalter, was granted Irish denization on 5 July 1631. [IPR]

HAMILTON, JAMES, in Donagheady, barony of Strabane, County Tyrone, probate 1637

HAMILTON, JAMES, born in 1600, second son of Gavin Hamilton a merchant in Coleraine, and grandson of Reverend Hans Hamilton in Dunlop, Ayrshire, graduated MA from Glasgow University in 1620, a minister in County Down from 1622 to 1638, died in Edinburgh on 10 March 1666, husband of (1) Elizabeth, daughter of Reverend David Watson in Killeavy, County Down, (2) Anna, daughter of Sir James Pringle in Galashiels. [PHS]

HAMILTON, JAMES, merchant and sometime provost of Bangor, died 21 January 1649. [Old Abbey Church g/s, Bangor]

HAMILTON, JAMES, born 1613, died 20 December 1651. [Holywood g/s]

HAMILTON, JAMES, gentleman in township of Saule, Ballysugach, County Down, 1659. [C]

HAMILTON, JAMES, in Eriglee, County Monaghan, 1659. [C]

HAMILTON, JAMES, gentleman in Killeleagh castle, County Down, 1659. [C]

HAMILTON, JAMES, in the barony of Castlereagh, County Down, 1659. [C]

HAMILTON, JAMES, son of Mr Gavin Hamilton, Prebend in Drumholme in the Kingdom of Ireland, testament confirmed on 29 August 1672 with the Commissariot of Glasgow

HAMILTON, Sir JAMES, Manrior Eliestoun, County Tyrone, testament confirmed on 3 July 1696 with the Commissariot of Edinburgh

HAMILTON, JAMES, merchant in Belfast, admitted as a burgess and guildsbrother of Glasgow 6 September 1707. [GBR]

HAMILTON, JAMES, of Cloughmills, High Sheriff of County Antrim in 1717. [UJA.11.1.79]

HAMILTON, JAMES, LL.B., Rector of Knock and Killeleagh, died in 1729. [County Down, Knock g/s]

HAMILTON, JANE, widow of Claud Hamilton, with 2000 acres at Garotobber and Clonkine, County Cavan, 28 March 1619. [Carew#211/32]

HAMILTON, JANE, wife of William Moore of Ballybregagh, was granted Irish denization on 5 July 1631. [IPR]

HAMILTON, JANE, born 1652, wife of Hugh Montgomery of Balymagown, died 22 July 1689. [Grey Abbey g/s]

HAMILTON, or BOYLE, JOAN, a widow, was granted Irish denization on 28 November 1624. [IPR]

HAMILTON, JOHN, was granted Irish denization on 10 May 1605. [IPR]

HAMILTON, JOHN, son of Patrick Hamilton clerk, was granted Irish denization on 9 July 1616. [IPR]

HAMILTON, JOHN, of Raphoe, was granted Irish denization on 17 August 1616. [IPR]

HAMILTON, JOHN, of Ballimagan, was granted Irish denization on 20 May 1617. [IPR]

HAMILTON, JOHN, of Bally McCormoch, was granted Irish denization on 28 November 1617. [IPR]

HAMILTON, JOHN, with 1000 acres appeared at a muster in 1618 with 24 men, 3 muskets, 7 calivers, 12 pikes, and 24 swords. [Cal. SP.Ire.1618/501][BMAddMS#18735]

HAMILTON, JOHN, the elder of Dromanish, tenant of John Hamilton of Edenagh, Precinct of Fewes, 1618. [PU#567]

HAMILTON, JOHN, with 2500 acres in the barony of Fues, County Armagh, appeared at a muster in 1618 with 56 men, 7 muskets, 11 calivers, 32 pikes and 40 swords. [Cal.SP.Ire.1618/501]

HAMILTON, JOHN, the elder, tenant of John Hamilton of Edenagh, Precinct of Fewes, 1618. [PU#567]

HAMILTON, JOHN, tenant of John Hamilton of Edenagh, Precinct of Fewes, 1618. [PU#567]

HAMILTON, JOHN, with 1000 acres in Killochan, County Cavan, 28 March 1619, [Carew Mss#211/2]; of Corronery, County Cavan, was granted Irish denization 29 July 1629. [IPR]

HAMILTON, JOHN, of Loughesk, County Donegal, gentleman, was granted Irish denization 19 July 1631. [IPR]; Justice of the Peace for County Donegal in 1629. [Cal.SP.Ire.1629/1437]

HAMILTON, JOHN, of Latbeag, County Tyrone, gentleman, was granted Irish denization on 19 July 1633. [IPR]

HAMILTON, JOHN, in the barony of Ardes, County Down, 1659. [C]

HAMILTON, JOHN, born in Scotland, graduated MA from
Edinburgh University in 1650, minister at Donaghadee from
1658, died at the Siege of Londonderry in 1689. [FI#39]

HAMILTON, JOHN, Captain of the Earl of Eglinton's Regiment, in
Bangor 1642. [PRO.SP.18.120]

HAMILTON, JOHN, Lieutenant Colonel of the Earl of Lindsay's
Regiment, in Bangor 1642. [PRO.SP.28.120]

HAMILTON, JOHN, in Devonish, County Fermanagh, 1659. [C]

HAMILTON, JOHN, in Dungannon on 8 March 1667.
[Cal.SP.Ire.348/8]

HAMILTON, JOHN, in Callidon, County Tyrone, subscribed to his
will on 20 January 1713, reference to his wife, son and
unmarried daughter, sisters Elizabeth Leslie, Agnes and
Magdalene, probate 19 May 1716 Dublin

HAMILTON, JOHN, of Ballymenagh, born 1646, died 2 May 1722.
[Holywood g/s]

HAMILTON, JOHN, born in Sorbie, Scotland, during 1651, eldest
son of Reverend Archibald Hamilton, graduated MA from
Edinburgh University in 1668, minister in Ballee from 1673 to
1685, in Comber from 1685 to 1689, died on 17 October 1702,
husband of (1) Annie Reynolds 1673, (2) Jean, daughter of
Reverend Peter Blair in Jedburgh in 1696, (3) Maybel,
daughter of Hugh Campbell in Donaghadee in 1698, (4)
Elizabeth, daughter of Henry Cunningham in Carlung 1701.
[FI#65]

HAMILTON, JOSEPH, born in Scotland, graduated MA from
Edinburgh University in 1646, minister in Duneane and Grange
from 1655, died in April 1686. [FI#39]

HAMILTON, MALCOLM, of Portaferry, graduated MA at the
University of St Andrews 1600, Chancellor of Down 1612,
Archbishop of Cashel 1623. [UJA#13/15]

HAMILTON, MALCOLM, of Castleton, County Fermanagh, Was
granted Irish denization on 17 August 1616. [IPR]

HAMILTON, MALCOLM, with 1500 acres at Dermiefogher in the Precinct of Magheraboy, 28 March 1619. [Carew Mss#211/69]

HAMILTON, MALCOLM, a minister in the diocese of Clogher, 1622. [TCD.ms.E#3/6]

HAMILTON, or MONTGOMERY, MARGARET, was granted Irish denization on 13 May 1634. [IPR]

HAMILTON, MARION, wife of Hugh Hamilton of Lisrovin, County Tyrone, gentleman, was granted Irish denization on 19 July 1631. [IPR]

HAMILTON, N., petitioner in June 1624. [Cal.SP.Ire.1624/1226]

HAMILTON, PATRICK, clerk, was granted Irish denization on 9 July 1616. [IPR]; a minister in the diocese of Down, 1622. [TCD.ms.E#3/6]; possibly the Reverend Patrick Hamilton in Donagheady, probate 1635

HAMILTON, PATRICK, of Ballygrangagh, was granted Irish denization on 5 July 1631. [IPR]

HAMILTON, PATRICK, of Strabane, County Tyrone, merchant, was granted Irish denization on 19 July 1633. [IPR]

HAMILTON, PATRICK, born in Ireland son of Patrick Hamilton of Clanbowies, a trooper in HM Life Guards in Linlithgow 5 June 1678. [CA.1.xxxix]

HAMILTON, ROBERT, of Stonehouse, Lanarkshire, applied for 2000 acres in Ulster on 13 July 1609, [PU#140]; was granted Irish denization on 29 August 1610 and a grant of Dirrinefogher in the barony of Magheraboy, County Fermanagh, 29 August 1610, [IPR] [TCD.ms#N2/2]; Undertaker in the Precinct of Magheraboy, County Fermanagh, 1611. [Cal.SP.Ire.1611/384]

HAMILTON, ROBERT, son of Gilbert Hamilton of Raploch, applied for 2000 acres in Ulster on 27 July 1609. [PU#143]

HAMILTON, ROBERT, MD, was granted Irish denization on 9 July 1616. [IPR]

HAMILTON, ROBERT, of Carrickelle, County Tyrone, was granted Irish denization on 17 August 1616. [IPR][SBT#23]

HAMILTON, ROBERT, of Ballinikell, was granted Irish denization on 28 November 1617. [IPR]

HAMILTON, ROBERT, tenant of John Hamilton of Edenagh, Precinct of Fewes, 1618. [PU#567]

HAMILTON, ROBERT, minister in the Diocese of Armagh, 1622. [TCD.msE#3/6]

HAMILTON, ROBERT, son of John Hamilton of Priestfield, Blantyre, Lanarkshire, was granted the estate of Caledon, County Tyrone, ca.1630. [SBT#22]

HAMILTON, ROBERT, of Rathcoole, was granted Irish denization on 13 May 1634. [IPR]

HAMILTON, ROBERT, Captain of the Earl of Lindsay's Regiment, in Bangor 1642. [PRO.SP.28.120]

HAMILTON, ROBERT, in the barony of Ardes, County Down, 1659. [C]

HAMILTON, ROBERT, in County Fermanagh, 1659. [C]

HAMILTON, ROBERT, born in Scotland, graduated MA from Glasgow University in 1648, minister at Killead from 1655, died in December 1673. [FI#39]

HAMILTON, ROBERT, a merchant in Killyleagh, died on 3 June 1689; his wife Jean Philips died on 10 September 1699. [Killyleagh g/s, County Down]

HAMILTON, ROBERT, graduated MA from Edinburgh University in 1679, minister in Brigh, Ballyclug, in 1688. [FI#65]

HAMILTON, THOMAS, of Ramullin, was granted Irish denization on 28 November 1617. [IPR]

HAMILTON, URSILLA, wife of Robert Hamilton a merchant, died on 6 September 1663. [Killyleagh g/s, County Down]

HAMILTON, WILLIAM, born about 1577 in Wedderhill, Fife, grandson of John Hamilton, Archbishop of St Andrews, of Trien Itragh, barony of Strabane, County Tyrone, gentleman, was granted Irish denization on 9 July 1616. [IPR][SBT#31]

HAMILTON, WILLIAM, a merchant in Strabane, County Tyrone, was granted Irish denization 17 August 1616. [IPR][SBT#22/29]

HAMILTON, WILLIAM, son of John Hamilton of Priestfield, Blantyre, Lanarkshire, of Ballefetan, County Tyrone, was granted Irish denization 17 August 1616, married Janet Moore, parents of nine children, imprisoned by the rebels in Doe Castle, County Donegal, in 1641, suffered 'great prevations' and died in 1642 [IPR][SBT#22]

HAMILTON, WILLIAM, of Loghskenie, County Donegal, was granted Irish denization on 17 August 1616. [IPR]

HAMILTON, WILLIAM, of Ballyclochen, was granted Irish denization on 20 May 1617. [IPR]

HAMILTON, WILLIAM, of Bangor, was granted Irish denization on 28 November 1617. [IPR]

HAMILTON, WILLIAM, with 1000 acres in the barony of Clankye, County Cavan, appeared at a muster in 1618 with 24 men, 1 musket, 3 calivers, 14 pikes, and 15 swords. [Cal.SP.Ire.1618/501] [BMAddMS#18735]; in Dromyck, County Cavan, with 1000 acres on 28 March 1619. [Carew Mss#211/3]

HAMILTON, WILLIAM, a minister in the diocese of Raphoe, 1622. [TCD.ms.E#3/6]

HAMILTON, WILLIAM, of Rowbane, was granted Irish denization on 5 July 1631. [IPR]

HAMILTON, WILLIAM, 1636. [SP.Ire#255/144]

HAMILTON, WILLIAM, Captain of Sir Mungo Campbell of Lawers' Regiment, in Temple Patrick, 1642. [PRO.SP.18.120]

HAMILTON, WILLIAM, in township of Bright, County Down, 1659. [C]

HAMILTON, WILLIAM, in the barony of Ardes, County Down, 1659. [C]

HAMILTON, WILLIAM, a juryman at a Coroner's inquest held at Duncanalley, County Donegal, on 15 September 1660. [Cal.S.P.Ire.1660]

HAMILTON, Lieutenant Colonel WILLIAM, who had raised cavalry in Ireland and sent it to Scotland in 1648 to support King Charles I, petitioned the Scots Parliament for reimbursement in 1663. [APS]

HAMILTON, WILLIAM, in Dungannon on 8 March 1667. [Cal.SP.Ire.348/8]

HAMILTON, WILLIAM, of Killiragh, County Down, 18 January 1712. [NAS.GD25, sec.8/900]

HAMILTON, WILLIAM, of Bellymulin, born 1657, died 28 February 1720. [Bangor Abbey g/s]

HAMPTON, WILLIAM, from Aberdeenshire, a minister in Burt, Inch and Elagh from 1673 to 1688. [FI#66]

HANNAH, JOHN, merchant on the John of Donaghadee at the port of Irvine, Ayrshire, on 16 August 1682. [NAS.E72.12.5]

HANNA, SAMUEL, a merchant in Londonderry, 18 June 1690. [NAS.GD26.4.242]

HANNAY, DAVID, in Dublin Castle, 3 March 1628. [SP.Ire#246/949]

HANNAY, PATRICK, late servant to the late Earl of Dunbar appointed as clerk to the Council of Ireland on 7 June 1624, [Cal.SP.Ire.1624/1226]; was granted Irish denization on 31 July 1624. [IPR][SP.Ire#241/96]

HANNAY, ROBERT, made a free denizen of Ireland and granted lands in Glencapp, County Wicklow, on 8 May 1628. [SP.Ire#246/991]

HARE, SAMUEL, master of the John of Larne at the port of Irvine, Ayrshire, on 27 March 1691. [NAS.E72.12.18]

HARPER, ALEXANDER, in Donagheady, barony of Strabane, County Tyrone, probate 1636

HARPER, JOHN, of Donaghadie, was granted Irish denization on 20 May 1617. [IPR]

HARPER, JOHN, of Ballyhay, County Down, was granted Irish denization on 20 May 1617. [IPR]

HARPER, ROBERT, of Provoston, was granted Irish denization on 20 May 1617. [IPR]

HARRIS, WILLIAM, an Irish student at Glasgow University 1706. [MUG#184]

HART, GEORGE, a Scots-Irish student at Glasgow University 1709. [MUG#192]

HART, JOHN, born in Scotland during 1617, graduated MA from St Andrews University in 1637, a minister in Taughboyne, Monreagh, from 1656, died on 8 January 1687, buried at Taughboyne, [FI#40]; a non-conformist minister imprisoned at Lifford in 1669. [Cal.SP.Ire.]

HARTLEY, EDWARD, was granted Irish denization on 12 February 1618. [IPR]

HARTLEY, JOHN, an Anglo-Irish student at Edinburgh University 1688. [CEG]

HARVIE, JOHN, was granted Irish denization on 22 June 1615. [IPR]

HARVEY, JOHN, a Scots-Irish student at Glasgow University 1709. [MUG#192]

HARVIE, THOMAS, of Newton, was granted Irish denization on 28 November 1617. [IPR]

HARVEY, THOMAS, born in 1645, graduated MA from Glasgow University in 1665, minister in Ballyrashane from 1673 to 1680, in Carndonagh and Moville from 1700, died on 24 February 1718. [FI#67]

HASTIE, JOHN, master of the Mary of Belfast at the port of Irvine, Ayrshire, on 10 December 1685. [NAS.E72.12.11]

HASTIE, JOHN, master of the Elizabeth of Coleraine at the port of Irvine, Ayrshire, on 3 August 1689. [NAS.E72.12.15]

HASTIE, JOHN, a Scots-Irish student at Glasgow University 1708. [MUG#189]

HASTIE, ROBERT, merchant aboard the Elizabeth of Glenarme at the port of Irvine, Ayrshire, on 14 January 1691. [NAS.E72.12.17]

HATRICK, JAMES, Strabane, County Tyrone, was granted Irish denization on 17 August 1616. [IPR][SBT#22]

HAY, FRANCIE, a distressed person from Ireland, given two dollars on 9 February 1644 by Elgin Kirk Session, Morayshire. [Elgin Kirk Session Records]

HAY, Sir GEORGE, servant of the king, was granted Irish denization on 23 December 1618. [IPR]

HAY, GEORGE, son of Sir George Hay, was granted Irish denization on 23 December 1618. [IPR]

HAY, HENRY, Captain of Colonel Stanley's Regiment in Ireland, husband of Margaret..., 1715. [NAS.RD4.116.455]

HAY, JAMES, a distressed person from Ireland, given two dollars on 9 February 1644 by Elgin Kirk Session, Morayshire. [Elgin KSR]

HAY, JOHN, a distressed person from Ireland, given two dollars on 9
February 1644 by Elgin Kirk Session, Morayshire. [Elgin KSR]

HAY, MARGARET, a distressed person from Ireland, given two
dollars on 9 February 1644 by Elgin Kirk Session, Morayshire.
[Elgin KSR]

HAY, MARJORY, daughter of a minister who had been killed by the
rebels in Ireland, was given two dollars on 17 February 1643
by Elgin Kirk Session, Morayshire. [Elgin KSR]

HAY, PETER, son of Sir Geoge Hay, was granted Irish denization on
23 December 1618. [IPR]

HEIGATE, JAMES, a clerk, was granted Irish denization on 26
August 1629. [IPR]

HELM, DAVID, a Scots-Irish student at Glasgow University 1708.
[MUG#189]

HENDERSON, ALEXANDER, a Scots-Irish student at Glasgow
University 1714. [MUG#203]

HENDERSON, DAVID, burgess of Newton Ards, County Down,
1612. [Cal.SP.Ire.1613/614]

HENDERSON, JOHN, a tailor in Strabane, was granted Irish
denization on 17 August 1616. [IPR][SBT#22]

HENDERSON, JOHN, merchant aboard the Margaret of Belfast at
the port of Irvine, Ayrshire, on 23 August 1682.
[NAS.E72.12.5]

HENDERSON, JOHN. Margaret Walker, relict of John Henderson, a
wright in Newcastle, who had fought and died for King
William in Ireland, petitioned the Privy Council of Scotland on
29 December 1691. [RPCS.XVI.655]

HENDRIE, HUGH, master of the Mathew of Donaghadee at the port
of Irvine, Ayrshire, on 24 September 1690. [NAS.E72.12.16]

HENRISON, ALEXANDER, of Ramullin, was granted Irish
denization on 28 November 1617. [IPR]

HENRY, JOHN, of Raphoe, was granted Irish denization on 28
November 1617. [IPR]

HENRY, ROBERT, a Presbyterian minister in Northern Ireland who
petitioned the Queen in 1691. [CTB.#/III.1207, 1258]

HENRY, WILLIAM, graduated MA from Glasgow University in
1663, a minister in Donegal and Belleek from 1674. [FI#67]

HENRY, WILLIAM, a Scots-Irish student at Edinburgh University
1706. [CEG]

HEPBURN, ALEXANDER, of Bangla, applied for 2000 acres in
Ulster on 18 July 1609. [PU#140]

HEPBURN, Sir ROBERT, baronet, was granted Irish denization on
12 July 1610. [IPR]; grant of O'Carragan, Precinct of
Mountjoy, on 12 July 1610.
[EPR.8.10][TCD/msN2/2][PU#547]; Undertaker in Precinct of
Mountjoy, County Tyrone, 1611; with 1500 acres in the barony
of Dungannon, County Tyrone, appeared at a muster in 1618
with 23 men, 1 musket, 3 calivers, 10 pike, 1 halberd, and 8
swords. [Cal.SP.Ire.1611/384; 1618/501][BM.AddMS#18735];
with 1800 acres at Carraghan, Precinct of Mountjoy on 28
March 1619. [Carew Mss#211/144]

HEPBURN, ROBERT, Captain of Robert Home of the Heugh's
Regiment, in Carrickfergus, 1642. [PRO.SP.18.120]

HEPBURN, WILLIAM, in Bishop Gate Street, Londonderry, 1659.
[C]; a gentleman in Londonderry, 1666. [IWD]

HERIOTT, GEORGE, was granted Irish denization on 9 March 1611.
[IPR]

HERRIES, FRANCIS, of Inver, a juryman at a Coroner's inquest held
at Duncanalley, County Donegal, on 15 September 1660.
[Cal.S.P.Ire.1660]

HERRIES, JOHN, in County Antrim (?), son of John Herries of Little
Culloch, 31 July 1693. [NAS.RS.Dumfries.5.95]

HERRON, JOHN, born 1652, died 14 December 1716; his wife Janet
Carnahan, born 1665, died 18 May 1727. [Killinchy g/s,
County Down]

HERRON, JOHN, born 1682, a clothier, died on 4 December 1728.
[Killyleagh g/s, County Down]

HERVY, THOMAS, a Scots-Irish student at Edinburgh University in
1699. [CEG]

HESLET, JOHN, a Scots-Irish student at Glasgow University 1715.
[MUG#205]

HEWISON, JOHN, a merchant in Dublin, admitted as a burgess and
guildsbrother of Glasgow 15 December 1724, [GBR]

HEYGATE, JAMES, a clerk and preacher, was granted Irish
denization on 11 July 1619. [IPR]

HIGGINS, MARMADUKE, an Irish student at Glasgow University
1718. [MUG#213]

HILL, ADAM, in Claggan, 1698. [IWD]

HILL, SAMUEL, an Irish student at Glasgow University 1710.
[MUG#194]

HILL, THOMAS, a Captain in Stewart's Regiment of Foot, 1710.
[IWD]

HILLHOUSE, ABRAHAM, a merchant in Ardkellie, County
Londonderry, 1675. [NAS.GD8#871]

HODGE, DAVID, accused of murdering Sir John Wemyss, failed to
appear at the Court of the Chief Place in Ireland during 1627.
[SP.Ire.Docquet#14]

HOGG, ROBERT, of Bellilidie, was granted Irish denization on 28
November 1617. [IPR]

HOGGE, WILLIAM, of Rathgill, born 1665, died 29 September
1704. [Old Abbey Church g/s, Bangor]

HOGSHEAD, FRANCIS, in Strabane, County Tyrone, probate 1623

HOGSYARD, ROBERT, born in Scotland, graduated MA from Glasgow University in 1653, minister in Ballyrashane from 1657. [FI#40]

HOLMES, JAMES, master of the Two Brothers of Coleraine at the port of Irvine, Ayrshire, on 24 December 1685. [NAS.E72.12.11]

HOLMES, JOHN, master of the John and Isabel of Belfast at the port of Irvine, Ayrshire, on 25 August 1691. [NAS.E72.12.18]

HOMBLE, JAMES, a minister in Ballimore, in January 1650. [NAS.GD3.3.42.5]

HOME, ALEXANDER, of Crofts, Berwickshire, Undertaker in the Precinct of Magheraboy, County Fermanagh, 29 April 1611. [Cal.SP.Ire.1611/384][TCD.ms#N2/2]

HOME, GEORGE, with 1000 acres at Drumcos, Precinct of Magheraboy, 28 March 1619. [Carew Mss#211/69]

HOME, GEORGE of Whitefield, serviced as heir to his uncle Alexander, Bishop of Raphoe, Ireland, on 6 July 1703. [NAS.SH]

HOME, Sir JOHN, of North Berwick, son of Alexander Home of Manderston, Berwickshire, was granted Irish denization on 24 July 1610, was granted Ardgart in the barony of Magheryboy, County Fermanagh, 24 July 1610. [IPR][TCD.ms#N2/2]; with 1500 acres at Moyglass, and 2000 acres at Carrynroe, Precinct of Magheraboy, 28 March 1619, [Carew Mss#211/71, 73]

HOME, JOHN, Major of the Earl of Leven's Regiment, in Carrickfergus, 1642. [PRO.SP28/120]

HOME, JONATHAN, in Dunmurray, County Antrim, 29 September 1718. [NAS.RS.19.9.257-259]

HOME, PHOEBE, spouse of Dr Christopher Irvine of Castle Irvine, as factor for her husband, 13 April 1697. [NAS.RH9.17.445]

HOME, ROBERT, of Blackhills, brother of the laird of Aytoun, applied for 2000 acres in Ulster on 27 July 1609. [PU#143]

HOME, Colonel ROBERT, in Carrickfergus, 1642. [PRO.SP.18.120]

HOME, ROBERT, Captain of the Lifeguards of Foot in Donaghadee on 14 September 1642. [PRO.SP.16.539.1/105]

HONEYMAN, ALEXANDER, a merchant in Carrick, Ireland, admitted as a burgess and guildsbrother of Glasgow on 20 December 1716. [GBR]

HONIS (?), ANDREW, was granted Irish denization on 22 June 1615. [IPR]

HOOK, JOHN, born 1681, son of David Hook in Comber, died 23 May 1704. [Comber g/s]

HOPE, WILLIAM, tenant of John Hamilton of Edenagh, Precinct of Fewes, 1618. [PU#567]

HORNE, Sir JOHN, Undertaker in the Precinct of Magheraboy, County Fermanagh, 1611. [Cal.SP.Ire.1611/384]

HORSBURGH, ROBERT, of Broadland, was granted Irish denization on 13 May 1634. [IPR]

HOUSTON, ALEXANDER, of Ballemeachan, son of William Houston, was granted Irish denization on 28 November 1624. [IPR]

HOUSTON, ALEXANDER, a tenant on Adair's estate in County Antrim, 1630. [PRONI#D15237]

HOUSTON, DAVID, born in Renfrewshire during 1633, educated in Glasgow around 1650, a minister in Glenarm and Ballymoney from 1661 to 1672, died on 8 December 1696, buried at Connor. [FI#67]

HOUSTON, JOHN, of Ballemeachan, son of William Houston, was granted Irish denization on 28 November 1624. [IPR]

HOUSTON, JOHN, Captain of the Earl of Glencairn's Regiment, in Carrickfergus 1642. [PRO.SP.18.120]

HOUSTON, RICHARD, gentleman in Kilkeele parish, barony of Newry, County Down, 1659. [C]

HOUSTON, ROBERT, in Silver Street, Londonderry, 1659. [C]

HOUSTON, WILLIAM, of Ballemeachan, gentleman, was granted Irish denization on 28 November 1624. [IPR]

HOUSTON, WILLIAM, son of William Houston of Ballemeachan, was granted Irish denization on 28 November 1624. [IPR]

HOUSTON, WILLIAM, of Craigs Castle, High Sheriff of County Antrim, 1628. [UJA#11.1.79]

HOUSTON, WILLIAM, of Craigs Castle, High Sheriff of County Antrim in 1676. [UJA.11.1.79]

HOW, JAMES, a Scots-Irish student at Glasgow University 1707. [MUG#187]

HOWATSON, MOSES, of Belaghstoun, a gentleman in County Kildare, 1715. [NAS.RD2.104.1006]

HOWE, ALEXANDER, of Crofts, grant of 1000 acres at Drumcoast, Precinct of Magheryboy, County Fermanagh, by 1612. [Cal.SP.Ire.1612/608]

HOWE, Sir JOHN, of North Berwick, grant of 2000 acres at Ardgart, Precinct of Magheryboy, County Fermanagh, by 1612. [Cal.SP.Ire.1612/608]

HOWIE, ALEXANDER, merchant aboard the Mary of Glenarme at the port of Irvine, Ayrshire, on 14 November 1690. [NAS.E72.12.17]

HOWIE, JAMES, of Ballymulin, was granted Irish denization on 28 November 1617. [IPR]

HOWNE, PATRICK, was granted Irish denization on 12 February 1618. [IPR]

HUDGSON, GEORGE, was granted Irish denization on 22 June 1615. [IPR]

HUME, Sir JOHN, in Devonish, County Fermanagh, 1659, [C]; 1695. [IWD]

HUME, PATRICK, in Devonish, County Fermanagh, 1659. [C]

HUNTER, HENRY, tenant of John Hamilton of Edenagh, Precinct of Fewes, 1618. [PU#567]

HUNTER, HENRY, second son of Patrick Hunter of Hunterstone in West Kilbride, Ayrshire, graduated MA from Glasgow University in 1650, a minister in Drommore from 1660, died in November 1673. [FI#40][Hunter of Hunterstone MSS#24/28]

HUNTER, JOHN, son of Patrick Hunter of Hunterstone, West Kilbride, graduated MA from Glasgow University in 1655, minister in Magherally from 1672 to 1684, died in Scotland during January 1699. [FI#68]

HUNTER, JOHN, master of the Providence of Coleraine at the port of Irvine, Ayrshire, 25 April 1682. [NAS.E72.12.6]

HUNTER, NATHANIEL, master of the Speedwell of Glenarm at the port of Ayr 10 March 1690. [NAS.E72.3.23]

HUNTER, PATRICK, in Glenarme 8 February 1656. [NAS.GD3.2.46.25]

HUNTER, PATRICK, master of the Janet of Glenarme at the port of Irvine, Ayrshire, 3 January 1681 and 4 August 1681. [NAS.E72.12.5/6]

HUNTER, ROBERT, of Cargin, County Donegal, was granted Irish denization on 17 August 1616. [IPR]

HUNTER, ROBERT, merchant aboard the Charlemont of Belfast at the port of Ayr 18 June 1678. [NAS.E72.3.4]

HUNTER, WILLIAM of Donan, was granted Irish denization on 20 May 1617. [IPR]

HUNTER, WILLIAM, master of the Mary of Glenarme at the port of
Irvine, Ayrshire, 5 November 1683. [NAS.E72.12.8]

HUTCHISON, ALEXANDER, son of George Hutcheson in
Monkton, Ayrshire, educated at Glasgow University in 1650, a
minister in Down, resident of Drumalig, a minister in Dublin
from 1690 to 1692, died in Armagh on 11 November 1711,
father of Beatrix - wife of Hugh Wallace of Ballyobikin, and
John, minister of Downpatrick from 1690 to 1697 and Armagh
from 1607 to 1729, [FI#41]; in Drumalig, Tonaghneeve,
County Down, will subscribed on 25 September 1711, probate
26 January 1725 Dublin; a Presbyterian minister in Northern
Ireland who petitioned the Queen in 1691. [CTB.#/III.1207,
1258]

HUTCHISON, ANDREW, master of the Marie of Glencairn at the
port of Glasgow 28 March 1670. [NAS.E72.10.2]

HUTCHISON, JAMES, merchant aboard the Mayflower of Larne at
the port of Irvine, Ayrshire, on 1 September 1689.
[NAS.E72.12.14]

HUTCHISON, JAMES, in Macosquin parish, County Londonderry,
1715. [NAS.RD4.117.856]

HUTCHISON, ISOBEL, daughter of John Hutchison in Macosquin
parish, County Londonderry, wife of John Armstrong there,
1715, [NAS.RD4.117.856]

HUTCHISON, JOHN, in Macosquin parish, County Londonderry,
1715. [NAS.RD4.117.856]

HUTCHISON, MARGARET, daughter of John Hutchison in
Macosquin parish, County Londonderry, wife of Robert
Workman in Balteoch parish, County Londonderry, 1715.
[NAS.RD4.117.856]

HYGATE, JAMES, Archdeacon of Clogher, County Monaghan, Was
granted Irish denization on 20 May 1617. [IPR]; a minister in
the diocese of Clogher, 1622. [TCD.ms.E#3/6]

INGLIS, JOHN, of Moynagh, County Tyrone, yeoman, was granted Irish denization on 27 June 1634. [IPR]

INGLIS, NINIAN, merchant in Londonderry, was granted Irish denization on 9 July 1616. [IPR]

INGLIS, THOMAS, of Old Liston, applied for 2000 acres in Ulster on 4 August 1609. [PU#143]

INNES, WILLIAM, Captain of Lord Sinclair's Regiment, in Newry, 1642. [PRO.SP.18.120]

IRELAND, JOHN, in Drumconell, Ireland, husband of Margaret McGill, 27 May 1695. [NAS.GD117/128]

IRVING, ALEXANDER, a plumber in Dublin, subscribed to his will on 12 October 1709, probate 3 September 1715 Dublin

IRVINE, CHRISTOPHER, of Letramonie, County Fermanagh, was granted Irish denization on 17 August 1616. [IPR]

IRVINE, CHARLES, serviced as heir to his father Thomas Irvine, surgeon apothecary in Dublin on 28 April 1713. [NAS/SH]

IRVINE, CHRISTOPHER, of Castle Irvine, Ireland, serviced as heir to his cousin Dr Christopher Irvine of Castle Irvine on 12 August 1714. [NAS.SH]

IRVINE, Major CHRISTOPHER, of Castle Irvine, County Fermanagh, cousin of Dr Christopher Irvine, 1714. [NAS.RD3.143.79]

IRVINE, CHRISTOPHER, son of Thomas Irvine an apothecary in Dublin and grandson of John Irvine of Drumcoltran, 1714. [NAS.RD2.104.57]; 1715, [NAS.RD3.145.231]

IRVING, EDWARD, tenant of John Hamilton of Edenagh, Precinct of Fewes, 1618. [PU#567]

IRVINE, GERALD, in Dungannon on 8 March 1667. [Cal.SP.Ire.348/8]

IRVING, JAMES, in Ballybridge, County Roscommon, 1684. [IWD]

IRVING, ROBERT, at the Mill of Cowie, applied for 2000 acres in Ulster on 20 July 1609. [PU#141]

IRVING, THOMAS, of Ancrush, a juryman at a Coroner's inquest held at Duncanalley, County Donegal, on 15 September 1660. [Cal.S.P.Ire.1660]

IRVING, THOMAS, serviced as heir to his brother Christopher Irvine, son of Thomas Irvine surgeon in Dublin on 6 December 1715. [NAS.SH]; an apothecary in Dublin 1710. [IWD]

IRVINE, THOMAS, an apothecary in Dublin, son of John Irvine of Drumcoltran, 1714, 1715. [NAS.RD2.104.57; RD3.145.231]

IRVINE, WILLIAM, in Derryvolan, County Fermanagh, 1659. [C]

IRWIN, ALEXANDER, surveyor at the port of Dundalk, August 1712. [CTP.Vol.CLI]

JACK, GIDEON, born in Scotland, graduated MA from Edinburgh University in 1665, ordained in Wexford during 1681, married Judith Waulkets, a minister in Killeshands from 1702 to 1704. [FI#69]

JACK, WILLIAM, born in Scotland, graduated MA from Edinburgh University in 1649, a minister in Ireland from 1655 to 1692, died in Scotland after October 1699. [FI#42]

JACKSON, HENDRY, master of the Janet of Donaghadee at the port of Ayr 15 November 1689. [NAS.E72.3.21]

JACKSON, JAMES, in Newtown, County Down, subscribed to his will on 13 November 1711, reference to his brother John Jackson of Ballygregin and his son James, nephew Gilbert son of John Jackson of Ballyskeagh, nephew John Teat, James Neill tenant of Ballymasea, John Thompson and John Jackson both in the parish of Newtown, Elizabeth Cord and her sisters and brothers, and his servants James Sloane and Martha Wither, witnesses Thomas jackson, innkeeper in Newtown, John Thomson, merchant in Newtown, and John Mairs, minister in Newtown, probate 18 February 1712, Dublin

JACOBS, SAMUEL, an Anglo-Irish student at Glasgow University in 1705. [MUG#183]

JAMIESON, DUGALD, minister in Catterline, Kinneff, Kincardineshire, then in Carncastle and Killwaughter, Ireland, husband of Elizabeth Allan, 1714. [NAS.RD3.140.170]

JAMESON, JOHN, was granted Irish denization on 6 September 1605. [IPR]

JAMIESON, JOHN, master of the Mary of Donaghadee at the port of Glasgow 1 June 1670. [NAS.E72.10.2]

JOHNSON, ANDREW agent for Sir Robert McLellan of Bombay, in the Precinct of Boylagh, 29 July 1611. [Cal.SP.Ire.1611/203]

JOHNSON, ARCHIBALD, was granted Irish denization on 9 July 1616. [IPR]

JOHNSON, JAMES, was granted Irish denization on 28 November 1617. [IPR]

JOHNSON, ROBERT, was granted Irish denization on 20 January 1622. [Privy Seal Chancery, file 1930]

JOHNSTON, CHARLES, a Scots-Irish student at Glasgow University 1715. [MUG#206]

JOHNSTON, DAVID, in Donagh, County Monaghan, 1659. [C]

JOHNSTON, DAVID, in Devonish, County Fermanagh, 1659. [C]

JOHNSTON, GABRIEL, a Presbyterian minister who fled from Scotland to Ireland in 1669. [Cal.S.P.Ire.1669]

JOHNSTON, GEORGE, an Irish student at Glasgow University 1718. [MUG#212]

JOHNSTON, GILBERT, a merchant burgess of Ayr residing in Halywood, Ireland, husband of Janet Mason, 17 August 1625. [NAS.GD1.521.4]

JOHNSTON, JAMES, baillie of the Water of Leith, applied for 2000 acres in Ulster on 27 July 1609. [PU#143]

JOHNSTON, JAMES, of Dromedon, County Fermanagh, 17 August 1616. [IPR]

JOHNSTON, JAMES, a minister at Lisnakea from 1655 to 1661. [FI#42]

JOHNSTON, JAMES, a gentleman in Aghnacldony, County Fermanagh, 1676. [IWD]

JOHNSTON, JAMES, in Enniskillen, 1699. [IWD]

JOHNSTON, JAMES, in Aghanure, County Fermanagh 1693. [IWD]

JOHNSTON, JOHN, tenant of John Hamilton of Edenagh, Precinct of Fewes, 1618. [PU#567]

JOHNSTONE, JOHN, a merchant in Londonderry (?) 1643. [SP.Ire#307/104]

JOHNSTON, JOHN, in Devonish, County Fermanagh, 1659. [C]

JOHNSTON, JOHN, in Maghercoolmoney, County Fermanagh, 1659. [C]

JOHNSTON, JOHN, master of the .....of Carrickfergus at the port of Glasgow 31 October 1670. [NAS.E72.10.2]

JOHNSTON, JOHN, merchant in Belfast, 1714. [NAS.RD3.141.75]

JOHNSTON, JOHN, a Scots-Irish student at Glasgow University in 1713. [MUG#201]

JOHNSTON, RICHARD, master of the Anthony of Larne at the port of Irvine, Ayrshire, on 7 October 1689. [NAS.E72.12.13]

JOHNSTON, Ensign ROBERT, in Clenish, County Fermanagh, 1659. [C]

JOHNSTOUN, THOMAS, in Fermanagh, petitioned the Lord Deputy on 11 October 1628. [SP.Ire#243/491,1]

JOHNSTONE, WALTER, gentleman in Rademane township, County Down, 1659. [C]

JOHNSTON, WALTER, in Templecarne, County Fermanagh, 1659. [C]

JOHNSTON, WALTER, in Mewlick, County Fermanagh, 1693. [IWD]

JOHNSTON, WILLIAM, in Donagh, County Monaghan, 1659. [C]

JOHNSTONE, WILLIAM, of Glynn, High Sheriff of County Antrim in 1723. [UJA.11.1.79]

JONES, MOSES, master of the Merchants Adventure of Belfast, arrived in Port Glasgow from Barbados September 1682. [NAS.E72.19.5]

KALLYA, (?), JANET, born 1664, wife of John Kernochan of Bellynockes, died on 29 March 1714. [Saintfield g/s, County Down]

KEARNES, JOHN, of Parsontown, County Tyrone, gentleman, was granted Irish denization on 19 July 1633. [IPR]

KEELAND, JOHN, Londonderry, was granted Irish denization on 17 August 1616. [IPR]

KEISH, JOHN, gentleman , in the barony of Castlereagh, County Down, 1659. [C]

KEITH, ALEXANDER, minister of Strathbrock, husband of Margaret Hamilton, later in Ireland, 5 March 1657. [NAS.GD30.1339, 1349]

KEITH, GEORGE, a sergeant-major in Antrim on 19 May 1645. [SP.Ire#260/137]

KEITH, GEORGE, born in Aberdeen around 1639, graduated MA from Marischal College, Aberdeen, in 1657, minister of Drumglass from 1659 to 1676, converted to Quakerism and emigrated to America in 1684, later became an Anglican, died in England on 27 March 1716. [FI#48]

KELLO, JOHN, master of the John of Portaferry at the port of Irvine, Ayrshire, on 15 August 1686. [NAS.E72.12.12]

KELSOE, THOMAS, of Ballihacamer, was granted Irish denization on 28 November 1617. [IPR]

KELSO, JAMES, from Ireland, imprisoned in Glasgow Tolbooth, petitioned the Privy Council 5 June 1685. [RPCS.11.64]

KENNEDY, ALEXANDER, a merchant in Newry, County Down, 1702. [NAS.RD2.86.1.372]

KENNEDY, ALEXANDER, a merchant in Raphryland, Ireland, 1702. [NAS.RD2.86.1.64]

KENNEDY, ANTHONY, was granted Irish denization on 29 January 1611. [IPR]

KENNEDY, ANTHONY, of Ballununan-Utrogh, was granted Irish denization on 28 November 1617. [IPR]

KENNEDY, ANTONY, born in Ayrshire during 1614, graduated MA at the University of St Andrews 1640, minister at Templepark from 1646, died on 11 December 1697, buried in Templepark. [UJA#13/15][FI#43]

KENNEDY, ANTHONY, a Scots-Irish student at Edinburgh University 1695. [CEG]

KENNEDY, DAVID, burgess of Newton Ards, County Down, 1612. [Cal.SP.Ire.1613/614]; a minister in Newtownards 1638, fled to Scotland. [PHS]

KENNEDY, DAVID, of Mencloynt, was granted Irish denization on 20 May 1617. [IPR]

KENNEDY, DAVID, of Gortivillan, was granted Irish denization on 28 November 1617. [IPR]

KENNEDY, DAVID, with 1000 acres at Horteville, Precinct of Mountjoy, 28 March 1619. [Carew Mss#211/150]

KENNEDY, DAVID, in the barony of Castlereagh, County Down, 1659. [C]

KENNEDY, DAVID, in the barony of Ardes, County Down, 1659. [C]

KENNEDY, DAVID, in Ballycultra, County Down, 1699. [IWD]

KENNEDY, FERGUS, of Gortivilley, was granted Irish denization on 20 May 1617. [IPR]

KENNEDY, FERGUS, gentleman, in the barony of Castlereagh, County Down, 1659. [C]

KENNEDY, GEORGE, was granted Irish denization on 28 November 1617. [IPR]

KENNEDY, GILBERT, tenant of John Hamilton of Edenagh, Precinct of Fewes, 1618. [PU#567]

KENNEDY, GILBERT, born 1623, resident in Castle Beg, died 3 March 1699. [Comber g/s]

KENNEDY, GILBERT, born 1627, second son of Colonel Gilbert Kennedy of Ardmillan, Ayrshire, graduated MA from Glasgow University in 1647, minister in Dundonald and Holywood from 1670, died on 6 February 1688, buried in Dundonald. [FI#70]

KENNEDY, HUGH, doctor of physick in Ballycultra, County Down, 1685. [IWD]

KENNEDY, HUGH, in Derfraghrog, County Tyrone, 1695. [IWD]

KENNEDY, JAMES, a clerk in Donegal, 1662. [IWD]

KENNEDY, JOHN, a merchant in Strabane, County Tyrone, ca.1617. [SBT#29]

KENNEDY, JOHN, a constable of Donaghadee 1 January 1647. [SP.Ire.#263/3]

KENNEDY, JOHN, in Ballimcgown, County Tyrone, 1681. [IWD]

KENNEDY, JOHN, born 1687, died 5 March 1721. [Comber g/s]

KENNEDY, OLIVER, was granted Irish denization on 5 July 1631.
[IPR]

KENNEDY, QUENTIN, in Ireland, brother in law of George Corrie,
son and heir of George Corrie of Kelwood, 1655.
[NAS.GD180#103]

KENNEDY, ROBERT, Captain of Robert Home of the Heugh's
Regiment, in Carrickfergus, 1642. [PRO.SP.18.120]

KENNEDY, THOMAS, of Coleraine, was granted Irish denization on
28 November 1617. [IPR]

KENNEDY, THOMAS, of Auchbouy, County Antrim, husband of
Janet Shearer, 28 February 1628. [NAS.GD77.145]

KENNEDY, THOMAS, born in 1625, eldest son of Colonel Gilbert
Kennedy of Ardmillan, Ayrshire, graduated MA from Glasgow
University in 1643, a minister in Donaghmore, County Tyrone,
from 1646, died on 9 February 1716. [FI#44]

KENNEDY, WALTER, of Ballylough Beg, County Antrim, 28
August 1627, and his brothers Robert and William.
[SP.Ire#245/821]

KENNEDY, WILLIAM, a carpenter, was granted Irish denization on
17 August 1616; in Strabane County Tyrone, 1617.
[IPR][SBT#22]

KERNES, ALEXANDER, general agent for the Scottish undertakers
in the precinct of Boylagh and Banagh, 1611, [Cal.
SP.Ire.1611/251]; of Tirmakine, was granted Irish denization
on 28 November 1617. [IPR]

KERR, ELIZABETH, widow of John Kerr dean of Armagh, will
subscribed on 18 July 1719, probate 16 November 1723 Dublin

KERR, PATRICK, born in Ireland, son of Major General Thomas
Kerr, a trooper in HM Life Guards in Linlithgow, Scotland, on
5 June 1678. [CA.1.xxxviii]

KERR, WALTER, of Cockmylne, applied for 1500 acres in Ulster on 25 July 1609. [PU#141]

KERR, WILLIAM, Captain of the Earl of Lothian's Regiment, in Carrickfergus in 1642. [PRO.SP.28.120]

KILPATRICK, HUGH, merchant aboard the Janet of Holywood at the port of Irvine, Ayrshire, on 20 September 1682. [NAS.E72.12.5]

KILPATRICK, HUGH, born in Dumfriesshire, minister in Lurgan from 1685 to 1688, in Ballimoney from 1693, died on 1 April 1712. [FI#71]; minister in Belimoine, 1701. [NAS.GD18/4019]

KILPATRICK, JAMES, son of James Patrick Kilpatrick in Kilwinning, Ayrshire, a minister in Maghera from 1668 to 1688, married Helen Kerr, widow of Reverend George Johnston, died on 4 July 1696. [FI#70]

KILPATRICK, THOMAS, of Knochfergus, was granted Irish denization on 20 May 1617. [IPR]

KILPATRICK, WILLIAM, in Ireland, 1686. [RPCS.11.469]

KINASTON, ROBERT, 1643. [TCD#MS837, fo.8]

KINCAID, JOHN, 1636. [SP.Ire#255/144]

KING, JOHN, a weaver, was admitted as a burgess of Glasgow on 11 February 1641, settled in Ireland by 1655. [GBR]

KING, MATHEW, master of the James of Larne at the port of Irvine, Ayrshire, on 13 August 1685. [NAS.E72.12.9]

KING, MATTHEW, merchant aboard the Hopewell of Larne at the port of Irvine, Ayrshire, on 28 September 1685. [NAS.E72.12.9]

KINNEAR, JOHN, MA University of St Andrews 1622, curate of Kells, prebentary of Connor, 1637. [UJA#13/15]

KINNAMONTH (?), DAVID, with 1000 acres in Dungannon, County Tyrone, appeared at a muster in 1618 with 17 men, 1 musket, 1 caliver, 5 pikes, and 7 swords. [Cal.SP.Ire.1618/501] [BM.AddMS#18735]

KYNNAMOND, PATRICK, (?), was granted Irish denization on 12 May 1617. [IPR]

KIRK, JOHN, tenant of John Hamilton of Edenagh, Precinct of Fewes, 1618. [PU#567]

KIRKCART, KATHERINE, wife of William Adaire of Ballemeachan, was granted Irish denization on 28 November 1624. [IPR]

KIRKPATRICK, JOHN, merchant aboard the Goodwill of Larne at the port of Irvine, Ayrshire, 15 August 1683. [NAS.E72.12.8]

KIRKWOOD, JAMES, rector and prebentary of Kilskeery, Ireland, formerly a parson at Colmonell, 1694. [NAS.RD2.77.627]

KIRKWOOD, JOHN, master of the Ross of Belfast at the port of Ayr 21 August 1689. [NAS.E72.3.19]

KNIGHT, JANET, daughter of Alexander Knight in Ballachry, Coleraine, Ireland, cnf 8 January 1652 Commissariot of Glasgow

KNOX, ANDREW, Bishop of Raphoe and Privy Councillor in Ireland, Was granted Irish denization 22 September 1619. [IPR]

KNOX, CLAUD, a minister in the diocese of Raphoe, 1634. [TCD.ms.T#1/10]

KNOX, GEORGE, in Munimore, County Donegal, 1681. [IWD]

KNOX, JAMES, a Scots-Irish student at Glasgow University 1720. [MUG#217]

KNOX, JOHN, a minister in the diocese of Raphoe, 1622, 1634. [TCD.ms.E#3/6; ms.T#1/10]

KNOX, JOHN, a tenant farmer of 20 acres on the Agnew estate in 1645. [NAS.GD154/514]

KNOX, THOMAS, Bishop of the Islands of Scotland, was granted Irish denization on 22 September 1619. [IPR]; a minister in the diocese of Raphoe, 1622. [TCD.ms.E#3/6]

KNOX, THOMAS, in Belfast, High Sheriff of County Antrim in 1685. [UJA.11.1.79]

KNOX, THOMAS, a Scots-Irish student at Glasgow University 1711. [MUG#196]

KNOX, THOMAS, in Lougheaske, County Donegal, will subscribed on 15 September 1717, probate 1 July 1721 Dublin

KNOX, WILLIAM, Captain of the Earl of Glencairn's Regiment, in Carrickfergus 1642. [PRO.SP.18.120]

KYLE, JAMES, was granted Irish denization on 9 July 1616; a merchant in Strabane, County Tyrone. [IPR][SBT#29]

KYLE, ROBERT, of Ballymenane, was granted Irish denization on 28 November 1617. [IPR]

KYLE, WILLIAM, in Strabane, was granted Irish denization on 17 August 1616. [IPR][SBT#22]

KYLE, WILLIAM, a Scots-Irish student at Glasgow University 1708. [MUG#190]

LACKEY, WILLIAM, a Presbyterian preacher and schoolmaster, imprisoned on 22 May 1663. [Cal.SP.Ire.345/149]

LAIRD, JOHN, master of the Hopewell of Donaghadee at the port of Glasgow 20 March 1666. [NAS.E72.10.1]

LAIRD, JOHN, master of the Swan of Donaghadee at the port of Ayr 9 November 1689, bound for Belfast and then Virginia. [NAS.E72.3.19]

LAIRD, JOHN, master of the Andrew of Donaghadee at the port of Irvine 10 March 1691. [NAS.E72.12.18]

LAMOND, JOHN, master of the <u>Blessing of Belfast</u> at the port of
Ayr 1 May 1667. [NAS.E72.3.1]

LANDASS, ROBERT, born in Robroyston, Lanarkshire, during
January 1630, graduated MA from Glasgow University in
1658, married Janet Baillie in 1670, minister in Ballymoney
from 1673 to 1687, died in August 1707. [FI#71]

LANG, Mr ALEXANDER, a minister at Lochbricklein, Ireland,
brother of Finlay Lang, a wright in Kilpatrick, 22 April 1691.
[NAS.GD1.521.37]

LANG, GEORGE, born in Dumfriesshire, minister in Newry from
1665, died on 25 January 1702. [FI#71]

LAUDER, ALEXANDER, son of William Lauder in Belhaven, east
Lothian, applied for 2000 acres in Ulster on 4 August 1609.
[PU#143/566]

LAUDER, GEORGE, deputy for Sir James Douglas, in the Precinct
of Fewes, County Armagh, 29 July 1611.
[Cal.SP.Ire.1611/204]

LAUDER, WILLIAM, of Creichnes, was granted Irish denization and
a grant of Kilrudden in the barony of Fewes, County Armagh,
on 11 August 1610, [IPR][TCD.ms#N2/2]; Undertaker in
Precinct of Fewes, County Armagh, 1611. [SP.Ire.1611/384];
in County Armagh in February 1624. [Cal.SP.Ire.1624#1194]

LAUDERDALE, JANET, of Newton, was granted Irish denization on
9 February 1625. [IPR]

LAUDERDALE, ROBERT, in Devonish, County Fermanagh, 1659.
[C]

LAW, JOHN, minister in Desertoghill and Errigal (Garvagh), from
1658, a minister in Scotland from 1691 to 1694, died on 9 June
1694. [FI#44]

LAWMOUTH, ..., a Scot, in the parish of Camlin and Glenavy in
1638. [SP.Ire#256/89]

LAWRIE, JOHN, born in Scotland in 1656, graduated MA from Glasgow University in 1676, minister of Macosquin, Ireland, 1680 to 1689, then in Penpont, Dumfries, then Auchenleck, Ayrshire, 1695-1710, died in June 1710. [NAS.GD461/4][FI#71]

LAWSON, ALEXANDER, son of the Rector of Maghrafelt, Ireland, graduated from Marischal College, Aberdeen, 1713. [MCA.II.292]

LAWSON, JOHN, in Greenbridge of Kilkenny, Ireland, 1701. [NAS.RD2.85.311]

LAWSON, PETER, in Strabane, County Tyrone, was granted Irish denization on 17 August 1616, a merchant there in 1617. [IPR][SBT#22]

LAYCOCK, THOMAS, Lifford, was granted Irish denization on 17 August 1616. [IPR]

LEARMONTH, SUSANNA, relict of James Munro Writer to the Signet, in Ireland 1715. [NAS.RD2.104.821]

LEATHAM, WILLIAM, died 17 October 1672. [Comber g/s]

LECKIE, CHRISTIANA, wife of William McLennan of Moynevonnen, was granted Irish denization 28 November 1624. [IPR]

LECKIE, ROBERT, of Glassigonan, was granted Irish denization 20 May 1617. [IPR]

LEECH, ALEXANDER, a tenant farmer of 30 acres on the Agnew estate in 1645. [NAS.GD154/514]

LEECH, DAVID, tenant of John Hamilton of Edenagh, Precinct of Fewes, 1618. [PU#567]

LEGGATT, WILLIAM, born in Scotland, graduated MA from Glasgow University in 1661, minister in Dantry, Drum, from 1671 to 1675, in Dromore, County Down, from 1675 to 1689, and from 1691, died in 1697. [FI#72]; minister at Drummore, County Down, 1694. [NAS.RD2.77/2.50]

LENNOX, ALEXANDER, in the Corbet, Tanaghneue, County Down, 20 June 1682. [NAS.GD10.828]

LENNOX, JAMES, Captain of Sir Mungo Campbell of Lawers' Regiment, in Temple Patrick, 1642. [PRO.SP.18.120]

LENNOX, JAMES, a merchant in Silver Street, Londonderry, 1659. [C]

LENNOX, ROBERT, a merchant in Belfast, 19 March 1676. [NAS.GD10.819]

LENNOX, ROBERT, born 1661, a merchant in Belfast, died 17 February 1733. [Old Poorhouse g/s, Belfast]

LENNOX, ROBERT, in the Corbet, Tanaghneue, County Down, 20 June 1682. [NAS.GD10.828]

LENNOX, ROBERT, in parish of Drumboin, Ireland, 15 April 1685. [NAS.GD10.532]

LENNOX, SAMUEL, in Belfast, 19 March 1676. [NAS.GD10.819]

LERMOND, JAMES, of Killaman, County Tyrone, gentleman, was granted Irish denization on 19 July 1633. [IPR]

LERMOND, PATRICK, of Killaman, County Tyrone, gentleman, was granted Irish denization on 19 July 1633. [IPR]

LESLEY, HENRY, a minister in the Diocese of Armagh 1622. [TCD.msE#3/6]; Bishop of Down by September 1631. [SP.Ire#252/2020]

LESLEY, JAMES, in the parish of Dunsford, County Down, 1659.[C]

LESLEY, JAMES, Sheriff of County Down in 1683. [NAS.GD10.497]

LESLIE, JAMES, in Tarbert, County Kerry, 1724. [IWD]

LESLEY, JOHN, Bishop of Raphoe, late Bishop of Sodor, was granted Irish denization on 20 May 1633. [IPR]

LESLIE, JOHN, Captain of the Earl of Leven's Regiment, in Carrickfergus, 1642. [PRO.SP28/120]

LESLIE, JOHN, Captain of Major General Robert Monro's Regiment, in Carrickfergus 1642. [PRO.SP.18.120]

LESSLIE, JOHN, merchant aboard the Recovery of Coleraine at the port of Irvine, Ayrshire, on 18 June 1691. [NAS.E72.12.18]

LESLIE, JOHN, dean of Dromore, subscribed to his will on 11 July 1716, probate 6 November 1722 Dublin.

LESSLY, MARGARET, spouse to Patrick Home a merchant in Cork, petitioned the Privy Council of Scotland on 28 August 1690. [RPCS.15.413]

LESLIE, PATRICK, General Adjutant of Lord Sinclair's Regiment, in Newry, 1642. [PRO.SP.18.120]

LESLEY, WILLIAM, of Ballymoney, High Sheriff of County Antrim in 1671. [UJA.11.1.79]

LEWERS, MATTHEW, a butcher freeman of Newton, County Down, 1640. [Hunter of Hunterstone MS#8]

LIDDERDALE, JAMES, Captain of Major General Robert Monro's Regiment, in Carrickfergus 1642. [PRO.SP.18.120]

LINCKE, WILLIAM, was granted Irish denization on 22 June 1615. [IPR]

LINDSAY, ALEXANDER, Captain of the Earl of Lothian's Regiment, in Carrickfergus in 1642. [PRO.SP.28.120]

LINDSAY, ALEXANDER, an Anglo-Irish student at Glasgow University 1715.   [MUG#206]

LINDSAY, ANDREW, in Drumenan, County Donegal, subscribed to his will on 28 October 1712, reference to his wife Margaret, daughter Susanna Lindsay or Patterson, and his son-in-law Robert Patterson, probate 14 November 1715 Dublin

LINDSAY, BERNARD, late of Leith, son of Thomas Lindsay of
Kingswark, grant of part of Craig, Mountjoy Precinct, barony
of Dungannon, County Tyrone, 26 June 1610. [PRO, Signet
Office, Docquet Book, Privy Seal Chancery #1786]
[TCD.ms#N2/2]; Undertaker in Precinct of Mountjoy, County
Tyrone, 1611. [Cal.SP.Ire.1611/384]; was granted Irish
denization on 26 June 1610. [IPR][PU#546]; with 1000 acres in
the barony of Dungannon appeared at a muster in 1618 with 21
men, 5 muskets, 3 calivers, 10 pikes, 2 halberds and 20 swords.
[Cal.SP.Ire.1618/501] [BM.AddMS#18735]

LINDSAY, DAVID, keeper of Edinburgh Tolbooth, applied for 2000
acres in Ulster on 25 July 1609. [PU#141]

LINDSAY, ELLINOR, in Fermanagh 1632. [SP.Ire#253/2090]

LINDSAY, JAMES, yeoman in Magevlin, County Donegal, was
granted Irish denization on 17 August 1616. [IPR]

LINDSAY, JEREMY, in Leith, applied for 2000 acres in Ulster on 25
July 1609, [PU#141]; Undertaker in the Precinct of
Magheraboy, County Fermanagh, 1611.
[Cal.SP.Ire.1611/384][TCD.ms#N2/2]; was granted Irish
denization on 12 February 1618. [IPR]

LINDSAY, JOHN, of Bally McCormoch, was granted Irish
denization on 28 November 1617. [IPR]

LINDSAY, ROBERT, son of Thomas Lindsay of Kingswark in Leith,
applied for 2000 acres in Ulster on 25 July 1609, [PU#141];
grant of part of Tulloghoge, precinct of Mountjoy, barony of
Dungannon, County Tyrone, 24 June 1610. [PRO. Signet
Office, Docquet Book, Privy Seal Chancery, #1786]
[IPR][PU#546] [TCD.ms#N2/2]; his widow with 1000 acres at
Tulloghoge, precinct of Mountjoy, 28 March 1619. [Carew
Mss#211/147]

LINDSAY, ROBERT, was granted Irish denization on 9 July 1616.
[IPR]

LINDSAY, ROBERT, pardoned on 27 July 1629.
[SP.Dom.Sig.Off#I/476]

LINDSAY, ROBERT, was granted Irish denization on 1 January 1631. [IPR]

LINDSAY, THOMAS, gentleman in townland of Clogher, County Down, 1659. [C]

LINDSAY, ..., a Lieutenant of Captain Robert Adair's troop, to be cashiered on 6 August 1646. [SP.Ire#261/41]

LINNE, ANDREW, supplication by Andrew Linne who had lived in Ireland for 18 years and whose wife Elizabeth Redgatt and their four children had been murdered by rebels at Castle Cloch 1646. [RPCS.VIII.163]

LINTON, FERGUS, in County Tyrone, 2 December 1636. [NAS.GD10.743]

LISTON, WILLIAM, graduated MA from Glasgow University in 1659, minister in Waterford from 1673 to 1676, in Letterkenny from 1679, died on 1 June 1695. [FI#72]

LITHGOW, JOHN, born in 1620, second son of Thomas Lithgow of Redpath, Earlston, Berwickshire, and Isobel Haliburton, a minister in Ireland before 1646. [FI#45]

LITTLE, JOHN, of Ballyhanwood, son of William Little of Caricullan, died on 29 October 1724. [Killinchy g/s, County Down]

LITTLE, WILLIAM, of Caricullan, born 1673, died in 1730. [Killinchy g/s, County Down]

LIVINGSTON, Sir GEORGE, of Ogilface, applied for 2000 acres in Ulster on 25 July 1609. [PU#141]

LIVINGSTON, HENRY, born 1631, son of Reverend Henry Livingstone of Kippen, Stirlingshire, graduated MA from Glasgow University, minister of Drumbo from 1656, died 7 April 1697, his wife Grizell born 1636, died 11 September 1708; father of Reverend Henry Livingstone of Ballynahinch. [Drumbo g/s] [FI#45]

LIVINGSTONE, JOHN, born in Kilsyth, Stirlingshire, on 21 June 1603, son of William Livingstone minister of Kilsyth and Agnes Livingstone, educated at Glasgow University from 1617 to 1621, graduated MA in 1621, a minister in Killinchy from 1630, attempted to sail to New England on the Eagle Wing in 1638, died in Rotterdam on 9 August 1672, husband of Janet, daughter of Bartholemew Fleming in Edinburgh. [PHS]

LIVINGSTON, WILLIAM, son of Mr John Livingston in County Down, apprenticed to James Tait, goldsmith burgess of Edinburgh, 10 March 1714, [Edinburgh Apprentice Register]

LIVINGSTON, WILLIAM, born 1643, a merchant in Lisburn, died 28 April 1719, his wife Mary Woombles, born 1652, died 6 May 1709. [Drumbo g/s]

LOCHNORIES, Lord, Undertaker in Precinct of Mountjoy, County Tyrone, 1611. [Cal.SP.Ire.1611/384]

LOCKHART, Sir JAMES, Captain of the Earl of Lothian's Regiment, in Carrickfergus in 1642. [PRO.SP.28.120]

LOCKHART, STEVEN, of Wicketshaw, applied for 2000 acres in Ulster on 4 August 1609. [PU#143]

LOGAN, or BOYD, MARGARET, a widow, was granted Irish denization on 9 December 1633. [IPR]

LOGAN, MATHEW, was granted Irish denization on 22 June 1615. [IPR]

LOGAN, WALTER, of Proveston, was granted Irish denization on 20 May 1617. [IPR]

LOGAN, WALTER, of Broadland, was granted Irish denization on 13 May 1634. [IPR]

LOGY, JOHN, was granted Irish denization on 9 July 1616. [IPR]

LORIMER, JOHN, master of the Providence of Belfast at the port of Irvine, Ayrshire, on 22 June 1686. [NAS.E72.12.13]

LOTHER, ALEXANDER, of Clony, was granted Irish denization on 12 February 1618. [IPR]

LOTHER, GEORGE, of Dirrendragh, was granted Irish denization on 12 February 1618. [IPR]

LOTHER, or HAMBLETON, JANE, of Castlekelagh, was granted Irish denization on 12 February 1618. [IPR]

LOVE, JOHN, in Strabane, County Tyrone, probate 1629

LOVE, WILLIAM, was granted Irish denization on 9 July 1616. [IPR]

LOWRY, ALEXANDER, in Drumully, County Fermanagh, 1659. [C]

LUNDY, Colonel ROBERT, Governor of Londonderry, 1689. [NAS.GD26.7.37]

LUTFOOT, DAVID, graduated MA from University of St Andrews in 1627, later curate of Killeagh, County Antrim. [UJA#13/15]

LYMONT, JOHN, a barber in Lisburn, County Antrim, 1699. [NAS.RD2.82.140]

LYNN, DAVID, was granted Irish denization on 17 August 1616; in Dunnalong, barony of Strabane, County Tyrone, 1617. [IPR][SBT#23]

LYNN, JOHN, was granted Irish denization on 17 August 1616; in Dunnalong, barony of Strabane, County Tyrone, 1617. [IPR][SBT#23]

LYNNE, WILLIAM, gentleman in Londonderry, was granted Irish denization on 9 July 1616. [IPR]

LYON, ANDREW, Londonderry, was granted Irish denization on 17 August 1616. [IPR]

LYON, JOHN, master of the Bonadventure of Coleraine at the port of Glasgow 1 May 1666. [NAS.E72.10.1]

LYON, JOHN, master of the James of Belfast at the port of Irvine, Ayrshire, on 29 July 1685 and on 21 May 1686. [NAS.E72.12.9/12]

MCADAM, JAMES, in Belfast, County Antrim, 1698. [NAS.RD2.81.1817]

MCADAM, JOHN, in Tyrone, 1623. [see John Campbell's testament 1623, Commissariot of Glasgow]

MCADAM, JOHN, of Liskelle, County Tyrone, gentleman, was granted Irish denization on 19 July 1633. [IPR]

MCADAM, JOHN, Templepark. County Antrim, 1698. [NAS.RD2.81.1817]

MCALEXANDER, GEORGE, of Ballyshenog, was granted Irish denization on 28 November 1617. [IPR]

MCALEXANDER, THOMAS, gentleman, was granted Irish denization on 9 July 1616; Provost of Strabane, County Tyrone, in 1618, 1626 and 1633. [IPR][SBT#32]

MCALPINE, ALEXANDER, in Monaghan, County Monaghan, was admitted as a burgess and guildsbrother of Glasgow on 29 May 1718. [GBR]

MCAULA, ALEXANDER, of Durlin, Dunbartonshire, was granted Irish denization on 16 July 1610, agent for the Duke of Lennox. [IPR][TCD.ms#N2/2]; grant of Balliveagh, precinct of Portelogh, 16 July 1610. [EPR.8.40]; Undertaker in Precinct of Portlogh, County Donegal, 1611. [Cal.SP.Ire.1611/384]

MCAULAY, ALEXANDER, or Stewart, with 1000 acres at Ballynege, on 28 March 1619. [Carew MSS#211/88]

MACAULAY, ALEXANDER, Captain of the Marquis of Argyll's Regiment, in Ballycastle, 1642. [PRO.SP.16.492.58]

MACALLEY, PETER, was granted Irish denization on 1 July 1614. [IPR]

MCBLAIN, THOMAS, a merchant in Dublin, formerly in Enoch, 1702. [NAS.RD2.86.2.1716]

MCBRIDE, JOHN, in Magherlin, County Down, 1694. [IWD]

MCBROOM, JOHN, born in Scotland, graduated MA from Glasgow University in 1655, minister in Portpatrick from 1656 to 1662, in Anahilt from 1663, died on 7 July 1682. [FI#77]

MCBRYD, Mr JOHN, preacher in Belfast, admitted as a burgess and guildsbrother of Glasgow on 13 March 1704. [GBR]; in Belfast, 1718. [IWD]

MCBURNIE, JOHN, died 24 May 1661, his wife Bessie Jearden died 1665. [Comber g/s]

MCBURNEY, MARY, born 1652, wife of John Orr of Clantanacally, died 3 July 1692. [Comber g/s]

MCCAIE, HUGH, died 18 December 1685. [Comber g/s]

MCCALLA, GEORGE, died 1 May 1685. [Comber g/s]

MCCALLA, JAMES, son of George McCalla, died 27 July 1686. [Comber g/s]

MCCAMUELL, GAWEN, yeoman in Dromanan, County Donegal, was granted Irish denization on 17 August 1616. [IPR]

MACCARTNEY, GEORGE, Hugh Eales, and George MacCartney petitioned for compensation for the loss of their ship James of Belfast which was impressed into government service when in Antigua and subsequently taken by the French off Guadaloupe, where the ship's merchant, David Agnew, was wounded, 26 February 1668. [ActsPCCol.#755]

MCCARTNEY, GEORGE, merchant in Belfast, High Sheriff of County Antrim in 1681, [UJA.11.1.79]; at the port of Ayr on 20 February 1690. [NAS.E72.3.20]

MCCARTNEY, ISAAC, a merchant in Belfast, 1715. [NAS.RD2.105.77]; 1722, [NAS.AC9/849]

MCCARTNEY, JOHN, in Dromsavage, Mullaghbrack parish, County
Armagh, subscribed to his will on 21 May 1716, reference to
his wife Marion, sons James and Hugh, witnesses Thomas
Johnston in Armagh, Daniel MacDowell in Derrynaught, and
Arthur Graham in Ballyherriland, County Armagh, probate 18
November 1718 Dublin

MCCAYLEY, WILLIAM, a tenant farmer with 5 acres on the Agnew
Estate in 1645. [NAS.GD154/514]

MCCLACHY, JAMES, yeoman, was granted Irish denization on 9
December 1633. [IPR]

MCCLAIRNE, JOHN, of Raphoe, was granted Irish denization on 28
November 1617. [IPR]

MCCLELLAN, HERBERT, of Gregorie, applied for 2000 acres in
Ulster on 25 July 1609. [PU#143]

MCCLELLAND, JOHN, born in 1609, son of Michael McClelland in
Kirkcudbright, educated at Glasgow University from 1626,
graduated MA in 1629, a schoolmaster in County Down,
attempted to emigrate to New England on the Eagle Wing in
1636, returned to Scotland, died in 1650, husband of (1)
Marion, daughter of Bartholemew Fleming in Edinburgh, (2)
Isabel McClelland. [PHS]

MCCLELLAN, WILLIAM, Captain of the Earl of Leven's Regiment,
in Carrickfergus, 1642. [PRO.SP28/120]

MCCLELLANE, ..., Captain of the Marquis of Argyll's Regiment,
in Dunluce, 1642. [PRO.SP.16.492.58]

MCCLUIR, ANDREW, in Ireland 1621. [see Jean Campbell's
testament 1621, Commissariot of Glasgow]

MCCOMBIE, JAMES, Captain of the Earl of Eglinton's Regiment, in
Bangor 1642. [PRO.SP.18.120]

MCCONNELL, JAMES, master of the Marion of Loch Larne at the
port of Irvine, Ayrshire, on 11 June 1681 and on 29 March
1682. [NAS.E72.12.3/6]; master of the Helen of Larne at the
port of Ayr 26 August 1690. [NAS.E72.3.22]

MCCOOK, ARCHIBALD, a Scots-Irish student at Glasgow
University 1711. [MUG#196]

MCCORMICK, ANDREW, minister in Magherally from 1655, killed
at the Battle of Rullion Green, Scotland, on 28 November
1666. [FI#46]

MCCORMICK, DAVID, died on 7 February 1693. [Killyleagh g/s,
County Down]

MCCORMACK, GORLIE, freeman of Lifford, 1612.
[Cal. SP.Ire.1612/511]

MCCORQUADALE, ARCHIBALD, merchant in County Armagh,
Ireland, 1706. [NAS.RD2.92.503]; admitted as a burgess of
Inveraray, Argyll, on 12 February 1707. [Inveraray Burgess
Roll]

MCCOY, THOMAS, a tenant farmer of 7 acres on the Agnew estate
in 1645. [NAS.GD154/514]

MCCRACKEN, ALEXANDER, an Irish student at Edinburgh
University 1673.   [CEG]

MCCRAE, ALEXANDER, a merchant in Belfast, 1699.
[NAS.RD2.83.461; RD4.85.79, 859, 953, 954]

MCCRAGHAN, ARCHIBALD, of Ballemagory, was granted Irish
denization on 17 August 1616; in Ballymagorry, barony of
Strabane, County Tyrone, 1617. [IPR][SBT#23]

MCCRAGHAN, GILBERT, of Ballemagorie, County Tyrone, was
granted Irish denization on 17 August 1616; there in 1617.
[IPR][SBT#23]

MCCRAGHAN, PATRICK, of Ballemagorie, County Tyrome, was
granted Irish denization on 17 August 1616; there in 1617.
[IPR][SBT#23]

MCCRERY, ANDREW, a tenant of Sir William Stewart, around
1620. [PU#545]

MCCRERY, JAMES, an Irish student at Edinburgh University 1673. [CEG]

MCCREERIE, JOHN elder in Drumbo, died in March 1702, his wife Mary Hafisher, born 1672, died 10 March 1709. [Drumbo g/s]

MCCRORIE, ANDREW, in Tyrone 1623. [see John Campbell's, burgess of Ayr, testament 1623, Commissariot of Glasgow]

MCCUBBIN, JOHN, of Dunamuy, parish of Rashee, County Antrim, 1690. [NAS.GD180#216]

MCCULLOCH, JAMES, in Drummorrell, Wigtonshire, applied for 2000 acres in Ulster on 18 July 1609, [PU#140]; grant of part of Mullaveagh, barony of Baylagh and Bannagh, County Donegal, 20 July 1610. [EPR.8.3] [TCD.ms#N2/2]; Undertaker in the Precinct of Boylagh, County Donegal, 1611. [Cal.SP.Ire.1611/384]; was granted Irish denization 20 July 1610. [IPR]; with 1000 acres at Mullaghvegh, County Donegal, 28 March 1619. [Carew Mss#211/83]

MCCULLOCH, JAMES, and company of Belfast, owners of the Mary Galley, and James Mears, merchant there, their factor, against Robert Allan, a Belfast merchant, for demurrage and other damage incurred on a voyage undertaken for the defender from Belfast to Barbados and back to Glasgow, by being unduly detained in Barbados by the defender. [NAS.Admiralty Court, Vol.32, pp.116/213, 28 January and 15 February 1726]

MCCULLOCH, MICHAEL, a tenant of Sir William Stewart, around 1620. [PU#545]

MCCULLOCH, THOMAS, of Donan, County Donegal, was granted Irish denization 17 August 1616. [IPR]

MCCUTCHION, ADAM, a merchant in Belfast, subscribed to his will on 3 May 1712, reference to his children Thomas, Jane, Isabel and Margaret, his brother James, brother Robert's children, sister .. Craig, her son Archibald, brother in law Archibald Craig, brother in law Robert Allan, Joseph Innis, William Stevenson, witnesses Reverend Samuel Ross in Londonderry, James White cooper in Belfast, and John Hamilton apprentice to William Stevenson, pro. 1718 Dublin

MCDOUGALL, PATRICK, of Ballemeachan, gentleman, was granted Irish denization on 28 November 1624. [IPR]

MCDOUGALL, ROBERT, commander of Sir John Ogle's fleet at Wexford on 21 June 1626. [SP.Ire#242/355]

MCDOWELL, ALEXANDER, gentleman, in the barony of Castlereagh 1659. [C]

MCDOWELL, JOHN, an Irish student at Edinburgh University 1705. [CEG]

MCDOWELL, JOHN, born 1701, son of Robert McDowell of Ballyhanwood, died 18 January 1714. [Comber g/s]

MCDOWELL, JOHN, in the parish of Mullaghbrock, County Antrim, subscribed to his will on 12 February 1712, reference to his sons Daniel and John, grandson William McDowell, Hugh Grier's children, John Scott son of Quintin Scott, witnesses Alexander Ferguson, John Woods, George Williamson, all of Derrynaght, County Armagh, probate 22 June 1719 Dublin

MACDOWGALL, UTHRED, of Ballimaconnell, was granted Irish denization on 20 May 1617. [IPR]

MCGHEE, DAVID, of Strabane, County Tyrone, gentleman, was granted Irish denization on 19 July 1631. [IPR]

MCGIE, JAMES, a gentleman in Belfast, admitted as a burgess and guildsbrother of Glasgow on 14 September 1677, [GBR]

MCGIE, JOHN, master of the Marie of Portaferry at the port of Irvine, Ayrshire, on 15 June 1686. [NAS.E72.12.13]

MCGILL, DAVID, matriculated at St Leonard's College, University of St Andrews, 1617, curate of Gray Abbey. [UJA#13/15]

MCGILL, GEORGE, Captain of Robert Home of the Heugh's Regiment, in Carrickfergus, 1642. [PRO.SP.18.120]

MCGILL, HUGH, in the barony of Ardes, County Down, in 1659. [C]

MCGILL, JAMES, in the barony of Castlereagh, County Down, in
1659. [C]

MCGILL, JOHN, master of the Recovery of Donaghadee at the port
of Irvine, Ayrshire, on 12 June 1683. [NAS.E72.12.7]

MCGILL, Mr SAMUEL, burgess of Glasgow, applied for 2000 acres
in Ulster on 25 July 1609. [PU#142]

MCGREGOR, PATRICK, in Drumale, 1725. [IWD]

MCHUTCHEON, WILLIAM, master of the Friends Adventure of
Belfast at the port of Irvine, Ayrshire, on 26 June 1686; master
of the William and Joan of Belfast at the port of Irvine on 2
February 1689. [NAS.E72.12.13/15]

MCILVEYNE, DAVID, of Ballelegin, was granted Irish denization
on 28 November 1617. [IPR]

MCINCHE, MATHEW, was granted Irish denization on 16 June
1615. [IPR]

MCINTYRE, JOHN, in Strabane, was granted Irish denization on 17
August 1616, in Strabane, County Tyrone, 1617.
[IPR][SBT#22]

MCJETYRE, JOHN, a freeman of Lifford in 1612.
[Cal.SP.Ire.1612/511]

MCKEBIN, JOHN, of Belystorket, born 1653, died 22 May 1715, his
wife Isabella Bell born 1669, died 8 March 1741. [Comber g/s]

MCKEE, Sir PATRICK, of Large, Minnigaff, Wigtonshire, grant of
part of Cargie, barony of Baylagh and Bannagh, County
Donegal, 24 July 1610. [EPR.8.18][TCD.ms#N2/2];
Undertaker in the Precinct of Boylagh, County Donegal, 1611.
[Cal.SP.Ire.1611/384]; was granted Irish denization 24 July
1610. [IPR]

MCKENNY, JOHN, a merchant in Silver Street, Londonderry, during
1659. [C]

MCKEY, DANIEL, in Donagheady, County Tyrone, probate 1636

MCKIBBAIR, JOHN, a Scots-Irish student at Glasgow University during 1715. [MUG#206]

MCKINDLIS, ROBERT, master of the Providence of Belfast at the port of Irvine, Ayrshire, on 4 July 1682. [NAS.E72.12.6]

MCKITRICK, ALEXANDER, a tenant of Sir William Stewart, around 1620. [PU#545]

MCKITRICK, HUGH, a Scots-Irish student at Glasgow University 1706. [MUG#184]

MCKITTRICK, JOHN, master and merchant of the John of Portaferry at the port of Irvine, Ayrshire, on 25 April 1681. [NAS.E72.12.3]

MCKNIGHT, JOHN, a Scots-Irish student at Glasgow University 1707. [MUG#186]

MCKUN, JOHN, born 1667, died 29 April 1731. [Comber g/s]

MCKUN, ROBERT, born 1660, died 1 February 1668. [Comber g/s]

MCKYNNY, ALEXANDER, of Ramullin, was granted Irish denization on 28 November 1617. [IPR]

MCLAGHLIN, JAMES, a Scots-Irish student at Glasgow University 1706. [MUG#184]

MCLAIN, ARCHIBALD, a Scots-Irish student at Glasgow University 1713. [MUG#201]

MCLAINE, WILLIAM, master of the William of Belfast at the port of Ayr 22 July 1683. [NAS.E72.3.12]

MCLEAN, ALLAN, of Balleny, County Antrim, later in Uist, 1714. [NAS.RD4.114.327]

MACLELLAN, Sir ROBERT, of Bomby, Galloway, was granted Irish denization and a grant of Rosses in the barony of Boylagh and Bannagh, County Donegal, on 19 September 1610, [IPR]

[TCS.ms#N2/2]; 14 March 1618. [IPR]; chief tenant to the Ironmongers Company and to the Haberdashers Company of the City of Londonderry, appeared at a muster in 1618 with 37 men.[Cal.SP.Ire.1618/501][BMAddMS#18735]; 1629. [SP.Ire#249/1504]

MCLENNAN, WILLIAM, of Moynevonnen, gentleman, was granted Irish denization on 28 November 1624. [IPR]

MCLENTAGH, ALEXANDER, of Ratteine, was granted Irish denization on 20 May 1617. [IPR]

MCMAKENE, JAMES, of Donaghadie, was granted Irish denization on 20 May 1617. [IPR]

MCMATH, ANDREW, of Donegal, was granted Irish denization on 28 November 1617. [IPR]

MCMINN, FRANCIS, a merchant in Donaghadee, 1718. [NAS.GD10#246]

MCMORRAN, JAMES, a Scots-Irish student at Edinburgh University 1697. [CEG]

MCNAGHTEN, ALEXANDER, was granted Irish denization on 22 June 1615. [IPR]

MCNAUGHTON, JOHN, was granted Irish denization on 29 January 1611. [IPR]

MCNEIL, ARCHIBALD, of Clogar, Rector of Balentoy, Ireland, 2 June 1704. [NAS.RS9.3.418]

MCNEIL, GILCHRIST, was granted Irish denization on 9 July 1616. [IPR]

MCNEAL, HENRY, a Scots-Irish student at Glasgow University 1718. [MUG#213]

MCNEILL, HECTOR, of Culremony, a yeoman, was granted Irish denization on 9 February 1625. [IPR]

MCNEILL, JOHN, in Patneill, Ireland, 27 August 1722. [Argyll Sheriff Court Book, Vol.7, 6.9.1722]

MCNEILL, LAUCHLAN, of Ballighicone, County Antrim, 25 January 1729. [NAS.RS9.6.220]

MCNEILL, NEILL, an apothecary in Belfast, 9 May 1712, [Argyll Sheriff Court Book, Vol.7, 22.8.1722]; 28 December 1722 and 19 September 1724. [NAS.RS.Argyll.4/591; 5/173]

MCPHEDRICHE, GILBERT, was granted Irish denization on 29 January 1611. [IPR]

MCQUERNS, SAMUEL, in Ballymena, 9 August 1704. [NAS.GD135.891]

MCRALLAN, THOMAS, master of the Jean of Carrickfergus at the port of Glasgow 22 November 1666. [NAS.E72.10.1]

MCROBERT, JOHN, was granted Irish denization on 29 January 1611. [IPR]

MCRULLY, ROBERT, master of the Robert of Belfast at the port of Irvine, Ayrshire, on 14 July 1685. [NAS.E72.12.10]

MCSPARRAN, JAMES, a Scots-Irish student at Glasgow University 1709. [MUG#191]

MCVARICH, PATRICK, 'now in Ireland' 29 December 1720. [Argyll Sheriff Court Book, Vol.7, 29.12.1720]

MCWALTER, PARLANE, of Auchinvennel, applied for 2000 acres in Ulster on 11 July 1609. [PU#139]

MCWALTER, ..., in Ireland, 1630. [NAS.GD180#371]

MCWILLIAM, ANDREW, coroner in County Donegal on 15 September 1660. [Cal.S.P.Ire.1660]

MACKESON, GEORGE, MA, was granted Irish denization 29 October 1622. [IPR]

MACHAN, JAMES, of Drumcarne, County Donegal, Wwas granted Irish denization 20 May 1617. [IPR]

MACHELL, WILLIAM, of Damcliff, was granted Irish denization 28 November 1617. [IPR]

MAILEWAIN, THOMAS, a Scots-Irish student at Glasgow University in 1711. [MUG#196]

MAINE, HENRY, born in Linlithgow during 1625, graduated MA from Edinburgh University in 1645, a minister in Islandmagee from 1649, died in Houstoun, Renfrewshire in October 1651. [CEG][FI#45]

MAINE, JOHN, in Strabane, County Tyrone, probate 1638

MAIRS, JOHN, graduated MA from Glasgow University in 1676, married Margaret Gilchrist in Antrim in 1677, minister in Loughbrickland from 1687 to 1689, in Longford from 1697 to 1706, in Newtownards from 1707, died on 25 December 1718. [FI#78]

MAIRS, JOHN, an Anglo-Irish student at Glasgow University 1713. [MUG#201]

MAIRS, MARGARET, wife of Mr John Mairs, died on 15 February 1686. [Kllyleagh g/s, County Down]

MALCOLM, JOHN, graduated MA from Glasgow University in 1674, minister in Lower Gillead, Gartree, from 1687 to 1699, in Dunmurray from 1699, died on 17 May 1729.[FI#78]

MANSON, JAMES, a gentleman in Ballylymy, parish of Magharalin, County Down, 1659. [C]

MARJORYBANKS, THOMAS, son of Thomas Marjorybanks of Ratho, Midlothian, applied for 2000 acres in Ulster on 25 July1609. [PU#142]

MARKFORD, JOHN, master of the Janet of Larne at the port of Glasgow 12 March 1672. [NAS.E72.10.3]

MARR, GEORGE, was granted Irish denization 31 July 1614. [Signet Office Docquet Book, S.P. Dom. Docquets]

MARSHALL, JAMES, of Coleraine, was granted Irish denization on 22 February 1634. [IPR]

MARSHALL, MATTHEW, of Garvegulen, died on 28 April 169-, aged 71; his wife Catrina Andrew, born 1623, died on 15 March 1701. [Killinchy g/s, County Down]

MARTIN, GEORGE, merchant in Carrickfergus, Belfast, and Lisburn, died in 1639. [PROI#RC9/1, p37]

MARTIN, JOHN, of Dunnevill, was granted Irish denization on 28 November 1617. [IPR]

MARTIN, JOHN, master of the Joan of Donaghadee at the port of Glasgow 11 January 1666. [NAS.E72.10.1]

MARTIN, JOHN, master of the Mary of Belfast at the port of Ayr 15 February 1684. [NAS.E72.3.13]

MARTIN, ROBERT, master of the Agnes of Belfast at the port of Glasgow 1 January 1672. [NAS.E72.10.3]

MARTIN, THOMAS, born in 1643, a merchant in Belfast, died on 29 October 1685; his wife Florence, was born in 1655 daughter of John Stewart of Ballydraine, died on 27 April 1683. [Drumbeg g/s, County Down]

MARTIN, WILLIAM, master of the Swan of Donaghadee at the port of Irvine, Ayrshire, on 7 August 1691. [NAS.E72.12.18]

MARTLAND, HUGH, master of the Janet of Donaghadee at the port of Irvine, Ayrshire, on 16 August 1682. [NAS.E72.12.5]

MATHEIS, WILLIAM, merchant aboard the Elizabeth of Glenarme at the port of Irvine, Ayrshire, on 8 October 1683. [NAS.E72.12.7]

MATHEW, ..., merchant aboard the Mathew of Donaghadee at the port of Irvine, Ayrshire, on 24 September 1690. [NAS.E72.12.16]

MAULE, PATRICK, was granted Irish denization January 1618.
[Signet Office, Docquet Book]

MAULE, THOMAS, was granted Irish denization on 13 December
1627. [IPR]

MAWHINNIE, MATHEW, master of the Mary of Coleraine at the
port of Glasgow 24 July 1666. [NAS.E72.10.1]

MAXWELL, AGNES, a widow in Drombegg, 1684. [IWD]

MAXWELL, ALEXANDER, a tenant of Sir William Stewart, around
1620. [PU#545]

MAXWELL, ALEXANDER, a merchant in Cork, 1720. [IWD]

MAXWELL, ARCHIBALD, freeman of Lifford 1612.
[Cal.SP.Ire.1612/511]

MAXWELL, ARTHUR, in Drumbeg, County Down, subscribed to
his will on 2 November 1720, reference to his wife Anne, sister
Margaret Maxwell or Hamilton, her sons James a merchant in
Belfast, Arthur a merchant in Liverpool, Archibald a merchant
in Rotterdam, daughters Mary and Ann, grand-nephew
Maxwell Hamilton son of Arthur Hamilton in Liverpool, niece
Katherine Hamilton or Mankin, James Hamilton her brother,
her husband Michael and son Arthur, sister in law Mrs Elinor
Stewart and her daughter Anne, niece Ann Stewart of Newry
and children Arthur, Alexander, James and Katherine, niece
Katherine Rainey, ...
Probate 25 February 1721 Dublin

MAXWELL, COLIN, in the barony of Castlereagh, County Down,
1659. [C]

MAXWELL, COLIN, son of Robert Maxwell, in the barony of Ardes,
County Down, 1659. [C]

MAXWELL, EDWARD, of Dinover, was granted Irish denization 20
May 1617. [IPR]

MAXWELL, EDWARD, of Lisdromchor, was granted Irish
denization 12 February 1618. [IPR]

MAXWELL, EDWARD, of Conner, High Sheriff of County Antrim
in 1635. [UJA.11.1.179]

MAXWELL, FRANCIS, in the barony of Ardmagh, County Armagh,
1659. [C]

MAXWELL GABRIEL, a Presbyterian minister who fled from
Scotland to Ireland in 1669. [Cal.S.P.Ire.1669]

MAXWELL, HERBERT, leased lands of Mullaghvaney, Proluske
and part of Killany from Sir William Stewart on 1 June 1616
for 21 years. [PU#545]; agent for the Earl of Annandale in
Ulster in 1627. [SP.Dom.Sig.Off#I.5]

MAXWELL HERBERT, a mill-owner in County Down 1629.
[SP.Dom.Sig.Off#I.525]

MAXWELL, HENRY, a clerk in College Hall, County Armagh,
1709. [IWD]

MAXWELL, JAMES, in the barony of Castlereagh, County Down,
1659. [C]

MAXWELL, JAMES, in Anlow, barony of Kenaght, County
Londonderry, 1659. [C]

MAXWELL, JAMES, of Gransho, was granted Irish denization 20
May 1617. [IPR]

MAXWELL, JAMES, in the barony of Ardmagh, County Armagh,
1659. [C]

MAXWELL, JAMES, an usher at Kilmore school, County Cavan,
1673. [BM.Sloane#202]

MAXWELL, JAMES, gentleman in Drumbeg, County Down, 1682.
[IWD]; born 1611, died 20 March 1681; his wife Ann was born
1614 and died on 30 March 1684; his son Arthur was born in
1655 and died on 22 January 1729. [Drumbeg g/s, County
Down]

MAXWELL, JAMES, in Pettigo, Ireland, 1715. [NAS.RD4.117.876]

MAXWELL, JOHN, of Ballihalbert, was granted Irish denization 20 May 1617. [IPR]

MAXWELL, JOHN, Lieutenant Colonel of Robert Home of the Heugh's Regiment, in Carrickfergus, 1642. [PRO.SP.18.120]

MAXWELL, JOHN, in Ballyriskbegg, County Londonderry, 1715. [IWD]

MAXWELL, MARY, in Strabane, County Tyrone, 1709. [IWD]

MAXWELL, ROBERT, Dean of Armagh, was granted Irish denization 20 May 1617. [IPR]

MAXWELL, ROBERT, a minister in the Diocese of Armagh, 1622. [TCD.ms.E#3/6]

MAXWELL, ROBERT, of Tynan, County Armagh, clerk, was granted Irish denization 9 August 1633. [IPR]

MAXWELL, Lieutenant ROBERT, in Ireland, 1624. [Cal.SP.Ire]

MAXWELL, ROBERT, son of the Dean of Armagh, 1634. [TCD.ms.T#1/10]

MAXWELL, ROBERT, in the barony of Ardes, County Down, 1659. [C]

MAXWELL, Sir ROBERT, in Anlow, barony of Kenaght, County Londonderry, 1659. [C]

MAXWELL, ROBERT, a Scots-Irish student at Glasgow University 1709. [MUG#193]

MAXWELL, THOMAS, in Dungannon on 8 March 1667. [Cal.SP.Ire.348/8]

MAXWELL, THOMAS, a merchant in Strabane, 1702. [IWD]

MAXWELL, WILLIAM, a merchant in Strabane, County Tyrone, 1709. [IWD]

MAXWELL, Lord, Earl of Nithsdale, granted the Castle of Dromahaire with 5000 acres of land, on 31 October 1621. [Cal.SP.Ire.1621#794]

MEEN, JOHN, a tenant of Sir William Stewart, around 1620. [PU#545]

MEEN, ROGER, a tenant of Sir William Stewart, around 1620. [PU#545]

MEEN, WILLIAM, a tenant of Sir William Stewart, around 1620. [PU#545]

MEKEN, JAMES, of Ballyrickert, born 1634, died on 9 February 1707; his wife Elizabeth Mulesworth, born 1651, died 2 March 1723, their son James born 1685, died 4 August 1696. [Comber g/s]

MELDRUM, JOHN, brother of the laird of Legy, applied for 2000 acres in Ulster on 13 July 1609, [PU#140]; was granted lands in County Fermanagh originally was granted to James Traill, Thomas Moneypenny and George Smelholm, on 13 March 1617. [Cal.SP.Ire.1617/343]

MELVILLE, JAMES, son of John Melvill of Raith, applied for 2000 acres in Ulster on 25 July 1609. [PU#142]

MELVILLE, ROBERT, Captain of the Earl of Leven's Regiment, in Carrickfergus, 1642. [PRO.SP28/120]

MELVIN, ARTHUR, commander of the William of Londonderry, wrecked in the Bay of Skaill, Orkney, October 1723. [NAS.GD217.698]

MELVIN, JANE, of Ballymeaghan, was granted Irish denization 9 February 1625. [IPR]

MENIES, ELIAS, a Scots-Irish student at Glasgow University 1712. [MUG#198]

MENOCK, ALEXANDER, died 20 November 1668, [Comber g/s]

MERCER, ROBERT, son of John Mercer minister at Slains, Aberdeenshire, educated at Marischal College, Aberdeen, 1619, a schoolmaster in Ellon, Aberdeenshire, then a minister in Mullacreck, Ireland. [MCA#2.195]

MERCER, THOMAS, a Scots-Irish student at Glasgow University 1715. [MUG#206]

MILLER, DAVID, born 1689, died on 30 November 1719, [Killinchy g/s, County Down]

MILLER, HUGH, master of the Prince of Glenarme at the port of Glasgow 5 March 1666. [NAS.E72.10.1]

MILLER, JOHN, was granted Irish denization 22 June 1615. [IPR]

MILLER, JOHN, from Haughs, Ayrshire, now in Ireland, 1 January 1634. [NAS.RS.Ayr#6, 25.1.1634]

MILLER, JOHN, master of the Janet of Glenarme at the port of Glasgow 6 May 1667. [NAS.E72.10.1]

MILLER, ROBERT, in County Tyrone, was granted Irish denization 17 August 1616; in Dunnalong, barony of Strabane, County Tyrone, 1617. [IPR][SBT#23]

MILLER, THOMAS, an Irish student at Glasgow University 1705. [MUG#183]

MILLER, WILLIAM, an Irish student at Glasgow University 1705. [MUG#183]

MILLING, ALEXANDER, master of the Blessing of Donaghadee at the port of Irvine, Ayrshire, on 17 August 1683. [NAS.E72.12.7]

MILLING, ARCHIBALD, master of the Dove of Belfast at the port of Irvine, Ayrshire, on 19 August 1691. [NAS.E72.12.18]

MILLON, JOHN, master of the Blessing of Donaghadee at the port of Irvine, Ayrshire, on 16 November 1688. [NAS.E72.12.14]

MILNE, ANDREW, Lieutenant Colonel of Sir Mungo Campbell of Lawers' Regiment, in Temple Patrick, 1642. [PRO.SP.18.120]

MILNE, WILLIAM, born in Aberdeenshire, graduated MA from King's College, Aberdeen, in 1650, a minister in Islandmagee from 1658. [FI#45]

MILNE, WILLIAM, a travelling chapman in Ardmonich, Ireland, then in St Ninian's, Stirlingshire, cnf 22 November 1667 Commissariot of Stirling

MILNER, ALEXANDER, master and merchant of the Gift of Donaghadee at the port of Irvine, Ayrshire, on 19 April 1683. [NAS.E72.12.8]

MILNER, JOHN, master and merchant aboard the Blessing of Donaghadee at the port of Irvine, Ayrshire, on 19 April 1683. [NAS.E72.12.8]

MITCHELL, ANDREW, was granted Irish denization 16 June 1615. [IPR]

MITCHELL, ANDREW, in Kilbridie, parish of Damacose, Ireland, dead by 1698. [NAS.GD25.7.110]

MITCHELL, DAVID, in Glencush, barony of Strabane, County Tyrone, probate 1640

MITCHELL, HUGH, of Fermanagh, was granted Irish denization on 17 August 1616. [IPR]

MITCHELL, HUGH, with 1500 acres in Clougher, County Tyrone, appeared at a muster in 1618 with 21 men, 1 musket, 2 calivers, 5 pikes, 1 halberd and 3 swords. [Cal.SP.Ire.1618/501] [BMAddMS#18735]

MITCHELL, JAMES, sailor on the Nightingale of Donaghadee at the port of Ayr 19 November 1677. [NAS.E72.3.4]

MITCHELL, JAMES, master of the Helena of Glenarme at the port of Ayr 21 August 1689. [NAS.E72.3.19]

MITCHELL, JOHN, a tenant farmer of 16 acres on the Agnew estate in 1645. [NAS.GD154/514]

MITCHELL, JOHN, graduated MA from Glasgow University in 165- minister in Tyrone before 1689, died in Ochiltree, Ayrshire, on 29 April 1690. [FI#78]

MITCHELL, JOHN, an Irish student at Glasgow University 1707. [MUG#186]

MITCHELL, JOHN, gentleman in Machregorach, County Antrim, will subscribed 26 May 1724, probate 19 April 1725 Dublin

MODERWELL, ADAM, the elder, in the parish of Donaghmore, County Donegal, 1632. [IWD]

MODERWELL, JOHN, a merchant in Strabane, 1679. [IWD]

MOFFAT, JAMES, tenant of John Hamilton of Edenagh, Precinct of Fewes, 1618. [PU#567]

MOFFAT, THOMAS, a Scots-Irish student at Glasgow University in 1713. [MUG#201]

MONCREIFFE, DAVID, was granted Irish denization on 9 July 1616; a merchant in Strabane, County Tyrone. [IPR][SBT#29]

MONCRIEFF, JOHN, Captain of Sir Mungo Campbell of Lawers' Regiment, in Temple Patrick, 1642. [PRO.SP.18.120]

MONCRIEFF, THOMAS, a merchant in Diamond Street, Londonderry, 1659. [C]

MONEYPENNY, ANDREW, of Billy, graduated MA at the University of St Andrews 1605, Archdeacon of County Antrim. [UJA#13/15]; Archdeacon of Connor, was granted Irish denization 20 May 1617. [IPR]; petitioner in June 1624. [Cal.SP.Ire.1624/1226]; a justice of the peace in County Antrim in 1627. [SP.Ire#245/821]

MONEYPENNY, ARTHUR, matriculated at St Leonard's College, University of St Andrews, 1601, graduated MA there in 1605, minister at Kirkcubbin. [UJA#13/15]; a minister in the diocese of Down 1622 and Connor 1634.[TCD.ms.E#3/6;ms.T#1/10]

MONEYPENNY, ARTHUR, of Portaferry, was granted Irish denization on 28 November 1624. [IPR]

MONEYPENNY, ARTHUR, a gentleman in Kilkeele parish, barony of Newry, County Down, 1659. [C]

MONEYPENNY, HUGH, in the barony of Ardes, County Down, 1659. [C]

MONEYPENNY, JOHN, in the barony of Ardes, County Down, 1659. [C]

MONEYPENNY, THOMAS, Lord Kinkell, Fife, was granted Irish denization and a grant of Aghalaga in the barony of Knockinny, County Fermanagh, on 15 October 1610. [IPR]

MONFOD, HEW, master of the John of Glenarme at the port of Glasgow 24 July 1666. [NAS.E72.10.1]

MONKTON, WILLIAM, master of the James of Londonderry at the port of Irvine, Ayrshire, on 28 June 1686. [NAS.E72.12.12]

MONRO, DANIEL, in parish of Seapatrick, Ballyloch, County Down, 1659. [C]

MONRO, GEORGE, Lieutenant Colonel of the Earl of Leven's Regiment, in Carrickfergus, 1642. [PRO.SP28/120]

MUNRO, GEORGE, a Major General in Ireland, husband of Margaret Bruce, son of Sir Alexander Munro of Bearcroft, 1702. [NAS.RD4.90.445]

MUNRO, GEORGE, in Ireland, eldest son of John Munro, Writer to the Signet, 1715. [NAS.RD2.104.821]

MONRO, HUGH, a Scots-Irish student at Glasgow University 1717. [MUG#209]

MONRO, JAMES, a Scots-Irish student at Glasgow University 1709. [MUG#192]

MONRO, JAMES, Writer to the Signet, deceased, husband of
Susanna Learmonth in Ireland, 1715. [NAS.RD2.104.821]

MONRO, ROBERT, Colonel of Major General Robert Monro's
Regiment, in Carrickfergus 1642. [PRO.SP.18.120]

MONTEITH, ROBERT, was granted Irish denization on 11 July
1619. [IPR]

MONTGOMERY, ADAM, son of Adam Montgomery of McViehill a
merchant and guildsbrother of Edinburgh, sometime a
merchant in Ireland, then a Captain of the King's Lifeguards
who was killed at the Battle of Worcester 1651. His widow
Grissel Montgomery, and their daughters Agnes, Marie and
Jean, petitioned Edinburgh Burgh Council on 7 October 1659.
[Edinburgh Burgh Records]

MONTGOMERY, ALEXANDER, gentleman, a juryman at a
Coroner's inquest held at Duncanalley, County Donegal, on 15
September 1660. [Cal.S.P.Ire.1660]

MONTGOMERY, ALEXANDER, in Bathleck, County Monaghan,
subscribed to his will on 29 August 1721, probate 18 April
1722 Dublin.

MONTGOMERY, ARCHIBALD, constable of Donaghadee on 1
January 1647. [SP.Ire.#263/3]

MONTGOMERY, DAVID, of Killochtie, a juryman at a Coroner's
inquest held at Duncanalley, County Donegal, on 15 September
1660. [Cal.S.P.Ire.1660]

MONTGOMERY, Lady ELIZABETH, was granted Irish denization
on 18 February 1622. [IPR]

MONTGOMERY, or BARCLAY, ELIZABETH, was granted Irish
denization on 18 February 1622. [IPR]

MONTGOMERY, GEORGE, Captain of cavalry in Ulster 27 January
1646. [SP.Ire]

MONTGOMERY, GEORGE, in the barony of Castlereagh, County
Down, 1659. [C]

MONTGOMERY, GILBERT, of Tullonefert, County Tyrone, 17 August 1616. [IPR]

MONTGOMERY, Reverend HANS, born 1668, son of Hugh Montgomery of Ballymagown and Jane Hamilton, died 27 November 1726, husband of Elizabeth Townley. [Grey Abbey g/s]

MONTGOMERY, HARRY, born in Ireland son of Robert Montgomery of Cummingburn, a trooper in HM Life Guards in Linlithgow, Scotland, on 5 June 1678. [CA.1.xl]

MONTGOMERY, Sir HUGH, was granted Irish denization on 22 November 1605. [IPR]; of Newton, County Down, 1610. [NAS.GD180#194]

MONTGOMERY, HUGH, of Granghaghe, was granted Irish denization on 20 May 1617. [IPR]

MONTGOMERY, HUGH, in Donaghadee on 17 May 1652. [NAS.GD3.5.420]

MONTGOMERY, HUGH, gentleman, in the barony of Castlereagh, County Down, 1659. [C]

MONTGOMERY, HUGH, in the barony of Ardes, County Down, 1659. [C]
MONTGOMERY, HUGH, in Maghera, barony of Loghinshoun, County Londonderry, 1659. [C]

MONTGOMERY, HUGH, of Dunbarkly, County Down, 1674. [Dunsandle Papers, AH#15/394]

MONTGOMERY, HUGH, Earl of Mount Alexander, subscribed to his will on 21 January 1716, reference to Henry Montgomery, son Thomas, cousin James Montgomery of Rosemont and his son William, cousin Edmonston Montgomery brother of James, cousin Mrs Jane Shaw and her daughter Sarah Shaw or Montgomery, cousin Mr Justice Caulfield, friend Charles Campbell, servants Mrs Jane Meredith and John Meredith, James Johnston mariner, John Hepperson glover, witnesses Patrick Hamilton, Hugh Clement, Alexander Laing, and John

Meredith, probate 23 March 1716 Dublin

MONTGOMERY, HUGH, in Derrygonely, County Fermanagh, subscribed to his will on 10 February 1720, probate 8 March 1722 Dublin

MONTGOMERY, HUGH, of Ballymagown, born in 1635, died on 31 October 1707. [Grey Abbey g/s]

MONTGOMERY, JAMES, of Tullonefert, County Tyrone, 17 August 1616. [IPR]

MONTGOMERY, Lieutenant JAMES, in Ardstraw, barony of Strabane, County Tyrone, probate 1618.

MONTGOMERY, JAMES, Captain of the Earl of Eglinton's Regiment, in Bangor 1642. [PRO.SP.18.120]

MONTGOMERY, Colonel JAMES, in Ireland, 22 June 1648. [NAS.GD3.5.420]

MONTGOMERIE, JAMES, in the barony of Castlereagh 1659. [C]

MONTGOMERY, Sir JAMES, born 1631, second son of Hugh, Lord Viscount Montgomery of Ardes, husband of (1) Katherine Stewart 1631, (2) Margaret Cole 163-, (3) Francesse St Laurence 1647, died 1693. [Grey Abbey g/s]

MONTGOMERY, Sir JAMES, a Cavalry officer in Ulster 27 January 1646. [SP.Ire]

MONTGOMERY, J., a Colonel in Antrim on 19 May 1645. [SP.Ire#260/137]

MONTGOMERY, JOHN, of Ballevegley, County Antrim, went to Scotland to join the army of Charles II, fought in the King's Life Guard at Dunbar 1 September 1650, late fought at Warrington and at Worcester in September 1651 where he was captured and later shipped to Virginia, as a former Cornet in Royal Service he petitioned for the grant of ferries on the River Shannon in February 1661. [SP.Ire#306/959]

MONTGOMERY, JAMES, of Rosemount, County Down, husband of
Elizabeth Edmonstone, 1698, 1699. [NAS.RD3.89.457/462;
RD3.92.375]; son of Sir James Montgomery, married
Elizabeth, eldest daughter of Archibald Edmonstone of
Dunstreth, 1687. [Grey Abbey g/s]

MONTGOMERY, JANE, wife of Hugh Montgomery, son of the
Right Honourable Lord Viscount Montgomery of the Ards, was
granted Irish denization 28 November 1626. [IPR]

MONTGOMERY, JOHN, of Ballinacrosse, was granted Irish
denization on 20 May 1617. [IPR]

MONTGOMERY, JOHN, of Ballymagorrye, was granted Irish
denization on 20 May 1617. [IPR]

MONTGOMERY, JOHN, of the Redene, was granted Irish denization
on 20 May 1617. [IPR]

MONTGOMERY, JOHN, a tenant of Sir William Stewart, around
1620. [PU#545]

MONTGOMERY, JOHN, a Scots-Irish student at Glasgow
University 1708. [MUG#189]

MONTGOMERY, JOHN, in Maghera, barony of Loghinshoulin,
County Londonderry, 1659. [C]

MONTGOMERIE, JOSEPH, master of the John of Glenarme at the
port of Irvine, Ayrshire, on 28 December 1682.
[NAS.E72.12.7]

MONTGOMERIE, JOSIAS, master of the John of Glenarme at the
port of Irvine, Ayrshire, on 8 July 1682. [NAS.E72.12.5]

MONTGOMERY, MATHEW, of Donaghadie, was granted Irish
denization on 28 November 1617. [IPR]

MONTGOMERY, NATHANIEL, master of the Relief of Glenarme
at the port of Irvine, Ayrshire, on 16 February 1681.
[NAS.E72.12.6]

MONTGOMERY, NICHOLAS, in Derrybrusk, County Fermanagh, 1659. [C]

MONTGOMERIE, PATRICK, of Ballyraboy, was granted Irish denization on 20 May 1617. [IPR]

MONTGOMERY, PATRICK, in the barony of Ardes, County Down, 1659. [C]

MONTGOMERY, ROBERT, of Kirkton, applied as an Undertaker for 2000 acres in Ulster on 4 July 1609, which was was granted. [PU#138]

MONTGOMERY, ROBERT, burgess of Newton Ards, County Down, 1612. [Cal.SP.Ire.1613/614]

MONTGOMERY, ROBERT, of Aughenlogher, County Fermanagh, was granted Irish denization on 17 August 1616. [IPR]

MONTGOMERY, ROBERT, matriculated at St Leonard's College, University of St Andrews, 1617, curate of Newtonards. [UJA#13/15]

MONTGOMERY, ROBERT, of Donaghdie, was granted Irish denization on 20 May 1617. [IPR]

MONTGOMERY, ROBERT, of Edenacananay, was granted Irish denization on 28 November 1617. [IPR]

MONTGOMERY, ROBERT, of Moneyglass, was granted Irish denization on 28 November 1617. [IPR]

MONTGOMERY, ROBERT, of Heslett in Scotland, was granted Irish denization on 12 May 1624. [IPR]

MONTGOMERY, ROBERT, a minister in the diocese of Down, 1622 and 1634. [TCD.ms.E#3/6; ms.T#1/10]

MONTGOMERIE, ROBERT, Captain of the Earl of Eglinton's Regiment, in Bangor 1642. [PRO.SP.18.120]

MONTGOMERIE, ROBERT, master of the Janet of Glenarme at the port of Irvine, Ayrshire, on 29 December 1683. [NAS.E72.12.7]

MONTGOMERY, SARAH, Viscountess of the Ards, was granted Irish denization on 28 November 1626. [IPR]

MONTGOMERY, THOMAS, provost of Newtown Ards, County Down, 1612. [Cal.SP.Ire.1613/614]

MONTGOMERY, THOMAS, of Knockfergus, was granted Irish denization on 20 May 1617. [IPR]

MONTGOMERY, THOMAS, master of the John of Belfast at the port of Glasgow 29 August 1672. [NAS.E72.10.3]

MONTGOMERY, WILLIAM, of Donaghdie, was granted Irish denization on 20 May 1617. [IPR]

MONTGOMERY, WILLIAM, in the barony of Ardes, County Down, 1659. [C]

MONTGOMERIE, WILLIAM, master of the Mary of Glenarme at the port of Irvine, Ayrshire, on 8 July 1682 and on 13 November 1684. [NAS.E72.12.5/9]

MONTGOMERY, WILLIAM, of Rosemount, born 1633, died 7 January 1707, his wife Elizabeth born 1635, died 15 November 1677. [Grey Abbey g/s]

MONTGOMERY, WILLIAM, merchant in Dublin, was admitted as a burgess and guildsbrother of Glasgow on 4 January 1717. [GBR]

MOORE, ALEXANDER, Captain of the Earl of Eglinton's Regiment, in Bangor 1642. [PRO.SP.18.120]

MOOR, ALEXANDER, an Irish student at Glasgow University 1705. [MUG#183]

MOORE, ALLAN, of Castledromne, County Tyrone, gentleman, was granted Irish denization on 19 July 1633. [IPR]

MOORE, ARCHIBALD, born in Scotland, was granted Irish
denization on 5 May 1605. [IPR]

MOORE, ARCHIBALD, with 1000 acres in County Cavan on 28
March 1619. [Carew Mss#211/28]

MOORE, ARCHIBALD, in the barony of Ardes, County Down,
1659. [C]

MOORE, CHARLES, a Scots-Irish student at Glasgow University
1715. [MUG#206]

MOORE, CHARLES, born in Armagh, licensed by the Presbytery of
Dunfermline in 1713, minister in Culross 1715-1718, and in
Stirling 1718-1736, died 30 November 1736. [F#7.325]

MOORE, HECTOR, of Donan, was granted Irish denization on 20
May 1617. [IPR]

MOORE, JAMES, of Cloghoum, County Down, was granted Irish
denization on 22 February 1634. [IPR]

MOORE, JOHN, was granted Irish denization on 22 June 1615. [IPR]

MOORE, JOHN, a seaman, was granted Irish denization on 9 July
1616. [IPR]

MOORE, JOHN, of Donaghadie, was granted Irish denization on 20
May 1617. [IPR]

MOORE, JOHN, of Raphoe, was granted Irish denization on 28
November 1617. [IPR]

MOORE, JOHN, in Strabane, County Tyrone, probate 1617

MOORE, JOHN, in the barony of Ardes, County Down, 1659. [C]

MOOR, JOHN, master of the John of Glenarm at the port of Ayr
2 August 1673. [NAS.E72.3.3]

MOORE, PATRICK, in the barony of Ardes, County Down, 1659.
[C]

MOORE, QUINTIN, was granted Irish denization on 20 May 1617. [IPR]

MOORE, ROBERT, of Whitchurch, was granted Irish denization on 5 July 1631. [IPR]

MOORE, THOMAS, a Scots-Irish student at Glasgow University 1719. [MUG#215]

MOORE, WILLIAM, of Milntown, was granted Irish denization on 20 May 1617. [IPR]

MOORE, WILLIAM, preacher at Newton, was granted Irish denization on 28 November 1617. [IPR]

MOORE, WILLIAM, of Bellybregagh, was granted Irish denization on 5 July 1631. [IPR]

MOORE, WILLIAM, of Annaghlaghbane, parish of Clogher, County Tyrone, senior, gentleman, was granted Irish denization on 19 July 1633. [IPR]

MOOREHEAD, WILLIAM, was granted Irish denization on 28 November 1617. [IPR]

MOOREHEAD, WILLIAM, of Terrell's Pace, County Westmeath, was granted Irish denization on 9 December 1633. [IPR]

MORISON, DAVID, was granted Irish denization on 17 August 1616; in Strabane, County Tyrone, 1617. [IPR][SBT#22]

MORISON, JOHN, a Scots-Irish student at Edinburgh University 1688. [CEG]

MORRISON, ROBERT, a merchant at the Diamond, Londonderry, 1659. [C]

MORRISON, SAMUEl, a gentleman in Dublin, 1724. [IWD]

MORTON, CONSTANTIN, was granted Irish denization on 9 July 1616. [IPR]

MORTON, WILLIAM, Captain of the Earl of Lindsay's Regiment, in Bangor 1642. [PRO.SP.28.120]

MOWAT, ANDREW, Captain of Colonel Murray's Regiment of Foot in Ireland, husband of Margaret Preston, 1702. [NAS.RD4.90.829]

MOWAT, JAMES, gentleman, was granted Irish denization on 28 November 1626. [IPR]

MOWBRAY, WILLIAM, son of John Mowbray of Croftangrie, applied for 2000 acres in Ulster on 18 July 1609. [PU#140]

MOWLEN, JOHN, of Crownerston, was granted Irish denization on 20 May 1617. [IPR]

MOWTRAY, WILLIAM, a yeoman, was granted Irish denization on 9 December 1633. [IPR]

MUIR, ALEXANDER, a merchant in Belfast, nephew of John Craig a merchant burgess of Glasgow, was admitted as a burgess and guildsbrother of Glasgow 27 March 1694. [GBR]

MUIR, CHARLES, in the Corbet, Tanaghneue, County Down, 20 June 1682, and 19 December 1683. [NAS.GD10.828/830]

MUIR, CHICHESTER, Antrim, 17 January 1736. [NAS.RS10.7.196]

MUIR, Mr JOHN, merchant in Dublin, burgess and guildsbrother of Glasgow 6 August 1717. [GBR]

MUIR, ROBERT, of Corronary, brother of James Muir of Thornton deceased by 1 July 1680. [NAS.GD21.48]

MUIRHEAD, HENRY, was granted Irish denization on 16 June 1615. [IPR]

MUIRHEAD, JOHN, of Drumreagh, born 1649, died 29 December 1717; his first wife Mary Patton born 1657, died 10 December 1703; his second wife Barbara Dickson born 1679, died 1715. [Killinchy g/s, County Down]

MUNN, ROBERT, master of the John of Belfast at the port of
Glasgow on 15 September 1670. [NAS.E72.10.2]

MUNOPENSE, JOHN, a tenant farmer of 18 acres on the Agnew
estate in 1645. [NAS.GD154/514]

MUNRO, GEORGE, in Ireland, eldest son of John Munro, Writer to
the Signet, 1715. [NAS.RD2.104.821]

MUNRO, HENRY, of Drumnascaugh, County Down, ca.1682.
[NAS.RS36{Inverness}.5.303/591]

MUNRO, JOHN, born in Scotland, minister in Carnmoney from 1685
to 1688, died in Scotland in March 1696. [FI#78]

MUNRO, JOHN, Welsetoun, County West Meath, deceased, his
widow Susanna, wife of Charles Stewart, 1715.
[NAS.RD4.116.779]

MUNRO, ROBERT, in the barony of Castlereagh 1659. [C]

MURCHLAND, ROBERT, master of the Relief of Glenarm at the
port of Irvine, Ayrshire, on 6 December 1668. [NAS.E72.12.1]

MURDOCH, MATTHEW, in Camus, barony of Strabane, County
Tyrone, probate 1631

MURDOCH, ROBERT, leased lands from Sir William Stewart on 1
May 1620 for 5 years. [PU#545]

MURE, CAIN, a tenant farmer on the Agnew estate in 1645.
[NAS.GD154/514]

MURE, HUGH, born 1654, died 20 September 1711. [Killinchy g/s,
County Down]

MURE, JAMES, portioner of Bothkennar, applied for 2000 acres in
Ulster on 25 July 1609. [PU#142]

MURE, Mr WILLIAM, advocate, eldest son of James Mure of
Rhoddans in Ireland, and nephew of William Mure of
Cauldwell, contracted to marry Anna Stewart, relict of James
Maxwell of Blawarthill, and daughter of Sir James Stewart sr.

of Goodtrees, late HM Advocate, 12 February 1711.[NAS.RH9.7.305]

MURRAY, ALEXANDER, murdered by George, William, Andrew and Alexander Cunningham, Charles Murray, James Lindsay, John walker and John Craig, in County Donegal 1660. [Cal.S.P.Ire.1660#304/11]

MURRAY, ALEXANDER, minister at Harr parish in Virginia, 1668, later Dean of Killaley, Ireland, by 1675. [NAS.AC7/4]

MURRAY, ANDREW, was granted Irish denization on 12 February 1618. [IPR]

MURRAY, ANDREW, a minister in the diocese of Raphoe, 1622. [TCD.ms.E#3/6]

MURRAY, ANDREW, in Ulster 1627. [SP.Dom.Sig.Off#I.5]

MURRAY, CHARLES, a gentleman in County Donegal, subscribed to his will on 2 November 1708, reference to his wife Frances Nesbitt or Murray, his executors Alexander Murray in Broughton, Thomas Knox in Mount Charles, Captain Thomas Knox in Lougheaske, and his brother in law Captain Albert Nesbitt, probate 9 March 1712 Dublin

MURRAY, GEORGE, of Broughton, Whithorn, Galloway, applied for 2000 acres in Ulster on 13 July 1609, [PU#139]; grant of Boylaghyeightra, barony of Boylagh and Bannagh, County Donegal, 12 July 1610. [EPR.8.10][TCD.ms#N2/2]; was granted Irish denization 12 July 1610. [IPR]

MURRAY, GIDEON, Captain of the Earl of Lothian's Regiment, in Carrickfergus in 1642. [PRO.SP.28.120]

MURRAY, JOHN, with 1000 acres at Boilagh and Bainage in County Donegal, 28 March 1619. [Carew Mss#211/75]

MURRAY, JOHN, one of the King's Bedchamber, was granted Irish denization on 13 December 1620. [IPR]

MURRAY, Sir JOHN, Captain of the Earl of Lothian's Regiment, in Carrickfergus in 1642. [PRO.SP.28.120]

MURRAY, JOHN, murdered by George, William, Andrew and Alexander Cunningham, Charles Murray, James Lindsay, John walker and John Craig, in County Donegal 1660. [Cal.S.P.Ire.1660, #304/11]

MURRAY, Sir PATRICK, second son of Sir John Murray, Earl of Tullibardine, was granted Irish denization on 28 July 1613. [IPR]

MURRAY, MUNGO, Captain of the Earl of Lindsay's Regiment, in Bangor 1642. [PRO.SP.28.120]

MURRY, PATRICK A., of Carikmanan, born 1653, died 3 January 1723. [Comber g/s]

MURRAY, Sir PATRICK, born in Scotland, was granted Irish denization on 19 December 1615. [IPR]; grant of lands in Munster 16 June 1614. [Cal.SP.Ire.1614/838]

MURRAY, RICHARD, of Broughton, in Castlemurray, County Donegal, 1664. [NAS.GD214.525]

MURRAY, RICHARD, late Sheriff of County Donegal, 13 March 1672; Captain of a militia troop of horse in County Donegal 19 December 1678. [NAS.GD10.495/496/1380]

MURRAY, Sir ROBERT, or Creighton, in Castlemurray, County Donegal, 1664. [NAS.GD214#525]

MURRAY, THOMAS, minister of Killyleagh around 1640, murdered in 1641, husband of Anna Griffith. [PHS]

MURTLAND, ROBERT, merchant aboard the James of Carrickfergus at the port of Ayr 25 June 1673. [NAS.E72.3.3]

NAPIER, ARCHIBALD, in the barony of Tirerill, County Sligo, 1659. [C]

NEIL, HENRY, a merchant in Pomp Street, Londonderry, 1659. [C]

NEILSON, JAMES, a Scots-Irish student at Glasgow University 1719. [MUG#215]

NEILSON, ROBERT, in Dungannon on 8 March 1667.
[Cal.SP.Ire.348/8]

NEISH, AGNES, wife of Reverend John Lothian, in Dundonnell,
Ireland, later in Monklands, Scotland, and now in Ireland, cnf
20 February 1658 Commissariot of Glasgow

NELSON, WILLIAM, of Ramullin, County Donegal, was granted
Irish denization on 28 November 1617. [IPR]

NEISBIT, ALBERT, in Toberdally, King's County, subscribed to his
will on 5 January 1709, probate 29 March 1720 Dublin

NEISBIT, ROBERT, in the barony of Tarranney, County Armagh,
1659. [C]

NESBIT, JAMES, of Tullaghdonnell, was granted Irish denization on
28 November 1617. [IPR]

NESBIT, JAMES, of Woodhill, County Down, 1732.
[NAS.GD10#945]

NESBIT, JOHN, in Aghaveigh, County Fermanagh, 1659. [C]

NESMITH, JAMES, a merchant in Pomp Street, Londonderry, 1659.
[C]

NEVIN, THOMAS, of Ballicopland, was granted Irish denization on
20 May 1617. [IPR]

NEVIN, THOMAS, in the barony of Ardes, County Down, 1659. [C]

NEWBURGH, W, a sheriff, in Dungannon on 8 March 1667.
[Cal.SP.Ire.348/8]

NICOLSON, HUGH, of Ballenaghie, died 16..., his widow Isobel
Orr died in 1696. [Old Abbey Church g/s, Bangor]

NICOLSON, JOHN, merchant in Dublin, was admitted as a burgess
and guildsbrother of Glasgow on 15 December 1724, [GBR]

NISBET, GEORGE, glasswright, son of George Nisbet in parish of Rapho, Donegal, former apprentice of James Elphinstone a glasswright burgess, was admitted as a burgess and guildsbrother of Glasgow 24 May 1677, [GBR]

NISBET, JAMES, a merchant in Glasgow then in Inver, County Donegal, 1715. [NAS.RD2.105.220]

NISBET, JOHN, in Strabane, 1673. [NAS.GD10#447]

NOBLE, WILLIAM, of Cashell, County Donegal, gentleman, was granted Irish denization on 19 July 1631. [IPR]

NORTON, SAMUEL, a Scots-Irish student at Glasgow University 1718. [MUG#213]

OGNEEVE, GILBERT, of Inver, a yeoman, was granted Irish denization on 9 February 1625. [IPR]

OGNEEVE, JOHN, of Ballegreenlaw, was granted Irish denization on 9 February 1625. [IPR]

O'HAMILL, NEILL, of Ballihemlinge, was granted Irish denization on 28 November 1617. [IPR]

ONG, FRANCIS, Dublin, was admitted as a burgess and guildsbrother of Glasgow on 6 October 1718. [GBR]

ORR, JAMES, of Raphoe, was granted Irish denization on 28 November 1617. [IPR]

ORR, JAMES, of Munlough, born 1756, died 13 April 1728. [Comber g/s]

ORR, JOHN, son of late Thomas Orr, in Barcosh, deceased in Ireland, cnf 9 July 1629 Commissariot of Glasgow

ORR, JOHN, master of the Fortune of Coleraine at the port of Irvine, Ayrshire, on 29 April 1682. [NAS.E72.12.6]

ORR, JOHN, of Clantanacally, born 1651, died 22 May 1722. [Comber g/s]

ORR, SAMUEL, a Scots-Irish student at Glasgow University 1706.
[MUG#184]

ORR, THOMAS, a Scots-Irish student at Edinburgh University 1699.
[CEG]

ORROCK, Captain DAVID, applied for 2000 acres in Ulster on 20
July 1609. [PU#140]

OSBORNE, ELIZABETH, eldest daughter of Captain Henry
Osborne, alderman of Londonderry, relict of John Ross of
Dreghorn, Ayrshire, 1644. [RGS.X.72]

OSBORNE, ROBERT, was granted Irish denization on 19 March
1616. [IPR]

PARK, HUGH, a Scots-Irish student at Glasgow University in 1711.
[MUG#196]

PARKER, GEORGE, tenant of John Hamilton of Edenagh, Precinct
of Fewes, 1618. [PU#567]

PARRIS, THOMAS, of Dublin, gentleman, was granted Irish
denization on 19 July 1633. [IPR]

PATERSON, ADAM, servant to William Montgomerie, merchant in
Dublin, was admitted as a burgess and guildsbrother of
Glasgow on 24 July 1717. [GBR]

PATERSON, ALEXANDER, in County Tyrone, was granted Irish
denization on 17 August 1616. [IPR]

PATERSON, ALEXANDER, was granted Irish denization on 12
February 1618. [IPR]

PATERSON, JOHN, was granted Irish denization on 9 July 1616.
[IPR]

PATERSON, JOHN, in Devonish, County Fermanagh, 1659. [C]

PATTERSON, JOHN, of Burncronen, a juryman at a Coroner's
inquest held at Duncanalley, County Donegal, on 15 September
1660. [Cal.S.P.Ire.1660]

PATERSON, JOSIAS, a Scots-Irish student at Edinburgh University in 1705. [CEG]

PATTERSON, MATTHEW, of Raphoe, was granted Irish denization on 28 November 1617. [IPR]

PATTERSON, ROBERT, in Newton, County Tyrone, 1636. [SP.Ire#255/144]

PATTERSON, ROBERT, corporal of Viscount Claneboy's troop of horse on 25 April 1642. [SP.Ire#260/63]

PATERSON, WILLIAM, in Strabane, County Tyrone, was granted Irish denization on 17 August 1616; a merchant there in 1617. [IPR][SBT#22]

PATTON, ROBERT, graduated MA from Glasgow University in 1654, minister in Ballyclare from 1655, died in 1680. [FI#79]

PATON, WILLIAM, was granted Irish denization on 22 June 1615. [IPR]

PATON, WILLIAM, a minister in the diocese of Raphoe, 1622. [TCD.ms.E#3/6][British Museum.Add.MS4756/116]

PATTON, WILLIAM, a Scots-Irish student at Glasgow University in 1708. [MUG#189]

PATRICK, JOHN, was granted Irish denization on 16 June 1615. [IPR]

PAUL, WILLIAM, a cloth merchant, late of Larne, County Antrim, 16 May 1729. [NAS.SC20.33.11]

PEACOCK, JOHN, of Ballidonan, was granted Irish denization on 20 May 1617. [IPR]

PEACOCK, JOHN, in the barony of Ardes, County Down, 1659. [C]

PEACOCK, PATRICK, born 1627, son of Patrick Peacock in Newburgh, Fife, graduated MA from the University of St Andrews in 1648, minister in County Down after 1663, later in

Donaghadee, died on 20 October 1691. [FI#79]

PEACOCK, UPTON, a Scots-Irish student at Glasgow University in 1713. [MUG#201]

PEARSON, ARCHIBALD, of Westhall, former Chamberlain to the Earl of Annandale, in Ireland 1672. [NAS.GD214#526/527]

PEARSON, DAVID, in County Donegal 1693. [NAS.GD1.510.112]

PEARSON, EDWARD, of Machrie, Internon, County Donegal, 1715, and 9 June 1716. [NAS.RD3.144.498; RD4.117.876; GD10.863]

PEARSON, EDWARD, brother of Reverend James Pearson at Killybeggs, Donegal, 1715. [NAS.RD2.105.77]

PEARSON, JAMES, a minister at Killybeggs, Donegal, 1715. [NAS.RD2.105.77]

PEDEN, ALEXANDER, a Presbyterian minister who fled from Scotland to Ireland in 1669. [Cal.S.P.Ire.1669]

PEEBLES, HUGH, born in Mainshill, Ayrshire, educated at Glasgow University, graduated MA in 1624, a minister in Ireland from 1633 to 1657?. [PHS]

PEEBLES, JOHN, of Carrow Johnvoistie, was granted Irish denization on 28 November 1617. [IPR]

PEEBLES, JOHN, younger of Pethirland, a resident of Ballimony, County Antrim, 1632. [NAS.RS.Ayr#5. 1.11.1632]

PEEBLES, THOMAS, born in Scotland, graduated MA from Glasgow University in 1626, an army chaplain then minister in Dundonald and Holywood from 1645, died in 1670. [FI#47]

PENTLAND, GEORGE, son of George Pentland in Courthill, Ireland, apprenticed to Charles Batchelor, barber burgess of Edinburgh, 20 March 1706, [ERA]

PENTLAND, JOHN, son of George Pentland in Ireland, apprenticed to Thomas Weir, apothecary burgess of Edinburgh, 22 August 1701, [ERA]

PERRY, JAMES, of Tullarash, County Tyrone, yeoman, was granted Irish denization on 27 June 1634. [IPR]

PERRY, JOHN, of Roughan, County Tyrone, yeoman, was granted Irish denization on 27 June 1634. [IPR]

PETTERSON, ELIZABETH, born 1680, wife of James McGown in Tylear, died on 17 March 1706. [Comber g/s]

PETERSON, GAVIN, in Belymcrillie, born 1621, died 1 April 1683. [Killinchy g/s, County Down]

PETERSON, WILLIAM, in Bellymarillie, born 1661, died 3 December 1729. [Killinchy g/s, County Down]

PHILPOT, WILLIAM, merchant in Dublin, was admitted as a burgess and guildsbrother of Glasgow on 20 February 1724. [GBR]

PITCAIRN, Lieutenant JAMES, in Ireland 1624. [Cal.SP.Ire]

PITCAIRN, JAMES, born on 26 January 1648 son of William Pitcairn of Forthar and Ann Crichton, graduated MA from the University of St Andrews, minister of Ballymena from 1676 to 1687, married Elizabeth, daughter of Sir Francis Ruthven of Freeland, father of Alexander, Janet and David. [FI#79]

PITSCOTTIE, COLIN, Lieutenant Colonel of the Earl of Eglinton's Regiment, in Bangor 1642. [PRO.SP.18.120]

PITTALLOCH, JOHN, master of the John of Glenarme at the port of Glasgow 9 June 1666. [NAS.E72.10.1]

POLLOCK, AGNES, relict of Adam Galt in the Grange of Kildalloch, Balrishan parish, Ireland, heir to James Pollock, a messenger in Maybole, Ayrshire, 28 October 1698. [NAS.GD25.7.110]

POLLOCK, ANNA, relict of Andrew Mitchell, in Kilbridie, Damacose parish, Ireland, heir to James Pollock, a messenger in Maybole, Ayrshire, 28 October 1698. [NAS.GD25.7.110]

POLLOCK, JOHN, son of John Pollock in Ireland, apprenticed to John Wilson barber burgess of Edinburgh, on 16 June 1708. [ERA]

POLLOCK, DAVID, in Killeleagh, barony of Newry, County Down, 1659. [C]

POLLOCK, JOHN, in Dublin, 1714. [NAS.RD3.142.42]

PONT, ROBERT, a preacher, was granted Irish denization on 12 February 1618. [IPR]; son of Zachary Pont a minister in Bowar, Caithness, a minister in Ireland before 1639, husband of Isabel Stewart. [PHS]

PONT, Reverend TIMOTHY, applied for 2000 acres in Ulster on 25 July 1609. [PU#142]

POOKE, JAMES, was granted Irish denization on 17 August 1616, a merchant in Strabane, County Tyrone, 1617. [IPR][SBT#22]

POOLE, WILLIAM, an Anglo-Irish student at Glasgow University in 1706. [MUG#184]

PORTER, JAMES, died 25 December 1707. [Drumbo g/s]

PORTERFIELD, THOMAS, a Scots-Irish student at Glasgow University in 1710. [MUG#194]

POTTER, SUSANNA, born 1695, died 29 October 1718. [Killinchy g/s, County Down]

POTTER, THOMAS, of Killinchy, born 1631, died 28 February 1697. [Killinchy g/s, County Down]

POWER, JOHN, a merchant in Londonderry, was granted Irish denization on 17 August 1616.[IPR]

PRESTON, Sir RICHARD, Lord Dingwall, was granted Irish denization on 24 November 1614. [IPR]

PRINGLE, LEWIS, in Tuam, Ireland, serviced as heir to his cousins James Pringle of Buckholm and Janet Pringle, widow of James Gellie advocate, on 6 January 1719. [NAS.SH]

PRINGLE, THOMAS, tenant of John Hamilton of Edenagh, Precinct of Fewes, 1618. [PU#567]

PRINGLE, WILLIAM, of Calligarrie, was granted Irish denization on 28 November 1617. [IPR]

PRINGLE, WILLIAM, master of the Nightingale of Belfast at the port of Ayr on 11 June 1681. [NAS.E72.3.5]

PURDY, JOHN, the younger, born 1697, died on 10 March 1715. [Kilmore g/s, County Down]

PURVES, THOMAS, in Bold, applied for 1000 acres in Ulster on 20 July 1609. [PU#141]

RAE, ADAM, tenant of John Hamilton of Edenagh, Precinct of Fewes, 1618. [PU#567]

RAE, JOHN, merchant aboard the Mary of Glenarme at the port of Irvine, Ayrshire, on 5 November 1683. [NAS.E72.12.8]

RAE, WILLIAM, a Scots-Irish student at Glasgow University in 1710. [MUG#194]

RAINE, Mr WILLIAM, a merchant in Belfast, 1722. [NAS.AC9/849]

RALSTON, JOHN, son of the laird of Ralston, was granted Irish denization and a grant of 1000 acres at Kilcloghan in the barony of Clanchy, County Cavan, on 29 August 1610, [IPR][TCD.ms#N2/2]; Undertaker of the Precinct of Tullochone, County Cavan, 1611. [Cal.SP.Ire.1611/384; 1612/608]

RAMSAY, ALEXANDER, brother of Thomas Ramsay of Balmouth, applied for 2000 acres in Ulster on 25 July 1609. [PU#142]

RAMSAY, CHARLES, a Scots-Irish student at Glasgow University in 1708. [MUG#189]

RAMSAY, DAVID, the King's clockmaker, was granted Irish denization on 27 July 1619. [Signet Office Docquet Book]

RAMSAY, GILBERT, born in Scotland, a minister in Bangor from 1646, died in August 1670, buried in Bangor Abbey. [FI#47]

RAMSAY, WILLIAM, one of the king's bedchamber, was granted Irish denization on 1 July 1614. [IPR]

RANKIN, ARCHIBALD, servant of the king, was granted Irish denization on 24 July 1619. [Privy Seals Chancery, file 1904]

RANKIN, JOHN, skipper in Donnaghee County Down, 1696. [NAS.RD2.80.3]

RANKIN, WILLIAM, in County Donegal, was granted Irish denization on 17 August 1616. [IPR]

RAWLEY, WILLIAM, of Tullaghoge, County Tyrone, yeoman, was granted Irish denization on 27 June 1634. [IPR]

RAYNOLD, PAUL, of Bangor, was granted Irish denization on 5 July 1631. [IPR]

READ, ALEXANDER, corporal of Viscount Claneboy's troop of horse on 25 April 1642. [SP.Ire#260/63]

READ, Captain JAMES, of Union Park, Queens County, and of Tullychin, parish of Killyreagh, was born in 1675, and died in 1727; his wife Rose Hamilton, daughter of Gawen Hamilton of Killyreagh Castle, was born 1687 and died in 1733. [Killyreagh g/s, County Down]

REDGATE, THOMAS, a merchant in Londonderry, was granted Irish denization on 9 July 1616. [IPR]

REDDIE, JOHN, in Donegal, son and heir to John Reddie in Leuchatsbeath, 24 June 1656. [NAS.GD172.1525, 1526, 1527]

REID, ANDREW, of Bally McCormoch, was granted Irish denization on 28 November 1617. [IPR]

REID, JAMES, master of the <u>William of Portaferry</u> at the port of
Irvine, Ayrshire, 20 July 1681 and 12 August 1681.
[NAS.E72.12.3/5]

REID, JAMES, a merchant in Newry, County Down, 1702.
[NAS.RD2.86.1.372]

REID, Reverend JAMES, son of Reverend William Reid, minister of
Killinchy from 1702 to 1753. [Killinchy g/s, County Down]

REID, Reverend WILLIAM, born in Scotland, graduated MA from
Glasgow University in 1641, a minister in Ballywalter from
1660, and in Ballynahinch from 1696 to 1704, died on 7 May
1708, [FI#47]; a minister in Belliwalter, Ireland, 22 July 1681.
[RGS#10.217]; minister in Ballynahinch from 1676 to 1704.
[Killinchy g/s, County Down]

REMICK, MARTIN, an Irish student at Glasgow University in 1705.
[MUG#183]

RICHARDSON, ALEXANDER, of Balliarkie, was granted Irish
denization on 28 November 1617. [IPR]

RICHARDSON, ALEXANDER, with 1000 acres in Dungannon,
County Tyrone, appeared at a muster in 1618 with 19 men, 3
muskets, 5 calivers, 8 pikes and 9 swords.
[Cal.SP.Ire.1618/501] [BM.AddMS#18735]; with 1000 acres at
Craigenballi, Precinct of Mountjoy, 28 March 1619. [Carew
Mss#211/148]

RICHARDSON, ALEXANDER, was granted Irish denization on 16
December 1630. [IPR]; granted lands in Creige, Precinct of
Mountjoy, 1630. [PU#550]

RICHARDSON, ARCHIBALD, of Augher, County Tyrone, 11
December 1707. [NAS.GD124.15.729]

RICHARDSON, JAMES, in Dungannon on 8 March 1667.
[Cal.SP.Ire.348/8]

RICHARDSON, JAMES, brother of Archibald Richardson of
Augher, was at the Siege of Londonderry, 11 December 1707.
[NAS.GD124.15.729]

RICHARDSON, JOHN, of Fardrum, County Fermanagh, a juryman in Inniskillen on 28 February 1624. [Cal.SP.Ire.1624#1157]

RICHARDSON, JOHN, of Killdresse, County Tyrone, gentleman, was granted Irish denization on 19 July 1633. [IPR]

RICHARDSON, PATRICK, a Scots-Irish student at Edinburgh University in 1690. [CEG]

RICHARDSON, ROBERT, an Anglo-Irish student at Glasgow University in 1717. [MUG#210]

RICHARDSON, THOMAS, in Newry, 1641. [TCD#ms837/12]

RICHARDSON, W., in Dungannon on 8 March 1667. [Cal.SP.Ire.348/8]

RICHARDSON, WILLIAM, born in Scotland, graduated MA from Glasgow University in 1641, minister of Killyreagh from 1649 to 1670, died on 20 July 1680. [Killyreagh g/s, County Down] [FI#47]

RICHARDSON, WILLIAM, Tatukyl, Kildress, County Fermanagh, 1690. [IWD]

RICHIE, JOHN, merchant in Carnetallagh, County Donegal, was granted Irish denization on 17 August 1616. [IPR]

RICHMOND, DONALD, born in Scotland, graduated MA from Glasgow University in 1644, minister of Holywood from 1652. [FI#47]

RIDDELL, JAMES, Major of the Earl of Lothian's Regiment, in Carrickfergus in 1642. [PRO.SP.28.120]

RIDDLE, ROBERT, of Castle Beg, born 1631, died 31 July 1661. [Comber g/s]

RIDDELL, Sir WALTER, Captain of the Earl of Lothian's Regiment, in Carrickfergus in 1642. [PRO.SP.28.120]

RITCHIE, ADAM, matriculated at St Leonard's College, St Andrews, 1621, curate of Ramoan, Connor, 1634. [UJA#13/15]

RITCHIE, ADAM, a merchant burgess of Ayr now resident in Ireland 1643. [NAS.GD135.999]

RITCHIE, JOHN, in Castle Stewart, 1623. [see John Campbell's testament, Commissariot of Glasgow, 1623]

RITCHIE, PATRICK, tenant of John Hamilton of Edenagh, Precinct of Fewes, 1618. [PU#567]

RITCHIE, ROBERT, smith in Castle Stewart, 1623. [see John Campbell's testament, Commissariot of Glasgow, 1623]

ROBERTSON, ALEXANDER, second son of James Robertson of Newbigging, to Ireland by 18 July 1664. [NAS.GD172/2460]

ROBINSON, JOHN, of Artra, County Tyrone, yeoman, was granted Irish denization 27 June 1634. [IPR]

ROBINSON, BARTHOLEMEW, of Coleraine, County Londonderry, merchant, was granted Irish denization on 19 July 1631. [IPR]

ROBINSON, JOHN, in Killeleagh, barony of Newry, County Down, 1659. [C]

ROBISON, CUTHBERT, merchant, admitted as a burgess and guildsbrother of Glasgow on 25 December 1622, husband of Janet Miller, settled in Ireland before 1655. [GBR]

ROBISON, JOHN, merchant aboard the Marion of Glenarme at the port of Irvine, Ayrshire, on 15 May 1682. [NAS.E72.12.6]

ROBSON, PATRICK, of Raphoe, was granted Irish denization on 28 November 1617. [IPR]

RODGER, JOHN, master of the Margaret of Larne at the port of Glasgow 28 September 1672; master of the Anthony of Carrickfergus at the port of Irvine, Ayrshire, on 26 July 1682; master of the Mayflower of Larne at the port of Irvine, Ayrshire, 1 September 1689 and at the port of Ayr 26 August 1690. [NAS.E72.10.3; E72.12.5/14; E72.3.23]

RODGER, WILLIAM, skinner, eldest son of William Rodger a merchant burgess, admitted as a burgess and guildsbrother of Glasgow on 18 November 1647, settled in Ireland by 1655. [GBR]

ROE, ANDREW, an Anglo-Irish student at Glasgow University in 1712. [MUG#199]

ROGER, SUSANNA, born 1656, wife of James Orr of Belligoun, died 28 October 1720. [Comber g/s]

ROGERS, WILLIAM, a merchant in Londonderry, was granted Irish denization on 17 August 1616. [IPR]

ROSE, HUGH, a minister in the diocese of Connor, 1622. [TCD.ms.E#3/6]

ROSE, JOHN, a minister in the diocese of Raphoe, 1622. [TCD.ms.E#3/6]

ROSS, Mrs DOROTHY, born 1671, wife of John Ross a merchant in Coleraine, died on 11 December 1713. [Ballywillin g/s, County Antrim]

ROSS, GEORGE, in the barony of Ardes, County Down, 1659. [C]

ROSS, GEORGE, an Irish student at Edinburgh University in 1697. [CEG]

ROSS, GEORGE, of Karney, born 1649, died on 27 December 1704, his wife Ursula Hamilton, born 1647, died on 26 February 1730. [Slanes g/s, Ardes, County Down]

ROSS, HUGH, in Kilnawly, County Fermanagh, 1659. [C]

ROSS, JAMES, of Ballunuenane-Itragh, was granted Irish denization on 28 November 1617. [IPR]

ROSS, JAMES, in the barony of Ardes, County Down, 1659. [C]

ROSS, JAMES, of Portiroe, Ireland, 1694. [NAS.RD2.77/2.50]; in Portavo, County Down, 1696. [IWD]

ROSS, JAMES, a Scots-Irish student at Glasgow University in 1719. [MUG#215]

ROSS, JOHN, a burgess of Glasgow, applied for 1500 acres in Ulster on 6 July 1609. [PU#139]

ROSS, JOHN, gentleman, in the barony of Castlereagh, County Down, 1659. [C]

ROSS, ROBERT, of Bellifodelie, was granted Irish denization on 28 November 1617. [IPR]

ROSS, ROBERT, in the barony of Ardes, County Down, 1659. [C]

ROSS, ROBERT, in Clownish, County Fermanagh, 1659. [C]

ROSS, ROBERT, born in Ireland, in Poland 8 November 1661. [NAS.GD406.9695]

ROSS, ROBERT, merchant on the Blessing of Donaghadee at the port of Irvine, Ayrshire, on 16 November 1688. [NAS.E72.12.14]

ROSS, SAMUEL, a Scots-Irish student at Glasgow University in 1710. [MUG#194]

ROSS, WILLIAM, in Clownish, County Fermanagh, 1659. [C]

ROSS, WILLIAM, in Kilnawly, County Fermanagh, 1659. [C]

ROUCHE, JOHN, Captain of Lord Sinclair's Regiment, in Newry, 1642. [PRO.SP.18.120]

ROW, DAVID, born around 1600, son of Reverend John Row in Carnock, Fife, a minister in Ireland before 1640. [PHS]

ROW, SAMUEL, born in 1609, son of Reverend Archibald Row in Stobo, educated at Edinburgh University, graduated MA in 1629, a minister in Ireland from 1634 to 1638, died in Edinburgh in June 1665. [PHS]

ROWAN, ANDREW, eldest son of John Rowan of Greenhead,
Govan, minister in Clough, County Antrim, from 1659 to 1661,
rector of Dunaghy (Clough) from 1661, died in 1717, husband
of ..... McPhedris, (2) Alice Dunlop. [FI#48]

ROWAN, ANDREW, a Scots-Irish student at Edinburgh University
in 1707. [CEG]

ROWAN, ROBERT, son of John Rowan of Greenhead, Govan, a
minister in Maghera from 1658, rector of Maghera from 1661,
died after 18 August 1693. [FI#48]

ROWATT, JOHN, born in Scotland, educated at Glasgow and
Edinburgh universities, graduated MA from Edinburgh
University in 1662, minister in Badong´and Cappagh by 1672,
in Drumraer and Ternan McGurk from 1673 to 1677, in Lifford
from 1682, at the Siege of Londonderry in 1689, died in
Clonleigh on 4 January 1694. [FI#79]

RULE, ROBERT, son of Reverend George Rule of Longformacus,
Berwickshire, graduated MA from Edinburgh University in
1644, minister in Londonderry from 1672 to 1688, died in
September 1703. [FI#80]

RUSSELL, ALEXANDER, a tenant farmer of 30 acres on the Agnew
estate in 1645. [NAS.GD154/514]

RUSSELL, JAMES, was granted Irish denization on 22 June 1615.
[IPR]

RUSSEL, JOHN, of Edenderry, born 1669, died 13 August 1729.
[Drumbo g/s]

RUSSELL, ROBERT, in Londonderry, was granted Irish denization
on 17 August 1616. [IPR]

RUTHERFORD, ROBERT, a Scots-Irish student at Glasgow
University in 1708. [MUG#189]

RUTHERFORD, WILLIAM, in Antrim 1641. [SP.Ire#258/92]

SANDERSON, ALEXANDER, in Dungannon on 8 March 1667.
[Cal.SP.Ire.348/8]

SANDERSON, ALEXANDER, in Drumkeevill, County Cavan,
1706. [IWD]

SANDERSON, GEORGE, of Tullylegane, County Tyrone,
gentleman, was granted Irish denization on 27 June 1634. [IPR]

SANDERSON, JAMES, a merchant, 1642. [SP.Ire.307/100]

SANDERSON, ROBERT, a Lieutenant Colonel in Antrim on 19 May
1645. [SP.Ire#260/137]

SANDERSON, ROBERT, of Castle Sanderson, County Tyrone,
husband of Jean Leslie, 1714, [NAS.RD2.103/2.336]

SANDILANDS, JEAN, relict of Robert Byres, a merchant in Dublin,
cnf 4 August 1730 Commissariot of Aberdeen

SAUNDERSON, ALEXANDER, was granted Irish denization on 26
September 1614. [IPR]

SAUNDERSON, ALEXANDER, was granted Irish denization on 25
November 1631. [IPR]

SAUNDERSON, KATHERINE, wife of Alexander Saunderson of
Tullelegan, County Tyrone, gentleman, was granted Irish
denization on 19 July 1631. [IPR]

SAUNDERSON, Captain, with 1000 acres in the barony of
Dungannon, County Tyrone, appeared at a muster in 1618 with
23 men, 8 muskets, 4 calivers, 10 pikes, 1 halberd and 8
swords.
[Cal. SP.Ire.1618/501][BM.AddMS#18735]; with 1000 acres at
Tullylegan in the Precinct of Mountjoy on 28 March 1619.
[Carew Mss#11/146]

SAVAGE, HUGH, a gentleman in the barony of Castlereagh 1659.
[C]

SAVAGE, HUGH, in the barony of Ardes, County Down, 1659. [C]

SAVAGE, JAMES, in the barony of Ardes, County Down, 1659. [C]

SAVAGE, JOHN, in the barony of Ardes, County Down, 1659. [C]

SAVAGE, JOHN, a merchant in Dublin, subscribed to his will on 5 March 1710, reference to his wife Katherine Savage or Audley, eldest son William, second son Hugh, William Savage of Dunturkin, County Down, Patrick Savage of Portaferry, County Antrim, Hugh Savage of Drumrode, James Savage his brother, witnesses Rowland Savage in Portaferry, County Down, William Cochrane victualler in Dublin, Hugh Savage gentleman in Drumnaroad, County Down, and James Rogers gentleman in Dublin, probate 9 July 1716 Dublin

SAVAGE, PATRICK, in the barony of Ardes, County Down, 1659. [C]

SAVAGE, WILLIAM, in the barony of Castlereagh, County Down, 1659. [C]

SAWBRIDGE, THOMAS, an Anglo-Irish student at Glasgow University in 1708. [MUG#189]

SAWER, JAMES, of Moynegragan, gentleman, was granted Irish denization on 28 November 1624. [IPR]; [see George Campbell of Cessnock's testament 18 November 1624 Commissariot of Glasgow]

SCOTT, FRANCIS, born in County Cavan the son of William Scott, trooper in HM Life Guards, in Linlithgow, Scotland, on 5 June 1678. [CA.1.xxxvii]

SCOTT, GEORGE, in Teedawnett, County Monaghan, 1659. [C]

SCOTT, GEORGE, in Boagh, County Monaghan, 1697. [IWD]

SCOTT, HENRY, of Deriaghy, born 1635 and died on 24 May 1710; his wife Elizabeth Maxwell was born in 1631 and died on 14 March 1708. [Drumbeg g/s, County Down]

SCOTT, JAMES, a minister in the diocese of Raphoe, 1622. [TCD.ms.E#3/6]

SCOTT, JAMES, of Carne, a juryman at a Coroner's inquest held at
Duncanalley, County Donegal, on 15 September 1660.
[Cal.S.P.Ire.1660]

SCOTT, JAMES, master of the Margaret of Belfast at the port of Ayr
19 March 1673. [NAS.E72.3.3]

SCOTT, JOHN, chaplain to Major General Munro's Regiment in
Ireland 1642. [FI#48]

SCOT, JOHN, an Irish student at Edinburgh University in 1678.
[CEG]

SCOTT, JOHN, master of the Content of Belfast at the port of Ayr 13
September 1684. [NAS.E72.3.13]

SCOTT, MATTHEW, master of the James of Donaghadee at the port
of Irvine, Ayrshire, 12 January 1691. [NAS.E72.12.17]

SCOTT, PATRICK, of Raighe, gentleman, was granted Irish
denization in 28 November 1624. [IPR]

SCOTT, WALTER, Lieutenant Colonel of the Earl of Lothian's
Regiment, in Carrickfergus in 1642. [PRO.SP.28.120]

SCOTT, WILLIAM, in Dartrye, County Monaghan, 1659. [C]

SCOTT, WILLIAM, master of the Swan of Donaghadee at the port of
Glasgow 1 December 1665. [NAS.E72.10.1]

SCOTT, WILLIAM, master of the Joan of Portaferry at the port of
Irvine, Ayrshire, on 23 April 1683. [NAS.E72.12.8]

SCOTT, WILLIAM, in Lessiegellie, Ireland, 1699.
[NAS.RD4.85.223]

SCOTT, WILLIAM, a gentleman in Annahagh, County Monaghan,
subscribed to his will on 21 January 1721, reference to his son
John, probate 1721 Dublin

SCRIMGEOUR, ALEXANDER, was granted Irish denization on 22
June 1615. [IPR]

SCUPPARD, JAMES, was granted Irish denization on 16 June 1615. [IPR]

SEATON, CHRISTOPHER, parson of Kilskeeny, County Tyrone, on 24 July 1631. [SP.Ire#252/2003]

SEATON, DAVID, Captain of Lord Sinclair's Regiment, in Newry, 1642. [PRO.SP.18.120]

SEATON, GEORGE, DD, 2 January 1641. [SP.Dom.Sig.Off#III, 407]

SEATON, JANET, of Ercham, was granted Irish denization on 9 February 1625. [IPR]

SEMPILL, ANDREW, of Ballygrenie, was granted Irish denization on 28 November 1617. [IPR]

SEMPILL, ANDREW, late servant to Robert, Lord Sempill, now in Lettirmarkaward, 4 November 1672. [NAS.GD20.1.588]

SEMPLE, BRICE, gentleman, was granted Irish denization on 22 September 1619. [IPR]

SEMPILL, BRUCE, late of Paisley and Renfrew, possibly then in Connaught, 7 August 1641. [Cal.SP.Ire.1641/vol.260]

SEMPLE, GABRIEL, a Presbyterian minister who fled from Scotland to Ireland in 1669. [Cal.SP.Ire.1669]

SEMPLE, Sir JAMES, born in Scotland, was granted Irish denization on 27 June 1615. [IPR]

SEMPLE, JOHN, born in 1602, a minister in Carsphairn 1646, then a minister in County Down, died during 1677. [PHS]

SEMPLE, JOHN, master and merchant of the Anthony of Carrickfergus at the port of Irvine, Ayrshire, on 17 April 1683. [NAS.E72.12.8]

SEMPLE, ROBERT, of Carrickballidonie, was granted Irish denization on 20 May 1617. [IPR]

SEMPILL, ROBERT, a minister in the diocese of Derry, 1622.
[TCD.ms.E#3/6]

SEMPILL, ROBERT, of Donnogheddy, County Tyrone, clerk, was
granted Irish denization on 19 July 1631. [IPR]

SEMPILL, WILLIAM, Justice of the Peace for County Donegal,
1629. [Cal.SP.Ire.1629/1437]

SEMPLE, WILLIAM, a non-conformist minister imprisoned at
Lifford in 1669. [Cal.SP.Ire]

SHARPE, JAMES, clerk in Strabane, County Tyrone, was granted
Irish denization on 17 August 1616; a gentleman there in 1617.
[IPR][SBT#22]

SHARP, JOHN, a minister, was granted Irish denization on 28 March
1617. [IPR]

SHAW, ANTHONY, born in Ayrshire during 1619, graduated MA
from Edinburgh University in 1639, a minister in Belfast from
1646, in Ballywalter from 1656, later in Scotland, died on 20
September 1687, husband of (1) Agnes McCubbin, (2) Janet
Taylor. [FI#48]

SHAW, HUGH, in the barony of Ardes, County Down, 1659. [C]

SHAW, JAMES, of Ballygelly, a farmer, was granted Irish denization
on 9 February 1625. [IPR]

SHAW, JAMES, matriculated at St Leonard's College, University of
St Andrews, in 1648, graduated MA there during 1651, a
minister in Carnmoney 1655 and in Coole 1657, died in
December 1672. [UJA#13/15][FI#49]

SHAW, JOHN, of Carncastle, 16... [PRONI#D2977]

SHAW, JOHN, was granted Irish denization on 22 June 1615. [IPR]

SHAW, JOHN, of Balliquhosk, was granted Irish denization on 20
May 1617. [IPR]

SHAW, JOHN, of Carnefenoge, a farmer, was granted Irish
denization on 9 February 1625. [IPR]

SHAW, JOHN, from Greenock, arrived in County Down with Sir
Hugh Montgomery, granted 4 acres in the Ards, moved to
Ballygally in 1622, [PRONI#LPC1339, T815]; in the barony of
Ardes, County Down, 1659. [C]

SHAW, JOHN, of Bush, High Sheriff of County Antrim in 1660.
[UJA.11.1.79]

SHAW, JOHN, matriculated at St Salvador's College, University of St
Andrews, 1646, graduated MA there 1649, minister at Ahoghill
1658, died in 1674. [UJA#13/15][FI#49]

SHAW, JOHN, an Irish student at Edinburgh University in 1704.
[CEG]

SHAW, JOHN, merchant in Dublin, admitted as a burgess and
guildsbrother of Glasgow on 9 June 1719. [GBR]

SHAW, MARGARET, relict of William Shaw, Provost of Newton,
County Down, Ireland, 1658, [NAS.GD214#523]; cnf 4 August
1666 Commissariot of Glasgow

SHAW, PATRICK, burgess of Newton Ards, County Down, 1612.
[Cal.SP.Ire.1613/614]

SHAW, PATRICK, of Balliwalter, was granted Irish denization on 20
May 1617. [IPR]

SHAW, PATRICK, a gentleman in the parish of Killaid, County
Antrim, subscribed to his will on 5 July 1715, reference to his
daughter Mary and her guardians - his father William Shaw of
Bush, Patrick Agnew of Killwaughter, and his brother William
Shaw of Bush; brother John Shaw of Bush, brother-in-law John
Shaw of Glanway, and kinsman William McCulloch of
Grogen, probate 29 August 1715 Dublin

SHAW, ROBERT, a trader to Ireland, 1714. [NAS.RD2.103/2.110];
merchant traveller between Scotland and Ireland, 1715.
[NAS.RD2.104.489]

SHAW, SAMUEL, a Scots-Irish student at Glasgow University in 1712. [MUG#198]

SHAW, WILLIAM, of Ballykilconan, was granted Irish denization on 28 November 1617. [IPR]

SHAW, WILLIAM, MA, chaplain to the Queen Consort Anne, was granted Irish denization on 11 July 1615. [IPR]

SHAW, WILLIAM, graduated MA from Glasgow University in 1651, minister in Donegore from 1671 to 1687, died in 1688. [FI#81]

SHAW, WILLIAM, in the barony of Ardes, County Down, 1659. [C]

SHAW, WILLIAM, of Bush, High Sheriff of County Antrim in 1693 and in 1710. [UJA.11.1.79]

SHAW, WILLIAM of Ballygonway, County Down, subscribed to his will on 1 July 1707, reference to his wife, his son John, daughter Rose Haven, daughter Frances wife of Patrick Shaw, daughter Anne wife of Cornelius Crimble, grandaughter Jane Crimble, sister Elizabeth Gillespie, nephew Hugh Gillespie, William Shaw in Bush, County Antrim, and the children of William Catherwood of Newton, probate 25 August 1710 Dublin

SHAW, WILLIAM, of Garney, Ireland, 1715. [NAS.RD4.117.808]

SHAW, WILLIAM, born 1699, died 20 April 1724; his wife Janet Dickson died 15 August 1724. [Killaresy g/s, County Down]

SHEARER, JAMES, master of the Recovery of Donaghadee at the port of Irvine, Ayrshire, on 8 November 1688. [NAS.E72.12.14]

SHIELDS, GEORGE, of Carricknanan, born 1652, died 21 August 1726. [Killinchy g/s, County Down]

SIBBALD, JAMES, of Keir, son of Andrew Sibbald of Keir and Margaret Arbuthnott, educated at Marischal College and at King's College, Aberdeen, minister of St Nicholas, Aberdeen, 1625 to 1640, later in Dublin, died 1647. [F.6.37]

SIM, DAVID, a Scots-Irish student at Glasgow University in 1708. [MUG#189]

SIMPLE, ANDREW, of Balleheglie, was granted Irish denization on 28 November 1617. [IPR]

SIMPSON, GABRIEL, was granted Irish denization on 17 August 1616; in Ballymagorry, barony of Strabane, County Tyrone, 1617. [IPR][SBT#23]

SIMPSON, GILBERT, educated at Glasgow University around 1646, minister of Ballyclare from 1655, died around 1670. [FI#49]

SIMPSON, JAMES, son of Reverend Richard Simpson of Sprostoun, Roxburghshire, graduated MA from Edinburgh University in 1635, an army chaplain in Ireland from 1642 to 1645, a minister in Scotland from 1645 to 1660, arrested in Portpatrick during 1660 when he was on his way to settle in Ireland, imprisoned and released on condition of exile, died in Utrecht, the Netherlands, before August 1694. [FI#50]

SIMPSON, ROBERT, a carpenter, was granted Irish denization on 28 November 1617. [IPR]

SINCLAIR, ANNE, a widow in Strabane, County Tyrone, 1728. [IWD]

SINCLAIR, DAVID, of Newtown, County Tyrone, gentleman, was granted Irish denization on 19 July 1631. [IPR]

SINCLAIR, HENRY, Lieutenant Colonel of Lord Sinclair's Regiment, in Newry, 1642. [PRO.SP.18.120]

SINCLAIR, PATRICK, Captain of Lord Sinclair's Regiment, in Newry, 1642. [PRO.SP.18.120]

SINCLAIR, ROBERT, merchant, was admitted as a burgess of Glasgow 4 January 1649, settled in Ireland by 1655. [GBR]

SINKLER, ROBERT, born 1595, died 1666, his wife Giels Gordon born 1603, died 1677, son John born 1623, died 1684. [Comber g/s]

SINCLAIR, ROBERT, a Scots-Irish student at Edinburgh University in 1695. [CEG]

SKELTON, BENJAMIN, an Anglo-Irish student at Glasgow University in 1706. [MUG#184]

SLOAN, ALEXANDER, gentleman in parish of Killeleagh, County Down, 1659. [C]

SLOAN, HENRY, died on 15 May 1659. [Killyreagh g/s, County Down]

SLOAN, JOHN, died on 12 May 1660. [Killyreagh g/s, County Down]

SLOAN, WILLIAM, a Scots-Irish student at Edinburgh University in 1718. [CEG]

SMART, WILLIAM, was granted Irish denization on 10 November 1619. [Signet Office Docquet Book]

SMELHOLM, GEORGE, from Leith, resident in the precinct of Knockninny, County Fermanagh, 20 April 1610, [TCD.ms#N2/2]; was granted Irish denization on 12 February 1618. [IPR]; Undertaker in the Precinct of Knockinny, County Fermanagh, 1611. [Cal.SP.Ire.1611/384]

SMITH, ALEXANDER, corporal of Viscount Claneboy's troop of horse on 25 April 1642. [SP.Ire#260/63]

SMITH, ANDREW, a Scots-Irish student at Glasgow University in 1715. [MUG#206]

SMITH, DANIEL, a Scots-Irish student at Glasgow University in 1708. [MUG#189]

SMITH, DAVID, master of the Speedwell of Belfast at the port of Ayr 24 May 1689. [NAS.E72.3.18]

SMITH, HENRY, MA University of St Andrews 1620, curate of Cairncastle, County Antrim, 1634. [UJA#13/15]

SMITH, HENRY, merchant aboard the Merchant of Larne at the port of Irvine, Ayrshire, 6 February 1682. [NAS.E72.12.5]

SMITH, JOHN, of O'Boyleston, County Donegal, was granted Irish denization on 17 August 1616. [IPR]

SMITH, JAMES, a Scots-Irish student at Glasgow University in 1720. [MUG#217]

SMITH, JOHN, was granted Irish denization on 16 June 1615. [IPR]

SMITH, JOHN, of Raphoe, was granted Irish denization on 28 November 1617. [IPR]

SMITH, JOHN, merchant in Belfast, at the port of Ayr 27 February 1690. [NAS.E72.3.20]

SMITH, JOHN, master of the Merchant of Larne at the port of Irvine, Ayrshire, on 22 December 1682. [NAS.E72.12.7]

SMITH, JOHN, a Scots-Irish student at Edinburgh University in 1705. [CEG]

SMITH, JOHN, a Scots-Irish student at Glasgow University in 1713. [MUG#201]

SMITH, JOHN, a Scots-Irish student at Glasgow University in 1717. [MUG#210]

SMITH, WILLIAM, seaman on the Merchants Adventure of Belfast, master Moses Jones, arrived in Port Glasgow from Barbados in September 1682. [NAS.E72.19.5]

SMITH, WILLIAM, merchant in Ayr, sometime in Londonderry 1696, [NAS.RD2.89.682]; merchant and alderman of Londonderry, formerly in Ayr, 1698. [NAS.RD2.81.2.202; RD2.81.2.329]; a merchant in Londonderry, 26 October 1709, [NAS.GD25, sec.8/867a]; merchant and Alderman of Londonderry, 1715. [NAS.RD2.104.1107]

SMITH, WILLIAM, a Scots-Irish student at Glasgow University in 1712. [MUG#199]

SMITH, WILLIAM, a Scots-Irish student at Glasgow University in 1717. [MUG#209]

SMYLY, J., in Dungannon on 8 March 1667. [Cal.SP.Ire.348/8]

SNODDIE, JOHN, master of the Goodwill of Larne at the port of Irvine, Ayrshire, on 15 August 1683. [NAS.E72.12.8]

SOMERVILLE, JAMES, of Tillikatter, County Fermanagh, was granted Irish denization on 17 August 1616. [IPR]

SOMERVILLE, JOHN, graduated MA from Glasgow University in 1642, minister in Ballyclare from 1653, died in 1654. [FI#50]

SOMERVILLE, THOMAS, in Devonish, County Fermanagh, 1659. [C]

SPALDING, SAMUEL, a Scots-Irish student at Edinburgh University in 1688. [CEG]

SPEAR, SOLOMAN, an Irish student at Glasgow University in 1720. [MUG#218]

SPEIR, ALEXANDER, of Grey Abbey, County Down, was granted Irish denization on 28 November 1617. [IPR]

SPENCE, JAMES, minister of Castlemartin, Ireland, son of Reverend Alexander Spence in Birnie, 1715. [NAS.RD3.146.574]

SPENCE, MICHAEL, of Stankhouse, an attorney in the Court of Common Pleas in Dublin 1708. [NAS.RS29.iv.231]

SPENCE, ROBERT, of Ramullin, was granted Irish denization on 28 November 1617. [IPR]

SPOTSWOOD, AGNES, wife of Dr James Spotswood, Lord Bishop of Clogher, was granted Irish denization on 29 October 1622. [IPR]

SPOTSWOOD, or ERSKINE, BEATRIX, daughter of Dr James Spotswood, was granted Irish denization on 29 October 1622. [IPR]

SPOTSWOOD, HENRY, son of Dr James Spotswood, Bishop of Clogher, was granted Irish denization on 29 October 1622. [IPR]; castle and lands of Agher, County Tyrone, in 1626. [SP.Ire#243/508]

SPOTTISWOOD, Sir JOHN, was granted Irish denization on 26 July 1627. [IPR]; made a free denizen of Ireland and granted lands in Leitrim on 25 May 1625. [SP.Ire#241, docquet 13]

SPROTT, JANET, wife of John Gebey of Belykil, died 9 April 1683. [Comber g/s]

STANEHOUSE, WILLIAM, of Carbolzie, was granted Irish denization on 20 May 1617. [IPR]

STANNAGE, JAMES, an Irish student at Glasgow University in 1715. [MUG#205]

STEEL, JAMES, a Scots-Irish student at Glasgow University in 1717. [MUG#210]

STEILL, THOMAS, master of the Marion of Larne at the port of Irvine, Ayrshire, on 7 January 1683. [NAS.E72.12.7]

STEINSON, WILLIAM, of Bangor, was granted Irish denization on 28 November 1617. [IPR]

STEPHEN, WILLIAM, a Scots-Irish student at Glasgow University in 1709. [MUG#191]

STEPHEN of LITTLECOTT, WILLIAM, an Anglo-Irish student at Glasgow University in 1715. [MUG#205]

STEPHENSON, DAVID, was granted Irish denization on 17 August 1616, in Strabane, County Tyrone, 1617. [IPR][SBT#22]

STEPHENSON, JAMES, a Scots-Irish student at Glasgow University in 1710. [MUG#194]

STEPHENSON, JOHN, of Pakusbancke, (Peacocksbank), Strabane, 17 August 1616. [IPR][SBT#22]

STEPHENSON, JOHN, sr., was granted Irish denization on 17
August 1616; in Strabane 1617. [IPR][SBT#22]

STEPHENSON, JOHN, jr., was granted Irish denization on 9 July
1616, in Strabane 1617. [IPR][SBT#22]

STEPHENSON, JOHN, a minor, was granted Irish denization on 17
August 1616. [IPR]

STEPHENSON, JOHN, a minor, was granted Irish denization on 17
August 1616. [IPR]

STEPHENSON, THOMAS, was granted Irish denization on 9 July
1616. [IPR]

STEPHENSON, THOMAS, was granted Irish denization on 17
August 1616. [IPR]

STEPHENSON, THOMAS, a carpenter, was granted Irish denization
on 17 August 1616, in Strabane, County Tyrone, 1617,
possibly the Thomas Stevenson, carpenter, in Cullydrummond,
Urney parish, County Tyrone, probate 1622. [IPR][SBT#22]

STERLING, JOHN, a minister in the diocese of Connor, 1622.
[TCD.ms.E#3/6]

STERLING, JOHN, of Galloe, County Meath, clerk, was granted
Irish denization on 9 December 1633. [IPR]

STEVENSON, ALEXANDER, yeoman in Raphoe, County Donegal,
was granted Irish denization on 17August 1616. [IPR]

STEVENSON, ALEXANDER, page of the Bedchamber, was granted
Irish denization on March 1619. [Signet Office Docquet Book]

STEVENSON, Captain ALEXANDER, in Dublin, 1698.
[NAS.RD4.98.129]

STEVIN, JOHN, of Raphoe, was granted Irish denization on 28
November 1617. [IPR]

STEWART, ALEXANDER, was granted Irish denization on 29
January 1611. [IPR]

STEWART, ALEXANDER, of Lagry, Esq., was granted Irish denization on 9 July 1616. [IPR]

STEWART, ALEXANDER, of Figart, was granted Irish denization on 28 November 1617. [IPR]

STEWART, ALEXANDER, of Ballevembegg, gentleman, was granted Irish denization on 28 November 1624. [IPR]

STEWART, ALEXANDER, of Redbay, County Tyrone, gentleman, was granted Irish denization on 19 July 1633. [IPR]

STEWART, ALEXANDER, of Ballyrattaghan, County Antrim, gentleman, was granted Irish denization on 9 August 1633. [IPR]

STEWART, ALEXANDER, of Dromart, County Antrim, gentleman, was granted Irish denization on 27 June 1634. [IPR]

STEWART, ALEXANDER, of Ballintoy, High Sheriff of County Antrim in 1632. [UJA.11.1.79]

STEWART, ALEXANDER, born 1645, died 20 October 1723, his wife Elizabeth Fraser born 1652, died 12 May 1734. [Ballintoy g/s, County Antrim]

STEWART, ALEXANDER, a gentleman in Killinchy parish, barony of Kinallerly, County Down, 1659. [C]

STEWART, ALEXANDER, a saddler in Coleraine, subscribed to a contract of marriage with Isobel Campbell, daughter of Duncan Campbell of Elister, Argyll, at Elister on 18 June 1706. Reference to her brothers George, Colin, John and Alexander Campbell.
[Argyll Sheriff Court Book, Vol.6, 4.3.1720]

STEWART, ANDREW, Lord Ochiltree, applied for 2000 acres in Ulster on 20 July 1609, [PU#140]; was granted Irish denization on 14 August 1610 and a grant of Revelmowtra in the barony of Mountjoy. [IPR] [Cal.SP.Ire.1611/384] with 3000 acres in the barony of Dungannon, County Tyrone, appeared at a muster in 1618 with 31 men, 5 muskets, 6 calivers, 21 pikes, 3 halberds and 17 swords. [Cal.SP.Ire.1618/501]; with 3500 acres at Revelen, Precinct of Mountjoy, 28 March 1619. [Carew Mss#211/145]

STEWART, ANDREW, son of Lord Ochiltree, with 1000 acres at Ballekivan, Precinct of Mountjoy, 28 March 1619. [Carew Mss#211/149]

STEWART, ANDREW, born in Ayrshire during 1598, matriculated at St Leonard's College, University of St Andrews, 1618, minister at Donegore 1627-1634, died in July 1634, father of Andrew - minister of Donaghadee from 1645 to 1671, Janet - wife of Reverend Thomas Crawford, and Elizabeth - wife of Lieutenant Paul Cunningham. [UJA#13/15][PHS]

STEWART, ANDREW, born in 1624, son of Reverend Andrew Stewart in Dungore, a minister in Donaghadee, died on 2 January 1671. [FI#50]

STEWART, Sir ANDREW, was granted Irish denization on 26 February 1630. [IPR]

STEWART, ANDREW, of Donaghreske, County Tyrone, gentleman, was granted Irish denization on 19 July 1633. [IPR]; with 1000 acres in County Tyrone, appeared at a muster in 1618 with 16 men, 2 muskets, 5 calivers, 6 pikes and 14 swords. [Cal.SP.Ire.1618/501]

STEWART, ANDREW, of Stewarthill, County Tyrone, 1702. [NAS.RD3.100.219]

STEWART, ANTHONY, of Drummochill, was granted Irish denization on 20 May 1617. [IPR]

STEWART, ARCHIBALD, of Balleatoe, was granted Irish denization on 9 February 1625. [IPR]

STEWART, ARCHIBALD, in Carrickfergus on 28 October 1641. [SP.Ire#260/33]

STEWART, BARBARA, wife of William Darragh of County Tyrone, clerk, was granted Irish denization on 27 June 1634. [IPR]

STUART, CHARLES, High Sheriff of County Antrim in 1683.
[UJA.11.1.79]

STEWART, CHRISTIAN, of Carcarmehon, was granted Irish
denization on 9 February 1625. [IPR]

STEWART, DAIRD, of Bonnerclasie, was granted Irish denization
on 22 February 1634. [IPR]

STEWART, DOROTHY, wife of Archibald Sanderson gentleman in
County Tyrone, was granted Irish denization on 27 June 1634.
[IPR]

STEWART, ELIZABETH, sister and heir of Robert Stewart of Gass,
and spouse of Thomas Agnew in Grey Abbey, Ireland, 9 March
1627. [NAS.GD25.4.34]

STEWART, FRANCIS, eldest son of the late Earl of Bothwell,
petitioned King Charles I to be made printer to the king in
Ireland on 11 February 1637. [SP.Ire#256/9,1]

STEWART, GEORGE, of Moutlout, County Donegal, gentleman,
was granted Irish denization on 19 July 1631. [IPR]

STEWART, GEORGE, in Omagh, County Tyrone, 1729. [IWD]

STEWART, GRISSELL, wife of John Richardson of Kildresse,
County Tyrone, yeoman, was granted Irish denization on 27
June 1634. [IPR]

STEWART, HARRY, of Barskeming, applied for 2000 acres in
Ulster on 20 July 1609. [PU#140]

STEWART, HARRY, brought from Ireland and imprisoned in
Edinburgh Tolbooth on 8 September 1664, petitioned the Privy
Council on 7 December 1665. [RPCS]

STEWART, HELEN, wife of Robert Cathcart, was granted Irish
denization on 19 July 1633. [IPR]

STEWART, HENRY, was granted Irish denization on 3 March 1630.
[IPR]

STEWART, HENRY, and his wife Margaret, refused to take an oath of allegiance to King Charles I prescribed for people of Scottish origin with estates in Ireland on 7 September 1639. [Cal.SP.Ire.1641#257/33]

STEWART, JAMES, of Rosyth, Fife, applied for 2000 acres in Ulster on 27 July 1609. [PU#143]

STEWART, Sir JAMES, of Glengarnock, grant of Dacrosscroose in the barony of Raffoe, County Donegal, 20 July 1610. [IPR]

STEWART, Ensign JAMES, in Ireland 1624. [Cal.SP.Ire]

STEWART, JAMES, of Ballymanagh, County Tyrone, gentleman, was granted Irish denization on 19 July 1633. [IPR]

STEWART, JAMES, with 1000 acres in Strabane, County Tyrone, appeared at a muster in 1618 with 21 men, 3 muskets, 2 calivers, 10 pike and 20 swords. [Cal. SP.Ire.1618/501]; Justice of the Peace for Tyrone, 1630. [SP.Ire#257/1144]

STEWART, JAMES, of Le Grange of Tullaghoge, County Tyrone, yeoman, was granted Irish denization on 27 June 1634. [IPR]

STEWART, JAMES, of Sicon, County Antrim, gentleman, was granted Irish denization on 27 June 1634. [IPR]

STEWART, JAMES, quartermaster of Viscount Claneboy's troop of horse on 25 April 1642. [SP.Ire#260/63]

STEWART, JAMES, in Dungannon on 8 March 1667. [Cal.SP.Ire.348/8]

STEWART, JAMES, a merchant in Belfast, petitioned the Scottish Parliament in 1689. [APS]

STEWART, JAMES, a merchant in Belfast, 1702. [NAS.RD3.99.2.34]

STEWART, JOHN, of Ballynoren, father of Patrick died 1 October 1623, Thomas died 24 June 1631, Marion died 24 July 1631, Robert died 27 December 1634, Ludovick died 30 December 1635, Grisel died 11 August 1638, Anthony died 24 October

1641, and John the eldest who died 13 August 1642.
[Killyleagh Old g/s, County Down]

STEWART, JOHN, Undertaker in Precinct of Portlogh, County
Donegal, 1611. [Cal.SP.Ire.1611/384]

STEWART, JOHN, a grant of Lismougherie in the precinct of
Portelogh, barony of Raffoe, County Donegal, 23 July 1610,
was granted Irish denization on 20 May 1617. [IPR]

STEWART, JOHN, of Veaghvahe, gentleman, was granted Irish
denization on 28 November 1624. [IPR]

STEWART, JOHN, was born in 1621 and died on 4 November 1691,
son of Captain William Stewart, son of Lord Garlies, who was
killed at Kilcullin Bridge in 1641. [Drumbeg g/s, County
Down]

STEWART, JOHN MACANDREW, of Ballywilliam, County
Antrim, gentleman, was granted Irish denization on 9 August
1633. [IPR]

STEWART, JOHN, merchant aboard the Alexander of Belfast at the
port of Irvine, Ayrshire, 25 June 1683. [NAS.E72.12.7]

STEWART, JOHN, in Ballybregah, born 1622, died 11 October
1692; his wife Elinor Boll, born 1634, died 11 October 1714,
father of Reverend Samuel Stewart in Girvan, Ayrshire.
[Killinchy g/s, County Down]

STEWART, KATHERINE, relict of John Stewart of Ballilane,
Ireland, 24 December 1677. [NAS.RS9.1.222]

STEWART, JOHN, a Scot, grant of part of Lismolnoghery, precinct
of Portelogh, 23 July 1610. [EPR.8.3]

STEWART, JOHN, was granted Irish denization on 29 January 1611.
[IPR]

STEWART, JOHN, of Collaghie, was granted Irish denization on 20
May 1617. [IPR]

STEWART, Sir JOHN, in the precinct of Magheraboy on 28 March
1619. [Carew Mss#211/190]

STEWART, JOHN, was granted Irish denization on 9 May 1629.
[IPR]

STEWART, JOHN, gentleman in Killinchy parish, County Down,
1659. [C]

STEWART, JOHN, born in Ireland son of Alexander Stewart in
County Antrim, a trooper in HM Life Guards in Linlithgow,
Scotland, on 5 June 1678. [CA.1.xl]

STEWART, LODOWIC, of Lurgabowy, County Fermanagh, was
granted Irish denization on 17 August 1616. [IPR]

STEWART, Lieutenant LUDOVICK, in Ireland 1624. [Cal.SP.Ire]

STEWART, MATTHEW, of Dromonehill, County Donegal,
gentleman, was granted Irish denization on 19 July 1631. [IPR]

STEWART, NINIAN, born in Scotland, was granted Irish denization
on 18 January 1611. [IPR]

STEWART, NINIAN, of Ballymoy, County Antrim, gentleman, was
granted Irish denization on 9 August 1633. [IPR]

STEWART, NINIAN, of Dromnegess, County Antrim, gentleman,
was granted Irish denization on 9 August 1633. [IPR]

STEWART, PATRICK, was granted Irish denization on 12 February
1618. [IPR]

STEWART, PATRICK, gentleman in Pubble, barony of Strabane,
County Tyrone, probate 1633

STEWART, ROBERT, applied for 2000 acres in Ulster on 20 July
1609. [PU#140]

STEWART, ROBERT, of Hilton, Edinburgh, applied for 2000 acres
in Ulster on 20 July 1609, [PU#141]; was granted Irish
denization and a grant of Ballykevan in precinct of Mountjoy,
County Tyrone, 29 August 1610. [IPR][TCD.ms#N2/2];

Undertaker in Precinct of Mountjoy, County Tyrone, 1611. [PU#546] [Cal.SP.Ire.1611/384]

STEWART, ROBERT, of Rotton or Roberton, Lanarkshire, applied for 2000 acres in Ulster on 20 July 1609, [PU#140]; was granted Irish denization and a grant of Gortavilly in the precinct of Mountjoy, County Tyrone, on 29 August 1610, [IPR][TCD.ms#N2/2] [PU#546]; Undertaker in Precinct of Mountjoy, County Tyrone, 1611. [Cal.SP.Ire.1611/384]

STEWART, ROBERT, a Colonel in Antrim on 19 May 1645. [SP.Ire#260/137]

STEWART, SAMUEL, Captain of Robert Home of the Heugh's Regiment, in Carrickfergus, 1642. [PRO.SP.18.120]

STEWART, THOMAS, born 1660, son of John Stewart {1621-1691}, died on 11 July 1715; his daughters Ann born 1705 and died 8 June 1707, Margaret born 1702 and died on 19 June 1708. [Drumbeg g/s, County Down]

STEWART, Sir WALTER, of Minto, Roxburghshire, grant of Coragh in the precinct of Portalogh, County Donegal, was granted Irish denization on 20 July 1610. [IPR]; grant of part of Corragh, precinct of Portalough, County Donegal, EPR.8.10]

STEWART, WALTER, in Clownish, County Fermanagh, 1659. [C]

STEWART, WILLIAM, of Dunduff, applied for 2000 acres in Ulster on 20 July 1609, [PU#140]; was granted Irish denization on 29 August 1610. [IPR]; grant of part of Downconally, barony of Baylagh and Bannagh, County Donegal, 24 July 1610. [EPR.8.3] [TCD.ms#N2/2]; Undertaker in Precinct of Portlogh, County Donegal, 1611. [Cal.SP.Ire.1611/384]; with 1000 acres at Cole Laghie, precinct of Portloughe, 28 March 1619. [Carew Mss#211/187]

STEWART, Captain WILLIAM, servitor in the barony of Kilmacrenan, 1611, [Cal. SP.Ire.1611/251]; servitor in Ulster, later an Undertaker in Wexford, was granted James Hayes' lands in the barony of Strabane, 26 January 1613. [Cal.SP.Ire.1613/615]

STEWART, Sir WILLIAM, with 2000 acres in Clougher, County
Tyrone, appeared at a muster in 1618 with 24 men, 1 musket, 3
calivers, 15 pikes and 22 swords. [Cal. SP.Ire.1618/501]
[BMAddMS#18735]; with 1000 acres at Gortavaghie and 1000
acres at Rumalton in the precinct of Kilmacrenan on 28 March
1619. [Carew Mss#211/103]; Cavalry officer in Ulster 27
January 1646. [SP.Ire]

STEWART, WILLIAM, was granted Irish denization on 7 May 1629.
[IPR]

STEWART, Sir WILLIAM, was granted Irish denization on 26 June
1629. [IPR]

STEWART, WILLIAM, late of Drumduff, County Tyrone,
gentleman, , was granted Irish denization on 19 July 1633.
[IPR]

STEWART, WILLIAM, in Dungannon on 8 March 1667.
[Cal.SP.Ire.348/8]

STEWART, WILLIAM, in Fort Stewart, County Donegal, 1713.
[IWD]

STEWART, W., in Dungannon on 8 March 1667. [Cal.SP.Ire.348/8]

STINE, JOHN, died 22 February 1666, his wife Margaret Stevens
died 12 September 1686. [Comber g/s]

STIRLING, JOHN, a Scots-Irish student at Glasgow University in
1721. [MUG#220]

STIRLING, Sir ROBERT, sent to Ireland in 1641, a Royalist army
officer in Ireland from 1641 to 1648, a Royalist army officer in
Scotland 1651, banished from Scotland by Oliver Cromwell,
took refuge in Ireland, petitioned Charles II in 1660 for lands in
Ireland. [Cal.S.P.Ire.1660]

STIRLING, ROBERT, born in 1635, son of Alexander Stirling a
farmer in Stewarton, Ayrshire, graduated MA from Glasgow
University in 1654, minister in Derrykeichan, died in 1699,
husband of Marian Campbell, father of Reverend John Stirling
and Reverend Thomas Stirling. [FI#50]

STIRLING, WILLIAM, in the Liberty of Dunower, County Dublin, 1659. [C]

STOTT, ANNE, in Hillsboro', County Down, 1680. [IWD]

STRATON, Sir ALEXANDER, of Laurenceton, was granted Irish denization on 8 February 1611. [IPR]

STRATTON, ARTHUR, born in Aberdeenshire, educated at King's College, Aberdeen, from 1651 to 1655, graduated MA in 1662, minister in Portaferry from 1680 to 1689. [FI#81]

STRATTON, FRANCIS, in County Fermanagh, 1659. [C]

STUART, JAMES, a Scots-Irish student at Glasgow University in 1706. [MUG#184]

STUART, Sir ROBERT, a Cavalry officer in Ulster 27 January 1646. [SP.Ire]

STURGEON, ANDREW, of Corowmanin, was granted Irish denization on 12 February 1618. [IPR]

STURGEON, JOHN, of Cregans, was granted Irish denization on 12 February 1618. [IPR]

STYLES, WILLIAM, merchant in Dublin, admitted as a burgess and guildsbrother of Glasgow on 1 September 1718. [GBR]

SUTHERLAND, WILLIAM, in Roscommon, 1715. [NAS.RD2.104.897; RD4.116.263]

SWAN, WILLIAM, gentleman in Farlagh, County Tyrone, 1697. [IWD]

SYM, ALEXANDER, tenant of John Hamilton of Edenagh, Precinct of Fewes, 1618. [PU#567]

SYMINGTON, JOHN, was granted Irish denization on 16 December 1630. [IPR]; granted 1000 acres in Gortevelle, Precinct of Mountjoy, 1630. [PU#551]

TAILLEOUR, ROBERT, preacher at Kilcan, County Cavan, was granted Irish denization on 20 May 1617. [IPR]

TARBET, JAMES, servitor to Alexander, Earl of Dunfermline, applied for 1000 acres in Ulster on 4 August 1609. [PU#143]

TATE, PATRICK, of Dromwherne, County Tyrone, was granted Irish denization on 27 June 1634. [IPR]

TAYLOR, ISAAC, a Scots-Irish student at Glasgow University 1705. [MUG#183]

TAYLOR, JAMES, born in Morayshire, minister in Monea Enniskillen and Derryvilla from 1675 to 1680, in Glendermott from 1680 to 1683, died in 1694. [FI#81]

TAYLOR, JOHN, a Scots-Irish student at Glasgow University 1708. [MUG#190]

TEMPLE, JOHN, a settler in Antrim, died 1638. [PROI#RC9/1/41]

THOMAS, JONATHAN, merchant in Dublin, admitted as a burgess and guildsbrother of Glasgow on 20 February 1724. [GBR]

THOMSON, ANDREW, graduated MA at the University of St Andrews in 1607, vicar of Ballywillan and Ballyrashane 1607. [UJA#13/15]; a minister in the diocese of Connor 1622, 1634. [TCD.ms.E#3/6; ms.T#1/10]

THOMPSON, HUGH, merchant in Londonderry, was granted Irish denization on 17 August 1616, [IPR]; 5 January 1621. [NAS.RS9.1.139]; burgess of Londonderry 1621. [see Jean Campbell's testament 1621, Commissariot of Glasgow]

THOMSON, HEW, sometime of Rebegge, County Antrim, now in Halls of Bargowe, Ayrshire, 10 November 1642. [NAS.RS Ayr#7, 4.9.1642, 15.11.1642]

THOMSON, HUGH, in Salmache, parish of Rye, Ireland, 19 August 1650. [NAS.RS9.3.107]

THOMSON, HUGH, merchant aboard the Providence of Coleraine at the port of Irvine, Ayrshire, on 3 May 1683.[NAS.E72.12.8]

THOMPSON, HUGH, a Scots-Irish student at Glasgow University in 1717. [MUG#209]

THOMPSON, JAMES, of Lifford, County Donegal, was granted Irish denization 17 August 1616. [IPR]

THOMPSON, JAMES. Thomas Lutewidge, factor in Edinburgh, merchant in Whitehaven, against William Lowes, master of the Queen Anne, James Thompson, carpenter in Dublin, and Robert Corson, ropemaker, owners of the said ship, for bringing back a cargo of damaged tobacco from Virginia too late for market. [NAS.Admiralty Court, Vol.28, pp1118/1135; 12 November 1723]

THOMPSON, JOHN, of Blackabbey, was granted Irish denization on 20 May 1617. [IPR]

THOMPSON, JOHN, a mason, was granted Irish denization on 12 February 1618. [IPR]

THOMSON, JOHN, a shopkeeper in Coleraine, County Londonderry, 1659, [C]; a merchant in Coleraine, 6 December 1678. [RGS#10.90]

THOMSON, JOHN, merchant aboard the Fortune of Coleraine at the port of Irvine, Ayrshire, 29 April 1682; merchant aboard the Two Brothers of Coleraine at the port of Irvine 11 September 1689. [NAS.E72.12.6/14]

THOMSON, JOHN, a Scots-Irish student at Glasgow University in 1706. [MUG#184]

THOMSON, JOHN, merchant in Coleraine, County Londonderry, son of John Thomson of Seven Acres, 1714, [NAS.RD3.143.202]

THOMSON, JOHN, son of Robert Thomson a merchant in Coleraine, 1714. [NAS.RD3.143.202]

THOMSON, LAURENCE, graduated MA at the University of St Andrews in 1620, vicar of Dunlane, County Antrim, 1633. [UJA#13/15]

THOMSON, MATTHEW, a weaver freeman of Newtown, County
Down, 1640. [Hunter of Hunterstone MS#8]

THOMPSON, ROBERT, merchant in Londonderry, was granted Irish
denization on 17 August 1616. [IPR]

THOMPSON, ROBERT, was granted Irish denization on 14 October
1619. [Signet Office Docquet Book]

THOMSON, ROBERT, merchant aboard the Elizabeth of Coleraine
at the port of Irvine, Ayrshire, 3 August 1689.
[NAS.E72.12.15]

THOMSON, THOMAS, a Scots-Irish student at Glasgow University
in 1720. [MUG#218]

THOMPSON, [' Tampson'], WILLIAM, a tenant farmer of 30 acres
on the Agnew estate in 1645. [NAS.GD154/514]

THORBRAND, ALEXANDER, son of George Thorbrand, burgess of
Edinburgh, applied for 1500 acres in Ulster on 25 July 1609.
[PU#142]

THORBRAND, GEORGE, burgess of Edinburgh, applied for 2000
acres in Ulster on 25 July 1609. [PU#141]

THWAITES, EPHRAIM, an Anglo-Irish student at Glasgow
University in 1710. [MUG#194]

TODD, ALEXANDER, a Scots-Irish student at Glasgow University
in 1706. [MUG#184]

TODD, JOHN, hardware merchant in Belfast, then in Wigtown, cnf
1713 Commissariot of Wigtown

TOD, WILLIAM, a Scots-Irish student at Edinburgh University in
1695. [CEG]

TORRANCE, SAMUEL, an Anglo-Irish student at Glasgow
University in 1709. [MUG#192]

TOSHACH, CATHERINE, wife of Reverend David Young in Ireland, 1715. [NAS.RD3.144.530]

TRAILL, HANS, in Drumticonnor, County Down, 1692. [IWD]

TRAILL, JAMES, from Fife, was granted Irish denization and a grant of Drifternan in the barony of Knockinny, County Fermanagh, on 12 October 1610, [IPR][TCD.ms#N2/2]; Undertaker in the Precinct of Knockinny, County Fermanagh, 1611. [Cal.SP.Ire.1611/384]

TRAILL, Lieutenant Colonel JAMES, died in Tullachin on 18 May 166-; his wife Mary, daughter of John Hamilton of Hamilton's Bawn, County Armagh. [Killyreagh g/s, County Down]

TRAILL, WILLIAM, born in Elie, Fife, during September 1640, son of Reverend Robert Traill, graduated MA from Edinburgh University in 1658, minister in Lifford from 1673 to 1682, settled on the Potomac River in Maryland from 1684 to 1690, died in Scotland on 3 May 1714, husband of (1) Euphan Sword in 1671, (2) Eleanor Traill in 1679, (3) Jean Murray in 1701. [FI#81]

TRANE, BESSY, of Dunluce, was granted Irish denization on 9 February 1625. [IPR]

TRINCH, JAMES, preacher, was granted Irish denization on 12 February 1618. [IPR]

TROTTER, ROBERT, farrier to the Prince, was granted Irish denization on 18 February 1616. [IPR]

TROWSDELL, JAMES, an Anglo-Irish student at Glasgow University 1706. [MUG185]; also at Edinburgh University 1706. [CEG]

TRUMBLE, JOHN, tenant of John Hamilton of Edenagh, Precinct of Fewes, 1618. [PU#567]

TRUMBLE, JOHN, merchant aboard the Elizabeth of Larne at the port of Irvine, Ayrshire, 11 December 1689. [NAS.E72.12.16]

TULLOS, PATRICK of Ramoan, MA University of St Andrews
1605, a minister in Ballycastle, County Antrim, [UJA#13/15];
was granted Irish denization 9 February 1625. [IPR]; a minister
in the diocese of Connor 1622, 1634. [TCD.ms.E#3/6;
MS.T#1/10]

TURBET, JOHN, of Killybegs, a juryman at a Coroner's inquest held
at Duncanalley, County Donegal, on 15 September 1660.
[Cal.S.P.Ire.1660]

TURNER, JAMES, Major of Lord Sinclair's Regiment, in Newry,
1642. [PRO.SP.18.120]

TWADELL, JOHN, a shopkeeper in the barony of Coleraine, County
Londonderry, 1659. [C]

URQUHART, JOHN, gentleman, was granted Irish denization on 21
October 1618. [IPR]

USHER, Sir WILLIAM, Clerk of the Council of Ireland, 3 October
1630. [SP.Ire#251/1824]

VALLANCE, JAMES, of Possill, fled to Ireland in 1680.
[NAS.GD61/71]

VANSE, JOHN, clerk at Kilmacrenan, was granted Irish denization
on 28 November 1617. [IPR]

VANS, JOHN, in Drumindony, parish of Drumarah, County Down,
1659. [C]

VANS, KATHERINE, wife of William Houston of Ballemeachan,
was granted Irish denization on 28 November 1624. [IPR]

VANS, PATRICK, of Libragh, second son of Sir Patrick Vans of
Barnbarroch, Kirkinner, Wigtonshire, was granted Irish
denization on 11 August 1610, grant of Boylaghwotra in the
barony of Boylagh, County Donegal, [IPR][TCD.ms#N2/2];
Undertaker in the Precinct of Boylagh, County Donegal, 1611.
[Cal.SP.Ire.1611/384]

VAUGHN, JOHN, a Scots-Irish student at Edinburgh University in
1699. [CEG]

VAUS, JOHN, a minister in the diocese of Raphoe, 1622.
[TCD.ms.T#1/10]

VERNER, BENJAMIN, of Kilgavinache, County Antrim, 1694.
[NAS.RD2.77.584]

VESEY, THOMAS, minister in Ballyscullin and Maghera from 1629,
in Coleraine from 1641, and in Strabane 1654. [FI#51]

VINCENT, HELEN, wife of William Vincent gentleman, was granted
Irish denization on 24 October 1618. [IPR]

WADDELL, ALEXANDER, sr., in Ilanderry, parish of Drumore,
County Down, 1659. [C]

WALKER, ARCHIBALD, merchant in County Armagh, was granted
Irish denization on 28 November 1617. [IPR]

WALKER, WILLIAM, in Belfast, serviced as heir to his grandfather
Andrew Walker late baillie of Dunfermline on 25 June 1717.
[NAS.SH]

WALKINGSHAW, JAMES, second son of John Walkingshaw of
Walkingshaw, Renfrewshire, minister in Benburb from 1673 to
1677, husband of Margaret Maxwell. [FI#82]

WALLACE, GEORGE, graduated MA from Glasgow University in
1651, minister in Holywood, died in Virginia 1693. [FI#51]

WALLACE, HUGH, in the barony of Ardes, County Down, 1659.
[C]

WALLACE, HEW, master and merchant of the John of Larne at the
port of Irvine, Ayrshire, 26 April 1669. [NAS.E72.12.1]

WALLACE, HUGH, a gentleman in Ballyskibin, County Down,
subscribed to his will on 20 June 1716, reference to his wife
Beatrix, brother in law John Hutcheson in Ballyrea, County
Armagh, eldest son Alexander Wallace, son Hans Wallace,
eldest daughter Beatrix Wallace, daughters Jane and Sarah
Wallace, witnesses William Alexander MD in Belfast, Hugh
Catherwood surgeon in Kirkistown, County Down, Hugh

McWilliam in Ballyrea, County Armagh servant to said John Hutcheson, probate 29 November 1716 Dublin

WALLES, HUGH, died 20 February 1726. [Killinchy g/s, County Down]

WALLACE, JAMES, Captain of Major General Robert Monro's Regiment, in Carrickfergus 1642. [PRO.SP.18.120]

WALLACE, JAMES, graduated MA from Edinburgh University in 1643, minister in Urney, died in 1674, probate 1675. [FI#51]

WALLACE, JAMES, in the barony of Ardes, County Down, 1659. [C]

WALLACE, JOHN, sr., in Strabane, County Tyrone, was granted Irish denization on 17 August 1616. [IPR][SBT#22]

WALLACE, JOHN, a Scots-Irish student at Glasgow University in 1713. [MUG#201]

WALLACE, SAMUEL, merchant, admitted as a burgess and guildsbrother of Glasgow on 13 May 1642, husband of Bessie Wallace, settled in Ireland by 1655. [GBR]

WALLACE, WILLIAM, of Bellyobekane, was granted Irish denization on 20 May 1617. [IPR]

WALLACE, WILLIAM, graduated MA University of Glasgow 1607, matriculated at St Mary's College, University of St Andrews, 1607, curate of Portcoman and Dunluce 1614, vicar there 1630, curate of Derrykeighan 1634. [UJA#13/15]; was granted Irish denization on 9 February 1625. [IPR]; a minister in the diocese of Connor, 1622. [TCD.ms.E#3/6]

WALLACE, ..., in Antrim, 1700. [NAS.RD12.39.1199]

WALLWOOD, ANDREW, son of James Wallwood a minister in Ireland 1700. [NAS.NRAS.1368/260/4]

WALSH, JOHN, in County Armagh, was granted Irish denization on 28 November 1617. [IPR]

WARD, JOHN, master of the <u>Janet of Holywood</u> at the port of Glasgow 26 April 1673. [NAS.E72.10.4]

WARD, ROBERT, in the barony of Ardes, County Down, 1659. [C]

WARDLAW, ARCHIBALD, gentleman in Dromkeyes parish, barony of Kinallerly, County Down, 1659. [C]

WARDLAW, WILLIAM, of Lismullen, County Down, was granted Irish denization on 28 November 1617. [IPR]

WASSON, SAMUEL, a Scots-Irish student at Glasgow University 1706. [MUG#184]

WATSON, DAVID, parson of Kilclere, 1615. [Cal.SP.Ire#34]; Rector of Kilsleve, was granted Irish denization 20 May 1617. [IPR]; born in Scotland, a minister in Killeavy Newry from 1617, died imprisoned in Mingarie Castle during March 1645, husband of Isabella Philis Kerr of Drumquin. [PHS]

WATSON, JAMES, portioner of Sauchton, applied for 2000 acres in Ulster on 18 July 1609. [PU#140]

WATSON, JAMES, minister in Magheralin from 1655. [FI#51]

WATSON, JOHN, a portioner of Saughtonhall, Edinburgh, applied for 2000 acres in Ulster on 6 July 1609. [PU#139]

WATSON, WILLIAM, of Auchend, a juryman at a Coroner's inquest held at Duncanalley, County Donegal, on 15 September 1660. [Cal.S.P.Ire.1660]

WATT, JOHN, in Holywood, born 1639, died 3 April 1702. [Holywood g/s]

WATT, WILLIAM, master of the <u>Rose of Belfast</u> at the port of Irvine, Ayrshire, 15 October 1691; at the port of Ayr 9 October 1690. [NAS.E72.12.18; E72.3.22]

WAUCHOPE, JAMES, of Ballygraphan, was granted Irish denization on 28 November 1617. [IPR]

WAUCHOPE, ROBERT, Captain of Major General Robert Monro's Regiment, in Carrickfergus 1642. [PRO.SP.18.120]

WAUGH, GEORGE, born in Perthshire during 1619, graduated MA from Edinburgh University during 1639, minister of Holywood from 1679 to 1689, died on 1 December 1691.[FI#82]

WAUGH, JAMES, in Clownish, County Fermanagh, 1659. [C]

WAUGH, WALTER, in Clownish, County Fermanagh, 1659. [C]

WEAR, ALEXANDER, of Castleton, County Fermanagh, gentleman, was granted Irish denization on 19 July 1631. [IPR]

WEIR, ALEXANDER, in Devonish, County Fermanagh, 1659. [C]

WEIR, ROBERT, in Devonish, County Fermanagh, 1659. [C]

WEIR, THOMAS, of Kirktoun, applied for 2000 acres in Ulster on 4 August 1609. [PU#143]

WEIR, WILLIAM, born in West Lothian during 1628, graduated MA from Edinburgh University in 1648, minister in Coleraine from 1674 to 1690, died in Linlithgow, Scotland, on 1 July 1695. [FI#82]

WELLWOOD, JOHN, minister in Glenavy from 1654. [FI#51]

WELSH, DAVID, born 1598, Provost of Killyreagh, died on 17 January 1658; his sons James born 1637, died 1639; Hans born 1643, died 1647, and David born 1650, died 1656. [Killyreagh g/s, County Down]

WELSH, JOSIAS, born in 1598, second son of Reverend John Welsh in Ayr and Elizabeth Knox, matriculated at St Leonard's College, University of St Andrews, 1620, MA there 1623, minister at Templepatrick, County Antrim, 1627-1634, died on 23 June 1634. [UJA#13/15][PRONI#T284] [PROI#RC9/1/41][PHS]; his widow Martha Pont and their three children John, Margaret and Loaz Welsh, settled in Stevenston, Ayrshire, during 1655. [NAS.RD615]

WELSH, JONAS, a minister in Connor by September 1631.
[SP.Ire#252/2020]

WEMYSS, Sir JOHN, former Sheriff of County Fermanagh, was
murdered before 14 April 1627, husband of Anne.
[SP.Ire#245/768; Docquets#638]

WEMYSS, Sir PATRICK, with 62 horsemen in Ireland 1647.
[SP.Ire#265/41-7]

WEMYSS, WILLIAM, of Newton, was granted Irish denization on
20 May 1617. [IPR]

WETHERSPOON, JAMES, a snapmaker in Strabane, County
Tyrone, probate 1623

WHITAKER, ROBERT, a minister in the diocese of Clogher, 1622.
[TCD.ms.E#3/6]

WHITE, ADAM, born in Scotland, graduated MA from Glasgow
University in 1648, minister in Clondevarrock from 1654 to
1672, in Ardstraw from 1672 to 1692, and in Billy from 1692,
died on 19 December 1708. [FI#51]; a non-conformist minister
imprisoned at Lifford in 1669. [Cal.SP.Ire]

WHITE, JAMES, a Scots-Irish student at Glasgow University 1711.
[MUG#196]

WHITE, JOHN, jr., an Irish student at Edinburgh University in 1704.
[CEG]

WHITE, ROBERT, master of the Alexander of Belfast at the port of
Irvine, Ayrshire, on 25 June 1683, and on 15 June 1685.
[NAS.E72.12.7/10]

WHITE, ROBERT, merchant aboard the James of Larne at the port of
Irvine, Ayrshire, on 27 March 1691. [NAS.E72.12.18]

WHYT, HUGH, brother of Alexander Whyt of Hill, educated at
Edinburgh University, graduated MA in 1676, denounced as a
fugitive on 5 May 1684, licensed as a Presbyterian minister in
Newtown, Ireland, on 31 January 1688, ordained 1690,
minister in Stirlingshire, died in 1716. [F.4.311]

WHITLAW, ANDREW, was granted Irish denization on 23
    December 1618. [IPR]

WILKIE, JOHN, burgess of Edinburgh, applied for 2000 acres in
    Ulster on 4 August 1609. [PU#143]

WILKIN, JOHN, of Carrickreagh, 1 November 1673.
    [NAS.GD1.273.1]

WILL, JOHN, born in Scotland, graduated MA from Glasgow
    University in 1645, minister in Glendermott from 1654 to
    1679, [FI#52]

WILLIAMSON, DAVID, in Killeleagh, barony of Kinallerly, County
    Down, 1659. [C]

WILLIAMSON, HUGH, a Scots-Irish student at Glasgow University
    1715. [MUG#205]

WILLIAMSON, JAMES, of Clay, was granted Irish denization on 20
    May 1617. [IPR]

WILLIAMSON, ROBERT, servant of Henry Robinson in
    Londonderry, 1615. [TCD.Stearne MSS#f3/15]

WILLOUGHBY, FRANCIS, an Anglo-Irish student at Edinburgh
    University 1704.   [CEG]

WILSON, ALLEN, was granted Irish denization on 28 November
    1617. [IPR]

WILSON, ANNA, daughter of the laird of Crogline, was born in
    1619, wife of John Stewart of Ballydrain, died on 25 December
    1682. [Drumbeg g/s, County Down]

WILSON, CLAUD, in Donagheady, barony of Strabane, County
    Tyrone, probate 1636

WILSON, GILBERT, clerk, was granted Irish denization on 22
    February 1621. [IPR]

WILSON, HILL, from Ireland, was admitted as a burgess and
guildsbrother of Glasgow on 4 July 1728, [GBR]

WILSON, HUGH, born in Scotland, educated at Glasgow University
in 1649, minister in Knock and Breda from 1649 to 1661, died
in Scotland during 1695. [FI#52]; a Presbyterian minister in
Northern Ireland who petitioned the Queen in 1691.
[CTB.#/III.1207, 1258]

WILSON, JAMES, of Letterkenny, was granted Irish denization on
28 November 1617. [IPR]

WILSON, JAMES, a merchant at the Diamond, Londonderry, 1659.
[C]

WILSON, JAMES, a merchant in Londonderry, husband of Jean
Birnie, daughter of John Birnie a merchant burgess of Ayr, 25
March 1674. [NAS.GD1.521.30]

WILSON, Mr JAMES, merchant in Newton, Ireland, was admitted as
a burgess and guildsbrother of Glasgow 4 July 1728, [GBR]

WILSON, JOHN, was granted Irish denization on 16 June 1615.
[IPR]

WILSON, JOHN, of Bangor, was granted Irish denization on 28
November 1617. [IPR]

WILSON, JOHN, a tenant of Sir William Stewart, around 1620.
[PU#545]

WILSON, JOHN, master of the Nightingale of Belfast at the port of
Ayr 26 July 1682. [NAS.E72.3.9]

WILSON, JOHN, master of the Speedwell of Glenarm at the port of
Ayr 17 July 1673; at the port of Irvine, Ayrshire, 24 January
1681 and 26 August 1681; at the port of Ayr 28 April 1690.
[NAS.E72.3.3/22; E72.12.3/5]

WILSON, JOHN, born in Ayrshire in 1653, graduated MA from
Edinburgh University in 1678, minister in Dunbire from 1684
to 1689, [FI#83]; serviced as heir to his brother James Wilson
a merchant in Abergavenny on 11 August 1716. [NAS.SH]

WILSON, JOHN, a Scots-Irish student at Glasgow University in 1720. [MUG#218]

WILSON, LANCELOT, merchant in Belfast, admitted as a burgess and guildsbrother of Glasgow on 29 June 1719. [GBR]

WILSON, NATHANIEL, a Scots-Irish student at Glasgow University in 1706. [MUG#184]

WILSON, NATHANIEL, in Belfast, 1727. [NAS.GD10#466]

WILSON, RICHARD, of Ballymanagh, County Tyrone, yeoman, was granted Irish denization on 27 June 1634. [IPR]

WILSON, RICHARD, born in Scotland, educated at Edinburgh and Glasgow universities, graduated MA from Edinburgh University in 1655, minister of Drumane Randalstown from 1672, died in June 1685. [FI#82]

WILSON, ROBERT, of Newton, was granted Irish denization on 20 May 1617. [IPR]

WILSON, ROBERT, of Lisnegate, was granted Irish denization on 12 February 1618. [IPR]

WILSON, ROBERT, born in Scotland, minister at Termin M'Gurk from 1655, died at the siege of Londonderry during 1689, father of Reverend Robert Wilson. [FI#52]

WILSON, ROBERT, master of the John of Belfast at the port of Ayr 14 September 1689. [NAS.E72.3.19]

WILSON, ROBERT, merchant in Belfast, admitted as a burgess and guildsbrother of Glasgow on 12 July 1703. [GBR]; 1722, [NAS.AC9/849]

WILSON, ROBERT, in Bikcomera, Seagoe parish, County Armagh, subscribed to his will on 14 December 1714, reference to his wife Elizabeth, sons Robert, Thomas, Ralph, William and Francis, daughters Margaret, Ann, Elizabeth and Judith, brother-in-law William Mathers, probate 16 November 1714 Dublin

WILSON, SAMUEL, a Scots-Irish student at Glasgow University in 1716. [MUG#208]

WILSON, THOMAS, of Corcrery, County Tyrone, gentleman, was granted Irish denization on 19 July 1633. [IPR]

WILSON, THOMAS, born in Blairgowrie, Perthshire, during 1640, graduated MA from the University of St Andrews in 1663, minister in Killibegs and Killachtie from 1676, emigrated to Maryland, died in Edinburgh on 13 June 1713. [FI#83]

WISHART, Sir JOHN, of Pittarro, Angus, grant of part of Latrim, precinct of Knockninny, County Fermanagh, 25 June 1610. [PRO.Signet Office Docquet Book, Privy Seal Chancery #1786]; was granted Irish denization on 25 June 1610. [IPR]

WISHART, JOHN, in Fermanagh, petitioned the Lord Deputy on 11 October 1628. [SP.Ire#243/491,1]

WISHART, JOHN, in Clownish, County Fermanagh, 1659. [C]

WITHERSPOON, ANDREW, Lifford, was granted Irish denization on 17 August 1616. [IPR]

WOOD, ANDREW, brother of John Wood of Geilston, applied for 2000 acres in Ulster on 20 July 1609. [PU#141]

WOODS, ANDREW, of Maymore, was granted Irish denization on 20 May 1617. [IPR]

WOOD, JAMES, of Meymore, County Donegal, was granted Irish denization on 17 August 1616. [IPR]

WOODDELL, ALEXANDER, of Ballinienagh, was granted Irish denization on 28 November 1617. [IPR]

WOODS, ANDREW, of Maymore, was granted Irish denization on 28 November 1617. [IPR]

WOODS, MICHAEL, senior, yeoman at the Falls, Belfast, 1 February 1678. [NAS.GD10/823]

WOODS, ROBERT, in Island Reagh, born 1655, died 18 July 1715; his widow Marion Watt, born 1664, died 14 February 1734. [Killinchy g/s, County Down]

WOOLLY, ROBERT, of Strabane, was granted Irish denization on 20 May 1617. [IPR]

WORKMAN, ROBERT, in Balteoch parish, Londonderry, 1715. [NAS.RD4.117.856]

WRIGHT, JOHN, a tenant of Sir William Stewart, around 1620. [PU#545]

WRIGHT, JOHN, master of the Catherine of Donaghadee at the port of Dumfries 1 September 1673. [NAS.E72.6.2]

WRIGHT, SAMUEL, master of the Janet of Holywood at the port of Irvine, Ayrshire, 3 October 1682. [NAS.E72.12.5]

WYLY, JOHN, of Ballihay, was granted Irish denization on 20 May 1617. [IPR]

WYLLIE, ALEXANDER, merchant aboard the Adventure of Coleraine at the port of Irvine, Ayrshire, 15 February 1689. [NAS.E72.12.14]

WYLLIE, JOHN, tenant of John Hamilton of Edenagh, Precinct of Fewes, 1618. [PU#567]

WYLLIE, JOHN, master of the Margaret of Larne at the port of Irvine, Ayrshire, 26 December 1668. [NAS.E72.12.1]

WYLLIE, THOMAS, born in Scotland during 1618, graduated MA from Edinburgh University in 1638, minister in Coleraine from 1669 to 1672, died in Scotland on 20 July 1676. [FI#84]

WYLLIE, WILLIAM, a Scots-Irish student at Glasgow University in 1717. [MUG#210]

YEATES, JOHN, a trunchmaker, born in Leedon, West Lothian, settled in Ireland before 29 July 1672. [IPR]

YONGE, THOMAS, in Strabane, County Tyrone, was granted Irish denization on 17 August 1616, probate 1635. [IPR][SBT#22]

YOUNG, ARCHIBALD, in Donagheady, County Tyrone, pro. 1638

YOUNG, ARCHIBALD, born in Scotland, graduated MA from Edinburgh University in 1663, minister in Downpatrick from 1673 to 1689. [FI#84]

YOUNG, ARCHIBALD, a Scots-Irish student at Edinburgh University in 1699. [CEG]

YOUNG, DAVID, a minister in Ireland, during 1715. [NAS.RD3.144.530]

YOUNG, JAMES, of Urny, barony of Strabane, County Tyrone, clerk, was granted Irish denization on 9 July 1616, there in 1617. [IPR][SBT#23]

YOUNG, JAMES, in Lilnane, Ireland, 1725. [NAS.GD10#454]

YOUNG, JOHN, professor of theology, royal chaplain, was granted Irish denization on 19 November 1616. [IPR]

YOUNG, JOHN, in the barony of Tarranney, County Armagh, 1659. [C]

YOUNG, JOHN, in Belfast, 13 August 1685. [NAS.GD10.832]

YOUNG, JOHN, in Castbine, Ireland, 1721. [NAS.GD10#450]

YOUNG, JOHN, a merchant in Belfast, will subscribed to on 29 August 1722, probate 4 June 1724 Dublin

YOUNG, ROBERT, agent for Sir James Cunningham of Glengarnoth, in the Precinct of Portlogh, 29 July 1611. [Cal.SP.Ire.1611/203]

YOUNG, ROBERT, of Culdrum, gentleman, was granted Irish denization on 28 November 1624. [IPR]

YOUNG, ROBERT, a yeoman, was granted Irish denization on 9 December 1633. [IPR]

YOUNG, WILLIAM, a clerk, was granted Irish denization on 18 October 1616. [IPR]

YOUNG, WILLIAM, merchant aboard the Mary of Glenarme at the port of Irvine, Ayrshire, 4 May 1691. [NAS.E72.12.18]